About the Authors

Dr Tony Lenehan is a senior executive with CERT, the state tourism training agency in Ireland. He is responsible for the strategic direction and implementation of management development, systematic training and quality initiatives within the tourism industry. He has also managed EU projects in South Asia, Eastern Europe and the Caribbean. Tony holds a PhD from the University of Surrey, an MSc in Management from Trinity College, Dublin; an MA in Management Learning from Lancaster University. His research interests include management learning and competences in service organisations. He has made presentations at a number of national and international conferences and seminars.

Dr Denis Harrington is a lecturer in management studies at the Business School at Waterford Institute of Technology, Waterford, Ireland. A commerce graduate of University College, Cork, Ireland, Denis has previously worked with Reuters, London and as a lecturer at South Bank University, London. He also holds an MBA from the University of Hull and a PhD from the Centre of International Business, South Bank University, London. His research interests include quality implementation in service industries and global service competition in hotel organisations. He has published a number of articles in the area and is currently working as an international consultant in the fields of education, training and quality management.

Managing Quality in Tourism

Theory and Practice

Tony Lenehan
Denis Harrington

Oak Tree Press
Dublin

Oak Tree Press
Merrion Building
Lower Merrion Street
Dublin 2, Ireland
http://www.oaktreepress.com

ISBN 1 86076 100 3

Printed in the Republic of Ireland by Colour Books Ltd.

Contents

List of Exhibits, Tables and Figures..*ix*

Foreword ....*xii*

Acknowledgements ....*xvii*

Preface..*xxi*

Chapter 1
Introduction to Quality Management

Introduction to Quality Management..1
Introduction..1
Significance of Textbooks on Quality Management 3
What is Quality 4
Changing Perspectives on Quality Management.......................8
Service (and Product) Quality..11
Disentangling Service Quality 12
Deficiencies in Quality Management.....................................15
Managing Quality in Tourism Organisations.........................19
Themes Addressed 29
Summary...29
Review Questions 30

Chapter 2
Strategic Analysis of the Hospitality Industry

Strategic Analysis of the Hospitality Industry............................31
Introduction..31
Hospitality and Economic Cycles..32
Characteristics of the Hospitality Industry 34
Consolidation within the Hospitality Industry 36
Growing Importance of Strategic Alliances 40
Management Contracts and Franchising.................................43
Impact of Technology...47

Emerging Developments 51
Research on the Tourism Industry 55
Importance of Quality 59
Summary...60
Review Questions 61

Chapter 3
Strategic Quality-Oriented Tourism Policies...............................63
Importance of Quality-Related Policies.......................................64
Quality at the Supra-national Scale..64
Quality and Quality Planning at the Destination Level............66
Case Study 3.1: Spain – Quality-Oriented Policies: a
Regionalised Approach 71
Case Study 3.2: Great Britain – How Quality Issues
Arrived on the Policy Agenda 75
Case Study 3.3: Republic of Ireland – Quality Initiatives
within the Tourism Sector 86
Summary...91
Review Questions 92

Chapter 4
Quality and Competitive Advantage 93
Introduction...93
Dynamics of Managing Quality...94
Strategic Nature of Quality Initiatives..97
Strategic Quality..105
Quality as Competitive Advantage..108
Benchmarking for Competitive Success 111
Benchmarking: A Practical Perspective.....................................113
Performance Measurement 116
Summary...122
Review Questions 122

Chapter 5
Hard and Soft Quality Management...125
Introduction...125
Quality Standards in Tourism Organisations............................126
Quality Standards – Help or Hindrance?..................................127
"Manufactured" Quality and Continuous Improvement.......130

Competitive Importance of "Soft" Quality 135
Contemporary Perspectives on TQM 137
Implications for Service Delivery 143
Internal Marketing..145
Information Technology Dimension.....................................151
Personal Service and Technological Efficiency:
    An Integrated Approach..156
Applying the Integrated Approach.....................................158
Summary 161
Review Questions 162

Chapter 6
Infrastructure for Quality Management **165**
Introduction..165
What is Human Resource Development? 166
Strategic HRD and the Tourism Sector...............................168
Quality Management Infrastructure: Challenges and
    Obstacles 175
    Senior Management 175
    "Top–Bottom" Integration 180
    Quality Culture...183
    Customer Orientation 191
    Employee Resourcefulness..196
Summary 206
Review Questions 208

Chapter 7
Evaluating Quality Management **209**
Introduction..209
Quality to Date 210
Strategic Quality: The Question of Implementation...............213
What Has Gone Wrong with Quality Implementation? 218
Challenges for Senior *and* Middle Management 225
Quality Implementation — Some Practical Issues...................229
Tensions in Quality Implementation 232
Summary 240
Review Questions 241

Chapter 8

Future Challenges for Quality Management 243

    Introduction 249

    Growing Importance of the Tourism Industry 244

    Quality: a New Method of Management 247

    Training for Quality 250

    Implementing the Quality Initiative 255

    Integration with Strategy 258

    Tensions, Complexities and Future Challenges for the
        Tourism Sector 263

    Summary 265

    Review Questions 267

Bibliography 269

Index 297

List of Tables, Figures and Exhibits

Tables

1.1	British Studies of Quality Management	17
1.2	Approaches to Examining Service Quality in Hospitality Firms	25
2.1	Examples of Strategic Partnerships Concluded within Hotel and Catering Industry, 1996	42
4.1	Development of Strategic Approach to Quality	106
7.1	Studies of Quality Implementation	224

Figures

3.1	Outline of Quality in Tourism	67
3.2	Steps of the Quality Evaluation Approach	68
3.3	Competitive Pressures in Tourism	78

Exhibits

1.1	Achieving Excellence in Practice	14
1.2	Quality Programmes Are Dead	17
1.3	Why TQM Doesn't Work . . . and What You can Do about It	19
1.4	So Much Work, So Little Time	22

1.5   What the French Really Fear: "Le Style Conran" 23
1.6   The Malcolm Baldrige National Quality Award 26

2.1   Know When to Change the Game 33
2.2   Accor Reports Success with Asian Growth Strategy 42
2.3   High Recognition Restaurants 46
2.4   It is Time to Enlarge the Pie 48
2.5   Rooms that Work 50
2.6   Quality and Competitive Advantage at Four Seasons
        Hotels 54
2.7   Comeback for the Full-service Hotel Strategy 59

4.1   Holiday Execs Hit the Road Promoting Service 98
4.2   Sweet Hospitality 104
4.3   End of the Traditional Pub Era 107
4.4   When 99 Per Cent Isn't Enough 110
4.5   Customer Feedback Methods 120

5.1   Lumpy Mashed Potatoes — Yuck! 130
5.2   Lake District Gets TQM Treatment 132
5.3   Service Delivery in the Restaurant Business 140
5.4   Las Vegas Resort Bets on Training and Wins 142
5.5   Managing Employees for Service Delivery at Sofitel 150
5.6   Room Service with a Difference 153
5.7   Service with a Smile 155

6.1   People Power Rises in Quality 167
6.2   Quality Management and HR Practices in
        UK Hotels 171
6.3   Commitment-Based Quality Management
        at Hampton Inn 177
6.4   Quality for the 1990s 182
6.5   Human Resources and the Quality Culture
        in US Hotels 185

6.6   Quality Culture as an All-embracing Code
of Practice...189

6.7   Training for Customer Care 192

6.8   Empowerment: Trendy Slogan or Effective
Management Tool?...198

6.9   Employee Resourcefulness — Risk and Reward?............200

6.10   Employee Recognition Programmes.................................201

6.11   Making Quality Work for Staff? 203

7.1   More Quality than You Think.................................210

7.2   Getting Down to the Basics of Quality
Management..212

7.3   Applying the Quality Philosophy 214

7.4   Driving the Quality Message 216

7.5   Quality Street...220

7.6   Problems with Quality Management.....................222

7.7   Teamwork in Practice! 226

7.8   When tqm becomes TQM.......................................230

7.9   Solutions for Maintaining Top Performance?...................234

7.10   Is Total Quality Fading as a Strategy? 237

8.1   Managing Change within the Irish Tourism
Industry..246

8.2   Tracking Customers' Expectations of Quality
Initiatives 250

8.3   Can't get this Big without HR Deluxe 251

8.4   Quality Focus Keeps Hands-on Host 100 Per Cent
Occupied 253

8.5   New Wave Management Techniques at Sabena 256

8.6   Reengineering Initiatives in the Tourism Sector 259

8.7   Management Competences in the Irish
Tourism Industry...261

Foreword

There has been an increased interest in quality initiatives in recent years. As the authors of this book correctly suggest, the emphasis on quality issues reflects a broader organisational concern for understanding and responding to the requirements of a transient and value-conscious consumer. It also reinforces the need for greater strategic awareness to achieve consistency in the provision of services. Quality has become a major strategic variable in the battle for market share and has emerged as one of the most potent means of reducing costs and improving overall organisational effectiveness. The perspective on quality has progressed from an initial operations focus on methodical improvement to a strategy-based one concerned with ways in which quality can be used to effect strategic advantage.

The European Organization for Quality (EOQ) and its sister organisation, the European Foundation for Quality Management (EFQM), have collaborated in the promotion of this customer-oriented quality as a strategic business methodology. Approaches using the European Business Excellence model, and indeed the various national award schemes based on the model, challenge senior managers to view their organisations strategically. I believe that this book will challenge its readers in a similar manner, while at the same time, it recognises important contributions and leading organisations and thinkers in the quality movement.

Specifically, the text focuses attention on the tourism industry. In the past, there was a reluctance on the part of researchers to address business and management issues in tourism organisations. The situation is entirely different today. The tourism industry is now one of the world's fastest growing industries and is already the world's largest service industry, generating, either directly or indirectly, more than ten per cent of world output, employment, investment and tax revenue. Tourism is an internationally traded service and an important source of economic and employment growth throughout the developed world. As the authors point out, by the turn of the century, it is estimated that the tourism, technology and telecommunications industries will constitute the three "super-industries" driving the global economy. Hence the importance of a text that addresses the management of quality within the tourism industry and related sectors.

The European Quality Award (Small and Medium Enterprises) in 1997 saw a German hotel as a finalist for the first time. This book will hopefully stimulate others in the tourism sector to follow this lead and in their own way to become role models.

Like other service industries, the pace and intensity of change has heightened in recent years within the tourism industry. Customers are growing in sophistication, markets are becoming more competitive and, with EMU, cost and price structures are becoming more transparent. In this environment, executives are challenged to keep abreast of current developments in the field and require timely and relevant information on a wide range of issues that affect them. No longer can practitioners rely solely on newspaper or article reports of business developments. Instead, they need to consult all available sources, particularly those that are comprehensive yet critical in nature and content. This book is significant in that regard.

Too often, accounts of quality management are prescriptive in approach and are not supported by research data and information. They lead the reader to believe that implementation is a relatively straightforward exercise achieved by adhering to a few basic fundamentals of management. This book offers a very different perspective on quality management than that provided in some of the more simplistic accounts of the subject. In line with the EOQ philosophy, the authors offer ideas and knowledge which will help organisations in their drive for competitiveness.

Equally, and importantly, the authors recognise and elaborate upon the problems which the quality movement has had to contend with in the past. There have been a number of critical studies in the area which to date have not received wide coverage in the business press. This book illuminates the problems with quality management in an insightful way using research and report data to support their thorough analyses. In doing so, it combines academic insight with an understanding of the difficulties faced by managers in implementing current thinking in practice.

Managing Quality in Tourism also traces the evolution of TQM in an interesting and innovative way. This account is significant because, for the first time, the importance of taking a strategic perspective on quality issues within the tourism sector has been emphasised. They recognise the imperative for tourism businesses of embracing change and modernisation if they are to meet changing consumer requirements and the challenges posed by increasing internationalisation. They present their arguments in a refreshing manner and integrate theory with practice in a way which should encourage students and executives to question current practices and think critically about their understanding of the subject.

The wide assortment of case examples and the well-developed academic arguments make this book conceptually sound. The critical insights are also to be commended, as are the chapters examining the necessary infrastructure for quality management. The objective is clear: to penetrate beneath the surface and examine quality in practice. In doing so, the authors have forced us to think carefully about applying theoretical principles in practice and through their work will doubtless stimulate further thinking in this important area.

Seán Conlan, President
European Organization for Quality
Switzerland, 1998

Acknowledgements

This book could not have been completed without the support and help provided by a large number of people. First, we wish to express our gratitude to our colleagues at CERT and the Waterford Institute of Technology, without whose encouragement this book could not have been written.

In the process of editing and writing this book, a number of people were especially helpful with their critical comments. We would like to extend our appreciation in particular to Duncan Tyler who toiled over numerous drafts of the text and provided important contributions in a number of areas. We are also very grateful to Brendan Rowe and Kevin Aylward for their support of this project and to the individuals who provided valuable case examples and insights into quality initiatives at their organisations. We owe a particular debt of gratitude to the publishing team at Oak Tree Press who have encouraged us through the publishing quagmire and particularly to David Givens, Janet Brown, Jenna Dowds and Brian Langan, who have worked with us through the evolution of the project. Together we have endeavoured to check all material and hope that no errors remain.

To Mary and Julette

Preface

Managing Quality in Tourism: Theory and Practice is written for undergraduate and postgraduate students of tourism management and for students on related business and management courses, as well as for managers in the tourism and hospitality industries. The textbook reflects the growing interest in quality management in tourism organisations and in service industries generally. It provides an up-to-date examination of theories and developments in quality management and takes account of the international nature of the tourism industry. The book also takes a critical perspective, as there has been a reluctance to question the effectiveness of quality management programmes.

In writing this text, we are attempting to bring together and make sense of the vast contributions in the area. Recent years have witnessed an increasing interest in the quality philosophy and there has been a large outpouring of articles on the subject. The interest in the quality movement has arisen as a consequence of the changed business and competitive environment within which organisations operate. The realities of change and ever-more differentiated markets and increasing competition have heightened the interest in quality management in a large number of organisations.

This is particularly the case in tourism organisations and other service industries. Increasingly, managers within these organisations are looking to the quality dimension in the search for customers and competitive advantage. Customers of tourism organisations are growing in sophistication and awareness and now expect high quality standards in every area of the business. Simultaneously, with increasing globalisation and the dominance of transnational corporations, the management of quality has become a key concern for domestic companies. Domestic firms must follow the lead set by these transnational companies if they are to compete successfully in the global market place. In addition, as the mature western economies shift from a manufacturing to a service base, governments have become interested in quality issues in order to gain advantage in attracting international investment monies and market share. Tourism now features strongly in these post-industrial economic development strategies. These are the key issues underlying our discussion of quality management.

We are interested in the challenges and complexities of applying quality management principles in this changing business environment. Of significant interest to our examination, therefore, are the practical realities associated with institutionalising a quality culture in tourism organisations. In this respect, the text maintains a strong practical emphasis. However, it is also important that the student of quality management should understand and be encouraged to reflect on the contributions in the area. Hence, the material is underpinned by critical discussion of relevant theories and developments. It aims to reconcile the need for careful examination of relevant theories in the area with a concern for developing a practical account of the challenges associated with the introduction of a quality philosophy to an organisation. Our contention is that if managers are to be encouraged to embrace the quality philosophy, they need to understand the implications of doing so fully. They need to be introduced to quality management principles, understand their strategic significance, appreciate the implementation challenges and critically evaluate the operation of quality programmes in their own organisations.

It is with the above concerns in mind that the current text has been developed.

Organisation of the Book

The first chapter elaborates on the development of the quality literature and examines the way in which the philosophy has evolved over the years. The main contributions are discussed and definitions of the quality concept are explored. Developing on this discussion, modern perspectives on quality management are presented and examined and the change in emphasis from product to service quality is discussed. The chapter also explores the quality management issues facing tourism firms and concludes with a discussion of the managerial benefits of subscribing to a quality orientation.

The second chapter reports on a review of the hospitality industry. This provides the context for the analysis undertaken in subsequent chapters. The economic significance of the industry is discussed and recent developments within the sector are examined. In this discussion, the importance of quality is set out and the rationale guiding the present examination is introduced. Recent research on quality management within the industry is presented and some practical issues associated with the application of quality management principles are examined.

Chapter 3 takes a wider, strategic perspective. It moves on from considerations of quality programme implementation within single organisations and addresses the issues raised when addressing quality issues on a sector-wide scale. The chapter focuses on the programmes devised by the Irish, British and Spanish governments and their associated tourism agencies in the mid-1990s. These accounts address the need to reinvigorate the tourism sector and outline strategic quality-related tourism approaches to achieving such objectives. The discussion concerns itself with the problems presented in trying to develop a quality ethic within a fragmented industry, and considers the need to address both product and service quality issues simultaneously.

Chapter 4 considers the issues and associated challenges of managing the quality dynamic. The notion of quality as an aspect of organisational strategy is introduced and the growing emphasis on the competitive benefits of quality practices are examined. The growing importance and usefulness of approaches such as benchmarking and performance measurement are examined and their significance in a strategic context explained.

Accounting for the importance attached to quality within the tourism industry, Chapter 5 distinguishes between "hard" and "soft" quality management. It takes as its starting point the notion of product quality and progresses to discuss quality standards in tourism organisations. The chapter also discusses the notion of "manufactured" or standardised approaches to managing quality and questions how these approaches fit with the growing sophistication and demands of customers.

Chapter 6 develops the discussion of "soft/hard" quality management further by discussing the necessary infrastructure for quality management. It considers human resource development and in particular its growing strategic importance within the tourism sector. From this, a quality management infrastructure is discussed and the practical challenges and obstacles in managing this within organisations are outlined.

Chapter 7 seeks to evaluate the prevalence and effectiveness of quality management practices within tourism organisations. It discusses the challenges and difficulties faced by those who are charged with implementing quality programmes and initiatives. Using research data, it also seeks to evaluate the reported accounts of quality implementation in different sectors world-wide and examines implications for the tourism sector.

On the basis of the comprehensive assessment of quality management undertaken, Chapter 8 presents our own analysis of the subject. It draws from and comments on themes developed in each of the other chapters and suggests possible areas where attention needs to be directed. The chapter concludes with a consideration of the challenges faced by managers in applying quality principles in practice.

Each chapter is structured such that it includes an overview of theoretical developments in the subject area, a critical examination of relevant perspectives and examples of practical application through the use of ongoing examples, questions and case exhibits. Each chapter ends with a summary and a set of review questions to aid understanding and application.

Chapter 1

Introduction to Quality Management

Introduction

The tourism industry has undergone significant reform in recent years. The combined effects of war in the Middle East and a world-wide economic recession and restructuring, together with the effects of having to adjust to increased pressure from techno-logical advancement and globalisation, have meant that main-taining the status quo has not been an option. Together these pressures have altered the possibilities for service delivery and heightened the importance of promoting a quality ethic. In line with developments in other service industries, greater emphasis has been placed on the positive business and competitive advan-tages of subscribing to the quality management philosophy. In addition there has been a general increase in the level of interest shown in the concept.

The upsurge of interest in quality management reflects the need across all sectors to respond to a more volatile and discern-ing consumer base. Customers of tourism companies now require a broad spectrum of convenient services at almost any time and at any place. The challenge to provide a flexible and convenient service has thus never been greater. With the influx of foreign op-erators, this requirement has intensified. Service expectations are now global and customers are more willing to compare offerings not only between companies but also across countries. Through-out the world-wide tourism industry, companies are striving to move towards a new model based on competitive advantage driven by quality.

> . . . [These] shifts and trends in the hotel, catering and tourism markets . . . indicate that changes do need to be made and that management practices do need to be changed if UK companies are to retain or improve their market position (Price, 1994: 58).

The changes occurring throughout the industry provide the impetus for the examination of total quality management reported in this text.

Studies of quality management in other industries (Wilkinson et al., 1993) have suggested the need for broad-based, comprehensive examinations of the quality concept. They have also identified the need to investigate the nature and application of these concepts and to determine whether quality has positive implications in business and competitive terms. Contributors also argue that there is a requirement to undertake more critical studies of the quality concept. As Wilkinson and Willmott (1995) discussed, there is a need to

> . . . open up quality management to questions and perspectives that are absent from the received wisdom of the quality literature . . . and to set the benefits associated with quality initiatives in a wider context so that their fragility and limits can also be appreciated (pp. 15–19).

In order to apply these conceptual developments to the tourism industry, it will be necessary to examine quality management from a number of perspectives. First, there will be a requirement to evaluate the role and nature of quality management within the sector. In particular, we will attempt to focus attention on the following:

• How widespread is quality management within the tourism industry?

- Who is involved in developing quality policy?

- By what means is quality measured?

- What role do employees play in managing quality?

- How effective are quality programmes?

- At what scale is tourism quality policy best made and implemented?

Much of the material on quality shares a concern for a greater understanding of the challenges associated with implementing quality initiatives. In their work examining new directions in the theory and practice of service quality management, Rust and Oliver (1994: 13) conclude:

> Managing service quality more effectively in the future requires developing a better understanding of how service quality works and capitalising on some fundamental, underlying trends that will create new areas of emphasis.

Similarly, Wilkinson and Willmott (1995: 1) considered that: "few studies . . . address its actual meaning, or reflect upon its practical implementation or social significance".

Consequently there is a need to examine:

- By what means is quality implementation achieved in practice?

- How do managers in hospitality firms approach quality implementation?

- Are there tensions in quality implementation?

- What are the practicalities of applying quality initiatives?

Significance of Textbooks on Quality Management

The material examined in this textbook is significant for a number of reasons. First, although increased significance has been at-

tached to the quality management philosophy within service industries in recent years, few studies, with some notable exceptions, have examined quality practices in the tourism industry.
This is an important consideration. As we will emphasise
throughout this text, tourism is an internationally traded service
and is a key contributor to economic and employment growth
throughout the developed world. It is estimated that by 2006, the
number of jobs in travel and tourism world-wide will have increased to 365 million. Within the European Union, tourism generates 19 million jobs and employs over ten per cent of the EU
workforce. The industry has changed immeasurably in the last
number of years. Tourism services have become international in
scope, are innovative and market-focused. Companies are under
increasing pressure to provide high-quality services to attract and
retain consumers.

Second, there has been a reluctance to address the question of
implementation of quality management. While the benefits of
quality management techniques have been widely publicised, and
the achievements of exemplary companies much lauded, the
challenges and associated difficulties with quality implementation have not been adequately addressed. The studies which have
addressed the quality concept have alluded to the difficulties of
implementing quality initiatives; however, these concerns have
not been examined in any great detail. These are issues which will
be examined in the chapters that follow. First, we begin by looking at the quality concept and how it has changed over time.

What is Quality?

The origins of the quality philosophy date back over three decades. In the early 1950s, three Americans, W. Edwards Deming,
Joseph Juran and Armand Feigenbaum began to introduce quality
control ideas to Japanese managers and educate them on the
benefits of adopting the quality philosophy. Previous to this, the

general perception was that investments in quality brought with it associated costs that couldn't be recouped. However, the founding fathers of the quality movement disabused managers of that notion. They argued that by attending continuously to the quality of a product or process, the organisation could save on time and money, reduce waste and deliver products faster to customers. Therefore, instead of focusing on results or outcomes, the quality management philosophy concentrates attention on the processes involved in delivering service to the customer. The quality movement argues that what is necessary is that organisations manage their service processes effectively so as to provide high quality for the customer.

However, like many new movements or ideas, thinking on quality took time to develop and be accepted. As a recent article in *Fortune* magazine (1995) reminds us:

> For years, Deming couldn't sell his message in the US. Then, on June 24, 1980, at 9.30 p.m., he appeared on an NBC show about Japanese quality called "If Japan can, why can't we?". A manager at Ford happened to be watching and brought Deming and his ideas to Ford. The result was "Team Taurus", a quality-driven project that helped Ford turn itself around and eventually led to the development of the company's best-selling car. . . . After that, quality spread widely throughout the rest of corporate America.

More recent years have witnessed a growing interest in the management of quality in business organisations. Research on quality management has evolved considerably in recognition of the fact that quality customer service is a prerequisite for competitive differentiation in a wide variety of markets. Since the mid-1980s, quality management has been given increased attention by both academics and practitioners, with organisations eager to understand ways in which the quality offered to external customers could be assessed and improved.

The initial interest in total quality was seen to evolve largely from manufacturing-based origins. In the traditional sense, quality was based on the physical characteristics of the product and was regarded as a reflection of the differences in measurable elements between products. According to this perspective, the quality of a product was assessed in terms of its conformance to a predetermined set of specifications. A number of influential writers propounded this view and emphasised the requirement for statistical control over the manufacturing process to ensure quality for the customer (Crosby, 1979; Deming, 1986; Juran, 1986).

Deming (1986) advocated the requirement for managers to take the initiative on quality matters and established a 14-point plan for improving quality. Similarly, Crosby (1979) also directed his attention at management and argued that management's lack of understanding contributed greatly to the problems with quality. Like Deming, he proposed a 14-point strategy for achieving zero defects. Juran (1986), however, defined quality from the perspective of the customer and emphasised a "fitness for use" approach. The argument being that the features of the product should be designed to meet customers' demands, not those of the manufacturer.

Central to this early quality management philosophy were a number of key principles. Firstly, the leading contributors argue the importance of getting things "right first time". Secondly, they share a concern for evaluating and benchmarking organisational processes in an overall attempt to improve the quality of a product or service delivered to the customer. Thirdly, and most importantly, they considered that quality management should be designed around what customers want. Processes, whether manufacturing or service, should be driven by a concern to provide customers with what they desire.

These early writers can be seen to converge on a number of key issues (Maxon, 1991):

- Quality is management's responsibility

- A consultative management style is necessary

- Improvement cannot be brought about in isolation from suppliers

- There are no easy routes to quality improvement

- The process is never-ending.

Moreover, regardless of the name which is ascribed to the concept or which writer's approach is adopted, quality can be understood as

> . . . an organisation-wide effort oriented to building and maintaining customer satisfaction and reducing costs by increasing the efficiency and reliability of all work processes (Levin and Gottlieb, 1993: 297).

As outlined earlier, Japanese managers were quick to align their organisations to these principles. Moreover, their interest in quality extended beyond its important role in improving production efficiency to an overall concern for developing an interest in the quality management philosophy at all levels within the organisation. In this sense, TQM was seen as a form of management behaviour based on the theories of continuous, incremental improvement and broad participation.

Flood (1995) summarises the strategic approach to developing an organisational concern for quality as follows:

- Senior managers must personally take charge of quality management implementation

- Personnel from all levels and functions of an organisation must undergo training in quality management

- Quality management must be continuous

- The workforce must participate in quality improvement.

Indeed, he suggests that a deficiency in the contributions of the leading thinkers in quality centres around their lack of concern for the management of the human dimension in quality management programmes. In particular, Flood (1995) comments that:

> Management of the human dimension of organisations is not at all clearly provided for. The gurus commonly declare their interest in managing people in their philosophies but on analysis offer few tangible principles and virtually no useable methods (p. 38).

Notwithstanding the above criticisms, it is fair to argue that the early contributors to the quality movement can be credited with developing the strong interest in quality which persists in organisations world-wide today. In fact, the "Total Quality" movement is now regarded as one of the most enduring management theories of recent years. Hodgetts (1996) makes the point when he writes:

> We are in the middle of a quality revolution that is rapidly spreading across the country . . . the word quality seems to crop up in just about everything that is being written about management . . . an increasing number of organisations seem to have taken quality to heart and are now prospering because of this strategic decision.

Changing Perspectives on Quality Management

With the increasing importance that was attached to services in the early 1980s, there was a concern to evolve service-based definitions of quality. The simultaneous concern for understanding quality in a service context evolved out of the increasing attention that was given to services marketing within the literature. In particular, it was argued that "conformance-to-specifications" and "fitness-for-use" approaches failed to take account of the unique characteristics of services (Lovelock, 1981). Although some writing from a manufacturing perspective emphasised the importance of customer concerns, the focus didn't embrace a discussion of the ways in which organisations should assess customer wants. The early contributions were thus dominated by theoretical debate concerning the appropriateness of applying manufacturing-based quality techniques to services.

Even so, Levitt (1972), in a controversial article, propounded the view that the failure of service organisations to achieve high quality was a product of their reluctance to adopt manufacturing techniques. Levitt (1972: 43) argued that to improve quality, companies should

> apply the kind of technocratic thinking which in other fields has replaced the high cost and erratic elegance of the artisan with the low-cost predictable munificence of the manufacturer.

In his view, the adoption of a manufacturing approach to the management of quality allowed for the provision of a consistently high level of service. He further emphasised the need to eliminate employee discretion in the service delivery process, arguing that "discretion is the enemy of order, standardisation, and quality" (Levitt, 1972: 44).

Others were critical of Levitt's proposition and argued that there were organisational issues which needed to be taken into account by service firms which were not applicable in other sectors. Firstly, they pointed out that most services were intangible and argued that it was difficult both for the firm to portray to customers what exactly was on offer and for the customer to evaluate the service prior to consumption.

Secondly, it was suggested that services were heterogeneous in the sense that they were different each time they are performed. Variation can be introduced to the service by either the provider or customer: the provider may not be able to achieve consistency in service provision while customer perceptions vary on a regular basis.

Thirdly, they pointed out that services were perishable. If a service (e.g. a hotel room) was not consumed by a customer at the time and location specified, it was lost. Thus, the process of managing for this aspect of service delivery would again vary between situations, and indeed organisations, which clearly has implications for the quality and consistency of the product offered.

Finally, reference was made to the fact that, with services, production and consumption occur simultaneously, which means that customers are given an opportunity to participate in the service delivery process. The service encounter, it was argued, was essentially a "moment of truth" wherein a potential customer relationship could be nurtured or lost forever.

Thus, taking account of these characteristics, Shostack (1977) pointed to the difficulties involved in transferring material product-based ideas to services, and highlighted the requirement to take account of the intangible nature of services. Specifically, she underlined the difficulties encountered when attempting to assess or quantify services, especially since "they cannot be touched, tried on for size, or displayed on a shelf" (Shostack, 1977: 73). This work formed the basis for a large outpouring of articles on services management, and although Shostack's (1977) argument did not address quality in a direct sense, future researchers used it as a foundation to challenge the notion of applying product-based techniques for controlling quality in service contexts.

From a tourism perspective, we can see that it is clearly inappropriate to apply solely product-oriented quality management philosophies to the tourism sector. With manufactured goods, a customer can test them out; for example, test driving a car before buying. One cannot, however, sample a holiday before reaching the destination. Customers' needs and wants, therefore, are vastly different between the two sectors. The tourist must be convinced by the tour operator, largely through brochure imagery and the personal knowledge of the travel agent, that a particular package and destination will meet their needs for relaxation, activity, culture or sporting experiences. The human touch in presenting the product to the prospective tourist is key to business success. If a customer does not get the service from the travel agent, no matter how good the holiday package may be in reality, the customer will buy from an agent where they are reassured that the product meets their requirements. The personal service element is inter-mingled with the product element at the point of sale. However, striking the balance between the two is difficult and depends upon the customer's perceptions of the supplier and its product quality (i.e. reputation) as much as the supplier's ability to per-suade the customer. Large travel agent chains linked to tour op-erators tend to rely on product reputation, whereas the smaller, less visible independents rely more on the service element.

Service (and Product) Quality

The difficulties in applying traditional manufacturing definitions in service contexts spawned a series of articles examining the service quality concept. Writers in this domain supported the idea of focusing attention on consumer-based definitions of quality. The early writings on the subject suggested that the quality con-cept was a subjective one whose effective management was de-pendent on an understanding of how the customer thinks about service quality. The general consensus was, therefore, that service quality was a function of the comparison which customers make between expectations of what an organisation should provide and perceptions of actual performance.

In this sense, service quality was a measure of how well the organisation's service level matched customer expectations. As Gronroos (1990: 37) remarked, "what counts is quality as it is per-ceived by the customers". Zeithaml et al. (1990: 16) also asserted that "the only criteria that count in evaluating service quality are defined by customers. Only customers judge quality: all other judgements are essentially irrelevant."

The main justification for examining quality in terms of whether a product and/or service meets/exceeds customer expectations is that it allows examination to be made of subjective factors (e.g. courtesy and appearance) in quality evaluations. Thus, the organisation monitors that which is significant to customers as opposed to developing specifications around internal judgements.

Disentangling Service Quality

As a consequence, greater consideration was given to the need to define the construct carefully and conceptualise quality management within a services marketing context. This was because of the growing importance of service quality both in the literature and in business practice and because of the need to include subjective elements as defined by the customer.

Work in this area has emanated primarily from the contributions of the American and Nordic schools of research. The American school of thought on service quality is represented by Parasuraman et al. (1985; 1988) and has been concerned to determine the criteria that customers use to evaluate service quality. Initially, they suggested a model of ten criteria for the evaluation of service quality; however, through further focus group research, they refined the model to five criteria known as SERVQUAL: tangibility, reliability, responsiveness, assurance and empathy (Parasuraman, 1988).

Their assessment of the dimensionality of service quality is also consistent with that outlined by Garvin (1987). He proposed similar criteria to the SERVQUAL approach: features, conformance, durability, reliability, performance, aesthetics and perceived quality. Simultaneously, the Nordic school conceptualised service quality to represent technical and functional dimensions and proposed six determining factors or criteria: professionalism and skills; attitudes and behaviour; accessibility and flexibility;

reliability and trustworthiness; reputation and credibility; and recovery. Indeed, taking the Nordic perspective, the various criteria can be examined on the basis of the emphasis placed on either "technical" (what) and "functional" (how) quality.

From a practical perspective, this research has stimulated considerable interest in the measurement of service quality and has formed the basis for measurement approaches in a number of different contexts. Parasuraman et al. (1993: 145) assert that, despite debate over the universal applicability of the SERVQUAL instrument, it nevertheless provides "core evaluation criteria that transcend specific companies and industries". It has been used to great effect by hotels, hospitals, banks and telecommunications companies.

The approach is all-encompassing in that organisations can include a number of different elements and weights in assessing customer expectations, emphasising the notion that firms will typically compete on different aspects of quality. Also, the customer expectations approach allows the organisation to maintain a strong focus on the marketplace and respond effectively to customer needs and wants (Garvin, 1994).

Such measurement now forms an important part of most service quality initiatives. Quality measurement systems based on these approaches exist in a large number of organisations. Indeed, the accurate measurement of customer satisfaction is essential if the hospitality industry is to deliver quality products and services. Some firms have developed sophisticated measurement systems to establish whether customer expectations have been met. Other organisations are using front-line staff to identify customer expectations and preferences. In Ireland, for example, the industry has introduced the Q Mark, which is essentially the Irish equivalent of BS5750. The Irish Hotels Federation (IHF) has launched a Quality Employer Scheme, the details of which are expanded upon later in the text; and the Restaurant Association of Ireland has introduced a Restaurant and Customer Charter to improve standards. All these have in some way been influenced by the initial work on quality measurement.

In fact, such is the importance of quality initiatives that they are now formally co-ordinated by organisations in many countries across the globe. In Ireland, Excellence Ireland provides this role to industry. A national quality organisation, its remit is to promote excellence across all areas of business and to enable and support organisations to become centres of excellence. The organisation has a membership of over 750 corporate organisations and 2,500 individuals. Exhibit 1.1 outlines details of a programme which the organisation is in the process of implementing, which aims to help companies take their first steps towards the systematic application of quality management. Again, it shows the importance which is attached to quality management within the business community in Ireland.

Exhibit 1.1: Achieving Excellence in Practice

Excellence Ireland's suite of business improvement and best practice frameworks now cater for the entire range of enterprises, from the largest multinational to the smallest organisations. The new business improvement programme ("Foundation Mark") is currently being piloted by companies in selected areas in the country. The Foundation Mark joins the Irish Business Excellence Model (IBEM), the revised Q Mark and the Hygiene Mark as key performance recognition and business improvement approaches provided by Excellence Ireland. The Foundation Mark is designed as a framework to help managers develop their business across all functions, with a focus on increasing efficiency, effectiveness, competitiveness and profitability. The approach also aims to create a working environment in which managers are constantly working towards continuous improvement of their organisation.

The Foundation Mark has five key elements. These are: leadership and planning; management of resources; people management; operations and process management; and results. The first four elements are known collectively as "management practices". Each element carries a score which is earned for evidence that the organisation demonstrates certain key practices.

The leadership criterion asks questions of the behaviour, working practices and processes employed by top management. People management covers issues such as terms and conditions of employment, training and communication practices. Achievement against the model will be recognised by Excellence Ireland. Following an initial pilot exercise, organisations will be assessed in accordance with the criteria set to ensure minimum levels of performance across all elements of the model.

Source: Excellence Ireland, Dublin.

Deficiencies in Quality Management

Despite the growing emphasis on services in general, and service quality management, there is a suggestion that quality has failed to take greater account of the softer/human resource issues and, for the most part, has tended to be dominated by discussions of quality management in manufacturing contexts. It has been difficult to gain an accurate picture of the prevalence and effectiveness of quality management initiatives in service organisations.

As a result, there is thus a very real need for a more broadly based perspective on quality management than is currently available. Contributors are beginning to question the nature and characteristics of quality management in different industry sectors (Wilkinson et al., 1993). From the studies which have been undertaken, the overriding picture shows that "most organisations are a long way from quality and are finding it difficult to get there" (Cruise O'Brien and Voss, 1992: 3).

For example, the findings from British research studies suggest that companies apply a mixture of approaches and techniques to achieve quality objectives and for the most part demonstrate a *partial* commitment to quality. Consider the accounts of the following reports on quality management. A study conducted by Kearney (1992) of over 100 British organisations showed that 80 per cent of quality programmes failed to produce any real benefits and, for the most part, these initiatives tended to fail because senior managers set unrealistic goals at the outset. Similarly, an Economist Intelligence Unit report (1996) concluded that quality initiatives failed because of their internal focus and the rigid and predetermined way in which they were operated. This latter finding is of particular significance to tourism operators.

Taking an internal focus to quality initiatives in the tourism industry is clearly too one-dimensional. When one is buying a holiday, one is in fact buying the expectation of an experience. This is intangible in two ways. First, an expectation may bear little resemblance to what one can in fact deliver (a holiday purchase has been described as buying a dream) and secondly, everyone's experience of a holiday and the destination is different — it may depend on the individual's own values, uncontrollable elements such as the weather or controllable elements such as the quality of food in a hotel. Quality programmes in tour operators must, therefore, focus on both the controllable elements, which can be seen as internal, and the uncontrollable elements. The focus on the latter must be in managing the customer's expectations of the holiday and not promising what one cannot deliver. It is because of poor practice in the latter that consumer protection laws within the European Union are very strict on tour operators' descriptions of hotels and resorts.

Another survey of quality management practices in 880 British firms found that only eight per cent reported a major improvement in sales due to a quality management programme and fewer than half claimed that their quality management programme had led to any improvements in sales or profitability (Redman et al., 1995a). Table 1.1 summarises the British studies of quality management.

Clearly, it is important to treat these results with care, especially since quality requires a long-term commitment from the organisation and the instances where failure is reported could sensibly be interpreted as meaning that the quality initiatives

Table 1.1: British Studies of Quality Management

Author	Research Findings
Cruise O'Brien and Voss (1992)	Report that British organisations are having difficulty with the introduction of quality initiatives.
Economist Intelligence Unit (1996)	Found that quality initiatives failed because of their internal focus.
Kearney (1992)	Study of 100 British organisations; 80% of quality programmes failed to produce any real benefit.
Zairi et al. (1994)	Report a strong association between quality and business performance.
Wilkinson et al. (1993) Redman et al. (1995)	Study of 880 British organisations; less than half reported major improvements in performance as a result of quality.

were not yet fully established. Indeed, Zairi et al. (1994), using data from 29 companies, suggested a strong association between quality implementation and business performance and argued that quality was a useful way in which to strengthen business operations and provide a platform for above-average business performance. Exhibit 1.2 places the above points in context and examines some evidence regarding the effectiveness of quality management programmes.

Exhibit 1.2: Quality Programmes Are Dead

Probably no one will argue with the importance of quality as a critical ingredient for competitiveness. But quality programmes — often called Total Quality Management (TQM) or something similar — have received sharp criticism for over-promising and under-performing. Consider these facts:

— a survey of 300 electronic firms showed that 73 per cent implemented TQM. Of these firms, 63 per cent reported less than a meagre 10 per cent improvement in product defects.

— a study by consultants Rath & Strong Inc. of 95 companies found that 38 per cent felt their quality efforts had failed.

— a survey of 500 executives conducted by Arthur D. Little Inc. reported two-thirds felt their quality programmes had not yielded significant results.

But quality programmes have helped! Turn the figures around from these reports: 37 per cent report more than ten per cent improvement in defects, 62 per cent of the companies felt their programme had not failed, and one-third of the executives indicated their programmes had yielded significant results. . . . It is both short-sighted and premature to believe quality programmes should be buried. Rather, some corrective surgery is necessary.

Source: Mark Frohman (1994), "Remything Management: the New Myths are Just as Counterproductive as the Old Ones", *Industry Week*, 21 March.

Notwithstanding these points, it is reasonable to suggest that a large number of British organisations operate partial quality initiatives and, although they report the adoption of quality practices, "in reality most schemes appear an ill-matched mixture of quality circles, employee involvement, quality tools and long-established quality assurance systems" (Hill and Wilkinson, 1995: 10). In fact, quality may have a different version or manifestation depending on the organisation and industry sector under investigation. Previously, it was thought that the quality prescription could be universally applied in any organisational setting, provided those who were responsible for implementation followed the appropriate procedures and techniques. However, commentators in the quality domain are beginning to question such assumptions, arguing that quality is not a "one size fits all" factor. It needs to take conditions at each company into account.

Quality is typically defined differently, depending on the organisation or customer under investigation. Within the organisation, certain characteristics of quality may be emphasised which are quite different to those valued by external customers. This clearly has implications for the quality and consistency of service provided to customers, especially if a particular department/

team strives for a high standard of internal quality to the detriment of building long-lasting relationships with customers. On the other hand, the quality criteria appropriate to meeting the needs of external customers may obstruct the proper functioning of quality internally: improving an internal process may affect speed and quality of service delivered to customers. Hence, managers and researchers must account for the trade-offs inherent in the different quality definitions used by relevant constituencies (see Exhibit 1.3).

Exhibit 1.3: Why TQM Doesn't Work . . . and What You can Do about It

Most TQM systems define quality as conformance to customer requirements. This is fine as far as it goes, but different departments within the same company, even different individuals, may have widely varying ideas of what customer requirements may be, depending on their operational outlook within the company. . . . TQM must start in the boardroom. People need to see where they are heading. What they need is a process vision — a clearly defined plan of where they are heading, how to get there, and what role they are to play in the process. . . . Continuous improvement depends on the ability of managers and employees to engage in creative and innovative problem-solving . . . fixing only what's broken is a seriously limiting view of continuous improvement.

Source: Industry Week, 3 January 1994.

The challenge is not to formulate one definition or model that attempts to account for all possible variables. Rather, the challenge is to develop models and definitions that are comparable, even cumulative, and account for many of the components neglected up to now.

Managing Quality in Tourism Organisations

Interest in quality within the tourism industry has tended to move in parallel with developments in other service industry sectors and the last decade has seen a growing interest in research on the subject. Studies of service quality in tourism organisations is, however, a comparatively recent phenomenon in comparison with other industry sectors. The initial interest in quality management within the tourism industry was prompted by pioneering research carried out by Nightingale (1985). This writer undertook research on the dimensionality of quality in a variety of hospitality organisations and suggested two quality components. The first was concerned with the service offering as perceived by the provider, while the second related to the service received as perceived by the customer. He argued that the effective management of service quality in hospitality organisations should be focused on these two key quality dimensions/criteria and implied a developing consensus between customers and providers as to what constitutes quality. This initial research stimulated much interest in the management of service quality in hotels, and writers showed a growing concern for understanding the implications of quality management for tourism organisations.

Since Nightingale's research on the subject, the large numbers of articles that have been published on quality management within the tourism sector have generally fallen into two main areas:

- Those contributions that have been concerned to examine quality measurement approaches in hospitality operations (Saleh and Ryan, 1991; and Callan, 1992; 1994; 1996);

- Those that are concerned with service encounter-related issues in tourism contexts (Randall and Senior, 1992; Lockwood and Ghillyer, 1996; and Guerrier, 1996b).

Accounts relating to quality measurement have been the most predominant. This is not surprising, since processes for stimulating and collecting customer information are critical to the successful management of quality initiatives. For example, in the US, hospitality managers view complaints and the process of collecting customer satisfaction data as a key consideration in the management of quality programmes. Industry associations such as the American Hotel and Motel Association regularly provide members with information and advice on the most effective means of evaluating customer satisfaction. There is industry-wide consensus that complaints and the measurement of customer satisfaction data are important ways of improving overall service standards.

The situation is different in European countries. For the most part, operators continue to use the "comment-card" approach to evaluate quality. They also experience problems dealing with complaints and do not have the procedures in place to respond with corrective action. In contrast, American firms empower their staff to deal with problems as and when they occur. Also, associations generally do not disseminate market-based information on a regular basis and that which is distributed is not used by hospitality managers. Recent evidence suggests that this is beginning to change, but only slowly. For example, in Ireland, Bord Fáilte (the Irish Tourist Board) now distribute monthly performance updates to hotels and also make available "Know your Market" guides for Britain, North America and Australia/New Zealand. Also, in Great Britain, the Hotel and Catering International Management Association (HCIMA) has launched a major quality initiative, "Hospitality Assured" (elaborated upon in later chapters), in an effort to address the deficiencies outlined above. This is encouraging, because if service failures and customer complaints are dealt with in an inefficient manner, this can have negative implications for the way in which customers perceive the quality of service. This is an area to which we will return in Chapter 4.

Exhibit 1.4 below provides an innovative perspective on quality measurement. Specifically, it shows how Bill Marriott manages the quality dynamic within the Marriott group and points to the importance of leading the quality effort from the very top of the organisation.

Exhibit 1.4: So Much Work, So Little Time

Bill Marriott, the CEO of Marriott International and a long-time road warrior keeps his breast pocket bulging with hand-written notes on each of the properties he plans to visit. After reading them en route to a site, he can recite a hotel's revenues or guest satisfaction rates with ease. . . . Marriott keeps his schedule like he runs his company. It's neat, compact and terribly practical. . . . On his whirlwind hotel visits, Bill Marriott makes a point of trudging through the bowels of his properties. He pokes around in the kitchen and takes pains to inspect carpets and bedspreads, constantly looking for input from everyone he meets. "My ideas come from being exposed," says Marriott.

Recently, for example, he heard from hotel guests sitting around a lobby lounge that they would prefer tables, along with the couches already there, to make working and snacking easier. There's another reason for all of Marriott's prowling: he's got ambassadorial shoes to fill. Marriott takes time to chat and pose with his cooks and sheet pressers — the troops who help ensure that customers come back. On one recent tour, Marriott posed for two dozen photographs in just ten minutes.

Source: Fortune, 3 February 1997.

In addition to the attention given to quality measurement in tourism, there has been strong interest in approaches adopted to manage service encounters with customers. Effective management of the service encounter is also critical in quality programmes. Research carried out in the hotels sector has traditionally had a strong operations focus. Despite recognising that the hospitality product is highly personalised, with satisfaction being judged on individual experience, the industry remains predominately operations-oriented (Gilpen, 1996: 145).

Significant as operations-based approaches are in allowing the organisation to focus on the various activities impacting the quality process, Guerrier (1996b) suggests that these approaches can often depersonalise to the extent that it can be easy to forget that there is a real human being at the end of the service delivery process, with a complex set of expectations and feelings and an identity outside their own work role. Tourism businesses are, however, changing. Responsiveness, flexibility, innovation and market focus are now order of the day for hospitality providers. Recognising this, CERT, the Irish State Training Agency for Tourism, has recently introduced a new programme, "Ireland's Best — Service Plus", to encourage businesses to be more proactive in planning and anticipating customer service requirements. Their argument is that, unless service encounters are planned for and managed dissatisfied customers will reduce the potential profits of tourism businesses.

This is an issue which has been taken very seriously by the British entrepreneur Sir Terence Conran in the design and management of service at his group of restaurants in Britain. Exhibit 1.5 shows how Conran is now exporting his formula to France and is challenging the traditional operations-focused hospitality businesses on their own turf. The evidence suggests that his youthful, anti-traditional style of design and service is destined to be as successful as his current ventures in Britain.

Exhibit 1.5: What the French Really Fear: "Le Style Conran"

France's top restaurateurs are already in a state of nervous excitement following a recent announcement that Sir Terence Conran intends to take them on at their own game, in their own backyard. The British entrepreneur plans to transform a defunct nightclub on the left bank of Paris into a high price, high snob-value restaurant, in the manner of Quaglino's, Bidendum and Bluebird in London. The spectacular success of the Conran restaurants in London has already shaken the French culinary establishment. The Conran formula, combining high quality food with a themed, youthful, anti-traditional style of design and service, is virtually unknown in France. The fear is that the new Conran restaurant will do something no French restaurant has yet done: combine excellent food with an atmosphere which is exciting, relaxed and young. As Conran himself points out: "The tradition of French cuisine is extraordinary but that is why in part it lacks flexibility. In London we have no homage to pay to the past".

The Conran invasion comes at an especially sensitive time. Several top-class provincial French restaurants have closed in recent years. The long economic chill, from which France is only now recovering, is partly to blame. But there is also a growing impatience among the well-heeled, young French professional classes with the stuffiness and lack of variety of the top-class restaurants in Paris. They do not want the chandelier-infested splendour of the old restaurants and hotels, with an atmosphere like a "morgue" or the look of an epic period movie. Nor do they want the "heliport and jacuzzi" approach of the stiffly modern newer restaurants. They want something "comfortable, something sympathetic and simple". Commentators also feel that French high-quality restaurants have not come to terms with a modern world where quality image and ambience are as important as the food. They are failing to turn gastronomy, based on gastronomic values alone, into a booming business proposition.

Source: *Independent*, 8 November 1997, p. 21.

Other contributions on quality in the tourism area are essentially attempts to review "mainstream" developments in quality management and examine in a conceptual sense the implications of such studies for tourism quality research (for instance, Johns, 1992; 1995; Lockwood et al., 1992; Gilbert and Joshi, 1992). Johns (1992; 1995) has been the most prolific writer in this area. In a number of different articles, the writer has sought to

> organise and synthesise the work on definition and specification of quality in the hospitality industry, in order to identify gaps in the existing knowledge and suggest avenues for future research (Johns, 1992: 14).

Gilbert and Joshi (1992) similarly attempt to "identify the major conceptual foundations which underpin the promulgation of quality management in the 1990s" (p. 149). These comprehensive overviews have heightened the significance of quality issues in academic and practitioner contexts and have greatly contributed to the development of research in the area. The various contributions are summarised in Table 1.2.

Table 1.2: Approaches to Examining Service Quality in Hospitality Firms

Authors	Research Area of Interest
Silvestro et al. (1989)	Examined quality measurement in a range of service industries
Callan (1989)	Investigated the use of hotel award schemes as a measure of service quality
Oberoi and Hales (1990)	Empirical examination of service quality within the conference hotel market
Saleh and Ryan (1991)	Analysed service quality in the hospitality industry using the SERVQUAL model
Johns (1992)	Reviewed the broad literature on service quality and addressed its application to the hospitality industry
Callan (1992)	Examined introduction of quality control at Avant Hotels
Randall and Senior (1992)	Examined the operation of services in NHS hospitals and outlined an approach for testing service quality initiatives in hospitals
Lockwood et al. (1992)	Presented an overview of the quality literature and discussed the influences which shape the development of a quality strategy
Senior and Morphew (1993)	Examined service quality within the British budget hotel sector; viewed service quality as a source of competitive strategy in economy hotel companies
Johns (1995)	Presented a critical review of the quality concept and identified future avenues for research
Lockwood and Ghillyer (1996)	Examined the concept of empowerment and its implications for service quality; emphasised the need to distinguish between static and dynamic quality
Callan (1996)	Reported an empirical investigation of an attributional analysis of customers' hotel selection by grading scheme categories

Another factor which served to heighten quality awareness within the industry was the Ritz-Carlton Hotel Company MBNQA (Malcolm Baldrige National Quality Award) in 1992. This prestigious award (see Exhibit 1.6), established by the United States Congress to promote national awareness of quality management in business and management, stimulated renewed interest in the quality concept within the hotel industry — especially since the Ritz-Carlton was the first hotel Baldrige winner since the initiation of the award in 1988. As a result, research on quality management was attached increased significance and the early 1990s witnessed a considerable number of articles on the subject.

Exhibit 1.6: The Malcolm Baldrige National Quality Award

Congress established the award programme in 1987 to raise awareness about quality management and to recognise US companies that have successful quality management systems.

The award programme focuses on quality as an integral part of today's business management practices. The award's criteria are widely accepted as the standard for quality excellence in business performance. They are designed to help companies deliver ever-improving value to customers and improve overall company performance and capabilities.

For many companies that make quality a part of doing business, the end result is better employee relations, higher productivity, greater customer satisfaction, increased market share and improved profitability. According to a recent report by the Conference Board, a business membership organisation, "A majority of large US firms have used the criteria of the Malcolm Baldrige National Quality Award for self-improvement, and the evidence suggests a long-term link between use of the Baldrige criteria and improved business performance".

The award is not given for specific products or services. Two awards may be given annually in each of the three categories: manufacturing, service and small business.

Source: The US Commerce Department's National Institute of Standards and Technology (NIST), which manages the award in close co-operation with the private sector.

Despite this upsurge of interest, in comparison to other service industry sectors the quality concept in tourism organisations remains understudied. There is a paucity of material on service quality in the hospitality sector and few studies have attempted to examine the operation and implementation of quality principles in hospitality settings.

The lack of considered study of quality issues in the tourism sector is not because of a lack of material. Many holiday companies do have product and service quality measurement schemes. In particular, tour operators closely monitor the reactions of holiday makers to their holidays, surveying them on return flights when they are a captive audience to avoid low response rates. Resort Condominiums International, the timeshare swap agency, monitors every holiday swap taken to every timeshare unit under their control. These are analysed and if any unit falls below standards and is not improved, it is withdrawn from the scheme. Such product quality control is particularly important in a sector of the industry which suffers from a poor image, even though it in itself does not sell timeshare.

Nevertheless, the academic evidence suggests that there remains much to be accomplished in our understanding of the management of quality in the 1990s. Commentators have argued that the quality concept is at an early stage of understanding and argue for a more rigorous analysis of the concept. For example, in early work on quality management in service industries, Johnston et al. (1990) expressed concern regarding the quality dimension in hotels and in particular the methods used to measure customer perceptions of hotel service quality. As Oberoi and Hales (1990: 701) remark in their work on quality within the hospitality industry: "In short, there is a clear need for further conceptual and methodological development in the area of service quality."

Significantly, recent research activities echo similar concerns regarding the quality concept. Ross (1994) suggests that thus far, service quality-related issues have received little research attention within the tourism/hospitality industry context. Additionally, Callan (1994: 496) offers support for undertaking studies of quality in hospitality organisations when he argues that

> . . . the years ahead will be a period when hospitality operations will serve an increasingly discerning public, who will not be prepared to accept poor quality services; they will complain and transfer allegiances to the providers of quality services. Hospitality providers must move along the road of "Total Quality Management".

Further, as Rees (1995) has pointed out in his research on hotel organisations, evidence suggests that hotel organisations are adopting "partial" quality management programmes:

> . . . while managers in Hotel Co. [case study example] were generally keen to stress how quality management has allowed employees to express their views more openly and take greater responsibility for their work, at the same time they acknowledge the clear trends towards the closer monitoring and tighter control of that work (Rees, 1995: 108).

Consequently, Olsen et al. (1995: 2), in a recent review, emphasise the need for fresh insights on service quality which question how organisations are utilising current concepts in an applied setting and contemplate new thoughts and applications. The fluid, albeit diverse, meanings associated with quality make it a "seductive and slippery philosophy" and point to the need for a greater understanding of its role and nature in service organisations. The management of quality

> . . . largely excludes consideration of ideas and evidence that might challenge or qualify its assumptions and prescriptions. To overcome this limitation, it is necessary to mobilise other traditions and perspectives, in order to acquire and develop a more measured . . . assessment of the theory and practice of managing quality (Wilkinson and Willmott, 1995: 15)

Themes Addressed

The material examined in this book is guided by the need to examine some of the deficiencies outlined above. Specifically, we recognise first the requirement to undertake a "broad-based examination" of quality management within the tourism industry in recognition of calls for a more comprehensive perspective on the quality dynamic. Secondly, the material is framed so as to take account of the growing number of contributions which suggest a "partial" dimension to the operation of quality management programmes in many organisations. While a large number of contributors have prescribed various approaches/guidelines to achieving a quality orientation, evidence from organisations involved in quality management programmes show that the exercise is far from straightforward. This is evidenced by the findings from research reports examined above and also in an article in *The Economist* (1992) which highlights the difficulties associated with the implementation of quality initiatives:

> ... despite some headline success stories ... there is mounting evidence that the quality programmes of many western companies are failing dismally.

The article poses the following question:

> If so many western companies believe they are at the mercy of quality, why are they finding it such a strain to get it right?

This question sets the tone for the material examined in this text. In particular, the authors are concerned to examine in a critical manner the practical realities of managing the "getting it right" philosophy.

Summary

There is a real need to understand the operation of quality management in contemporary tourism and hospitality organisations. Market realities of change and increased competitiveness have emphasised the importance of taking careful account of the quality message. Organisations across different industry sectors are showing a developing interest in the concept and in particular how they might apply quality principles for greater organisational advantage. This text aims to assist both students and managers by providing an up-to-date account of quality management issues: what is encompassed by quality and how might we apply it in practical organisational settings?

This chapter has attempted to place the material examined in this text in context. A starting point for any discussion of quality management is an introduction to the leading thinkers in the area. In this respect, we have tried to be thorough and have examined in detail developments in the area. The reader has been introduced to the quality philosophy and has been given an overview of how the philosophy has developed over the years. The discussion has also encompassed an outline of current perspectives on the subject and has throughout maintained a critical approach. Also, in keeping with the spirit of the text, readers are given the opportunity to apply some of the theoretical ideas in the review questions outlined below.

Review Questions

1. Consider some definitions of quality. How do these apply to a workplace of your choice?

2. How has thinking on quality developed over the years? Outline and appraise the various contributions.

3. Why has quality assumed importance in the 1990s? Why might an organisation consider evolving a quality orientation?

4. List organisations that you believe have achieved a quality focus. What explains their success?

5. Why is quality a difficult concept for the tourism and hospitality industry to define, measure and plan for?

Chapter 2

Strategic Analysis of the Hospitality Industry

Introduction

The tourism industry is one of the world's fastest growing industries and is already the world's largest service industry. In 1993, the World Tourist Organisation estimated growth in global travel from 450 million travellers in 1992 to 630 million by the year 2000. By the turn of the century, it is estimated that the tourism, technology and telecommunications industries will constitute the three "super-industries" driving the global economy. McRae (1995: 108) places the importance of the tourism industry in context when he writes:

> Tourism is the largest service industry of all and has enormous appetite for labour. In 1993, the tourism industry employed roughly 130 million people, more than any other industry in the world. Demand for tourism will continue to rise . . . all this growth will require yet more labour, often with new skills. . . .

The hospitality industry represents an important part of the wider tourism industry and in many countries has grown both in terms of the number of operational units and numbers employed within the sector. For example, in Ireland, tourism accounts for 8.5 per cent of GNP, generating over £3 billion in revenue and employing some 180,000 people. Similarly in Great Britain, the hotel industry accounts for roughly four per of GDP (National

Economic Development Office, 1992: 9). In 1992, approximately
1.3 million people were employed within the commercial sector of
the industry (restaurants, pubs, clubs, contract catering and hotels) while a further million worked in the non-commercial sector
(HCTC, 1994). In terms of employment, this amounts to almost
ten per cent of Great Britain's employed population and highlights the economic significance of the industry to the British
economy (Price, 1994).

Hospitality and Economic Cycles

However, in the last decade, the industry has been subject to the
inevitable downward spiral of business and property prices that
ensued after a decade of prosperity and rapid expansion in the
1980s. Between 1986 and 1992, the US hospitality industry lost
close to $14 billion. Commentators have described such a period as
one of the most difficult for the lodging industry in the twentieth
century. As well as declining property values, factors such as ex-
cessive debt, economic recession and the Gulf War crisis have all
contributed to the current situation. An article in *The Economist*
(1992) states the problem as follows:

> One in every two hotels in the country has been in trouble;
> three quarters of those built since 1986 have been in serious
> difficulty. Financial institutions are now America's biggest
> hotel owners — and most want to be shot of their investment.

A lot of investment was channelled into hotels in the 1980s, which
increased the room supply and property portfolios of many companies. Consequently, the ensuing slump of the early 1990s meant
that many hotels went into receivership:

> These are hard times for Europe's hoteliers. After several
> years of heady expansion in the 1980s, some of the region's
> leading hotel groups have been left with big financial head-
> aches. Now groups covering a much broader range of hotel

categories, such as France's Accor, are having to tighten their belts (*The Economist*, 12 June 1993, p. 77).

Consider the Marriott Corp., outlined in Exhibit 2.1 below. After rapid expansion of its hotel chains in the 1980s was stalled by a poor real estate market and the recession, Marriott had to evolve different strategic approaches to outmanoeuvre rivals.

Exhibit 2.1: Know When to Change the Game

Fast-growing hotelier Marriott was tearing along like a high-speed train during the 1980s when it was derailed by the triple whammy of a collapsed real estate market, an oversupply of hotel rooms, and a lingering recession. Between 1989 and 1992, profits tumbled by half, capital spending plunged from $1.4 billion to $210 million dollars, and Marriott was nearly buried under $3.6 billion debt. So Bill Marriott decided to trade on the company's most valuable asset — the Marriott brand name — and move into franchising. From a base of 21 per cent of hotels franchised in 1989, Marriott now franchises almost 27 per cent and plans to raise that to more than 50 per cent by the turn of the century.

For all its troubles, Marriott's basic operations have been sound. While industry occupancy rates have averaged less than the 66 per cent break-even point for several years, Marriott's have remained high at 75 per cent. In a recent survey conducted amongst *Fortune* readers, it was shown that between 1988 and 1992, the numbers who had checked into a Marriott hotel in the past twelve months had jumped from 47 per cent to 70 per cent (No. 2, Holiday Inn, fell from 48 per cent to 32 per cent).

Source: Fortune, 28 June 1993, p. 101

This contrasts sharply with current levels of tourism performance world-wide. In Ireland, for instance, the number of visitors have doubled since 1988 and the levels of investment in tourism infrastructure and facilities have been significant. Tourism has outperformed most other sectors and has contributed greatly to economic and employment growth. Similar performance levels have been reported within the British sector. In their review on developments within the industry, Pannel Kerr Forster (1995) reveal that occupancy rates in many markets have reached their highest level in over a decade. In Great Britain, for example, the average occupancy rate for 1995 was 81.9 per cent, up 2.2 points on 1994. The report states that:

> ... after crippling price competition and low occupancy rates around the world, only those regions dogged by political in- stability or terrorist activity, or experiencing economic slow- down, are still being squeezed (Pannel Kerr Forster, 1995).

Other indicators also suggested strong growth within the indus- try: again in Britain, the average achieved rate for occupied rooms increased by over five per cent compared with 1994; average rooms yield per available room increased by over 13 per cent on 1994. This is not specific to the British market. Occupancy rates have risen to some 60 per cent in continental Europe and 80–90 per cent in the US.

Indeed, the above findings have been borne out by other in- dustry reports. In its world-wide hotel study, Horwath and Hor- wath (1995) showed that British hotel operators were the most efficient in Europe, with the highest room occupancy, the highest gross operating profit and second-highest pre-tax income per available room (even though they charged the lowest average room rate). These developments have also been accompanied by changes in the nature and characteristics of the hospitality indus- try, to which we now turn our attention.

Characteristics of the Hospitality Industry

The hospitality industry comprises hotels, restaurants, pubs and clubs, guesthouses, self-catering operations, leisure and sports facilities. The largest sector within the hospitality industry is ac- counted for by hotels; hence the measure of discussion given to hotels within the text. These encompass a wide variety of accom- modation types, ranging from guesthouses and inns to hotels and motorway lodges. In Great Britain, independent operators account for 85 per cent of the total number of hotels and 65 per cent of the total number of bedrooms (Jordans Report, 1991). Although the total number of hotels within the industry is difficult to ascertain, it is estimated that there are some 20,000 hotels providing approximately 500,000 rooms. Over 70 per cent of hotels are estimated to have less than 25 rooms, with nearly 90 per cent having less than 50 rooms (Hotels Group Directory, 1992). It has also been pointed out that 87 per cent of all hotel establishments employ (on average) between one and ten people and 70 per cent of hotels are operated by self-employed owner-managers (HCTC, 1994: 23–4). Similarly, across Europe it is estimated that approximately two million rooms are offered by privately owned hotels, most of them small family-owned concerns (*The Economist*, 1992).

The US is commonly regarded as having one of the most highly developed hospitality industries. The sophisticated nature of the industry is shown by the high ownership concentration and strong levels of brand proliferation. The industry in the US is also noted for innovation and its adaptability to new concepts, ideas and best practices. Notable innovations within the industry in the US include the following:

- Establishment of the first US hotel management company by Western Hotels (now Westin);

- Sheraton's development of the "reservatron", the industry's first automated electronic reservations system, and the first toll-free reservations number;

- Development of the fast-food concept by Ray Kroc; and

- The accomplishments of the Ritz-Carlton hotel group in becoming the first hospitality company to win the prestigious Malcolm Baldrige National Quality Award (JHIC, 1998).

Edgar and Taylor (1996: 7) suggest the following characteristics common to hospitality organisations:

- Highly labour-intensive
- Operating in complex and dynamic environments
- Predominately composed of small independent enterprises
- Spatially disaggregated and fragmented.

Repeatedly, therefore, the literature makes reference to the fragmented nature of the hospitality industry, which is described by Porter (1980: 191) as "an industry in which no firm has a significant market share and can strongly influence industry outcome".

However, despite the emphasis which writers have placed on the fragmented nature of the industry, there is growing evidence to suggest that the industry is becoming more consolidated. The pressures for increased international presence, and market share, amongst hospitality companies has heightened competition within the industry and has led to a greater consolidation of ownership within the hotel sector. Writing about the changing nature of competition within the industry, Purcell (1993: 129) comments:

> Multidivisional and multinational organisations have become increasingly important and influential components of both the commercial and institutional sectors. Mergers and takeovers within the industry and the entry of "new players" has changed the structure of the industry, with the effect that a shrinking number of very large groups increasingly employ a growing proportion of the industry's workforce. Competition for customers and staff has become increasingly international.

Consolidation within the Hospitality Industry

Consolidation has been a major feature of the industry in recent years. Increased competition and the drive towards globalisation have forced companies to increase the size of their operations so as to achieve greater clout in marketing terms and gain scale economies by combining sales, systems, marketing activities and administration. Within the industry, the market leaders tend to be the chain groups where the pattern of acquisitions and takeovers has been witnessed on an increasing scale:

> The latter third of this century has witnessed a shift away from the entrepreneurial, independent operator to the dominance of complex, multinational and multidivisional hospitality firms. Today the hospitality organisation is rich in diversity of function and form (Becker and Olsen, 1995: 39).

The most significant development in recent years has been the £3.9 billion takeover of Forte, Britain's largest hotel group, by Granada, the British television and leisure company. With this deal, Granada hopes to integrate Forte's roadside restaurants and mid-market and budget hotels — Posthouse and Travelodge — with Granada's own operations. Other developments include Forte's purchase of Meridien in 1994 and Marriott International's 49 per cent stake in Ritz-Carlton, the Atlanta-based group. Further, ITT Sheraton Corp has recently acquired Ciga Hotels, the Italian luxury hotel chain, for an estimated $80 million. With this acquisition, Sheraton assumes the management responsibilities for Ciga's 38 hotels, most of which are located in Europe. The acquisition forms part of an overall strategy to position Sheraton as a major player in the luxury gambling sectors of the hospitality industry in Ireland.

Jurys Hotel Group, the largest publicly quoted hotel group in the Republic of Ireland, has decided to merge with the largest family-owned hotel group, the Doyle Hotel Group. This proposed combined group will contain a portfolio of 25 hotels under three separate brands located in the Republic of Ireland, Great Britain and the US.

The number of changes in brand affiliations has also grown in the last decade. Customers appear less concerned with changes in ownership and have more interest in quality, "value-for-money" exchanges. In fact, merger and brand affiliation changes are reported to have increased overall standards of service for the customer.

In Great Britain, publicly quoted hotel companies now constitute a quarter of total room stock, significantly higher than the European average of 14 per cent (Pizam and Knowles, 1994). As Harrison (1996) points out:

> Year on year, publicly quoted hotel chains have augmented their domination of UK hotel room supply, culminating with 34 per cent in 1993.

A recent study shows that between 1989 and 1992 the stock of hotel rooms in Europe belonging to publicly quoted groups grew by a fifth, to 340,000 (*The Economist*, 1993). This is a pattern that looks destined to continue. Commentators argue that, as quoted chains account for an average of only 14 per cent of hotel rooms on offer in EU countries, there is room for further growth and development. The Hyatt chain, for example, is currently attempting to grow its business and build a presence in Europe. Similarly, Choice Hotels International, another American group that specialises in hotel franchising, is gradually developing its operations across EU countries.

Recent hotel acquisitions point to a desire on behalf of the acquirer to restructure, rather than expand. Many hotels, for example, who in the 1980s acquired businesses in the hope of achieving economies of scale through increased diversity, are having to divest themselves of non-core activities in the race for competitive advantage. Examples here include the decision by Granada, on taking over Forte, to refocus efforts away from the bigger hotels to the middle range of the market. Granada intends to dispose of Forte's international hotels — the Exclusive and Meridien groups which have a value of £1.6 billion — and to sell Forte's stake (68 per cent) in the luxury Savoy group of hotels. Further examples include the decision by Four Seasons, the luxury Toronto-based hotel group, to divest itself of property assets and the divestment of Copthorne Hotels by Aer Lingus, the Irish state-owned airline.

Indeed, there is now a trend away from airline ownership of hotels, especially in the deregulated US industry. This trend is not specific to the American market. For example, after entering the hotel business in 1980 by establishing SWISSOTEL, a joint venture with Nestle, Swissair is considering reducing its involvement in hotels to focus increasingly on its core business. In a similar vein, Lufthansa has sold 22 per cent of its 42.6 per cent stake in Kempinski Hotels to Advanta Investors Group so as to achieve a sharper focus on its core business of air transport.

History may give us a little insight into why this position of "double peaking and troughing" of profits between airlines and hotels is prevalent. The first airline–hotel relationship was between Pan Am and Intercontinental Hotels. American economic expansion programmes required the development of business interests overseas, particularly into Mexico. American businessmen would not stay in Mexican hotels as they did not have the luxury and service they were used to. The American government approached Pan Am to develop the first transnational hotel chain. From the outset, the fortunes of the transnational hotel chain were intimately liked to the fortunes of the airline industry.

Other organisations have restructured through "demerger", so as to separate their hotel management and property management skills. For example, Marriott Corporation has split into two separate companies: Host Marriott, which deals with real estate and debt issues, and Marriott International, which deals with hotel management. This demerger illustrates the value that can be realised by separating hotel management and property skills. It also fits well with the current emphasis on demerger, where investors tend to value the parts of the company more than the whole, "partly because sharper focus is believed to enhance performance" (Daneshkhu, 1996).

Growing Importance of Strategic Alliances

There is no disputing the fact that the hotel industry is fast becoming a global industry, whereby hotel chains are developing
into giant multinational corporations with world-wide presence.
However, the industry has still some way to go in terms of globalisation. This adds weight to a recent Economist Intelligence Unit
(EIU, 1996) report which argues that, although cross-border ties
are becoming an increasing feature of the hotel industry, there is
still no hotel group that is truly global. The report revealed that
the most geographically widespread hotel companies were represented in less than a third of all countries; this shows that hotel
organisations have a significant way to go before claiming global
status.

This helps to explain the growing impetus towards creating an
international presence that exists within the hospitality sector. Go
and Pine's (1995) work highlights the increasing pace at which
alliances are being developed within the industry. The appeal of
alliances and joint ventures lies in the smaller amounts of equity
needed to finance such arrangements. Recent contributions suggest that strategic alliances will increase in importance and will be
driven by a variety of factors. These will include the ability to
plug gaps geographically and to strengthen particular segments,
whether at the upmarket, mid-market or budget end. In particular, the EIU report makes the following point concerning the
growing significance of strategic alliances:

> Such alliances allow companies to make cost savings because
> of their greater combined purchasing power and a lower re-
> quirement for investment in information technology for the
> development of reservation systems (EIU, 1996).

The trend for alliance building is not just limited to the hotel sector. Alliances and "buy-ins" have been a feature of the global airline industry throughout the late 1980s and 1990s. British Airways
has entered into strategic alliances with American Airlines on

transatlantic routes and on routes to Poland — here they share codes and frequent flyer benefits, and market jointly. Such alliances have been brought about by the need for airlines to be able to serve the global market whilst being restricted by access to air routes. The alliances allow for through-ticketing between airlines, the sharing of reservation systems and loyalty schemes. Such is the state of integration proposed by British Airways and American Airlines in 1998 that European competition ministers are studying merger proposals that would see these two carriers gaining a stranglehold on transatlantic flights.

Technological advances within the industry have also strengthened the case for focusing on strategic alliances. In technological terms, hotel organisations have to invest substantial amounts of money in an area that is outside their core skills and as a result the systems developed are often not sufficient to keep pace with customer demands in the marketplace. Smaller operators, in this instance, are finding it particularly difficult to stay abreast of technological developments and are having to ally themselves with other, mainly larger, companies to reap the benefits of central reservation systems. As Pizam and Knowles (1994: 291) point out: "The biggest companies are expanding fast at the expense of the smaller companies and independents".

Recent years have thus witnessed the announcement of a number of important strategic alliances within the world-wide hospitality industry: the Bonaparte hotel group has teamed up with Radisson SAS to benefit from its sophisticated reservation system, while at the same time allowing Radisson to move rapidly into southern Europe. Also, Intercontinental Hotels and Resorts has entered into an agreement with Southern Sun, South Africa's largest hotel group, to operate hotels in South Africa, while allowing Intercontinental rapid entry into an emerging economy. Exhibit 2.2 tracks the development of Accor's Asian growth strategy and serves to illustrate the international nature of the hospitality business.

Exhibit 2.2: Accor Reports Success with Asian Growth Strategy

Accor, which operates 114 hotels representing 17,000 rooms in the Asia-Pacific region, is in the process of building another 56 properties. Plans call for the company to be operating 170 hotels with over 31,000 rooms by the turn of the century. According to Ray Capdevila, the President of Accor's Asia Pacific Corp. (AAPC) a further increase in the size of Accor's portfolio will be no problem, as capital investment has been plentiful.

AAPC announced in mid-December a "business co-operation agreement" with Japan's The Hokke Club, "designed to create Japan's first international hotel chain aimed at the middle market". Announcing the agreement, Sadanao Kojima, chairman of the Hokke Club, said that his group had chosen AAPC as a partner because of its proven record of successful hotel management in the Asia Pacific region, and because the two companies shared a strategy focused on providing quality accommodation at affordable prices.

"The middle of the market is where the potential for growth lies in the Japanese hotel industry, now being far more complex and challenging than in the past", Kojima said. "To perform to an optimum level, we need the support of a company with international connections and a strong corporate philosophy".

Source: Hotel & Motel Management, 6 May 1996, p. 8.

Other significant strategic developments concluded in 1995 are summarised in Table 2.1 below.

Table 2.1: Examples of Strategic Partnerships Concluded within Hotel and Catering Industry, 1996

Companies	Amount (million £)
Granada/Pavillion	125
CDL/Copthorne Hotels	224
Compass/Eurest	580
Sodexho/Gardner Merchant	730
Whitbread/Marriott (franchised hotels)	180
Bass/Harvester (restaurant chain)	165
Barclay Brothers/Ritz Hotel (London)	75
Landmark/Regent Hotel (London)	70

Source: Adapted from Quest (1996).

These developments show the expansion of well-known British groups within Britain (Granada, Bass and Whitbread); the expansion of British groups overseas (Granada, Compass and Gardner Merchant) and the growing interest shown by overseas groups in the British hotel and catering industry (Sodexho, CDL and Landmark) (Quest, 1996).

Management Contracts and Franchising

Recent years have also witnessed the growth in popularity of management contracts as a means of expanding a company's influence in the market. Across the industry world-wide, the ownership of hotel properties is becoming separated from their management, which is being contracted out to big international hotel chains. During the recession, the fall in hotel asset values and the corresponding drop in occupancy levels meant that hotel organisations were shying away from investing in new property assets. As a result, management contracts grew in significance, with hoteliers favouring the notion of managing over owning. As the competition for capital went global, hoteliers were significantly more constrained in their development efforts. One observer makes the point when he writes:

> . . . the raising of development capital was once a question of one hotel company competing for funding against other similar organisations. This has changed. In today's global market, a hotel company may be competing with a textile plant in Taiwan, a chemical plant in Germany or an electronics plant in Belgium for the same capital. So there are constraints on development because of this competition (Hine, 1995: 26).

Instead, therefore, modern operators are seeking to expand principally through franchise or management contracts. In 1992, for example, Jarvis Hotels created a new hotel division, Jarvis International, armed with the task of acquiring management contracts from third parties such as banks and financial institutions. Similarly, Ladbroke, the hotels and betting company which owns Hilton International, split its company into property management and operational management to increase returns and improve performance. The decision to split the company was justified on the basis that Ladbrokes was more effective at operating hotels than managing assets.

However, pursuing growth through management contracts is becoming more competitive. Given the growth of popularity of the management contract, hotel owners have a wider choice of groups from which to select. Instead of being granted three per cent of turnover and ten per cent of gross operating profit, managing companies under the present competitive climate are more likely to settle for two per cent of turnover and eight per cent of gross operating profit. Additionally, investors now "demand that the operating company takes a partial equity stake or guarantees specific rates of return" (*Financial Times*, 1996). Some argue that recent developments are reminiscent of the 1950s, when investors generally brought in outside managers with a traditional leasehold contract. As a recent contribution points out:

> It certainly marks a break with the 25 go-go years before 1990.
> Now all that remains is for hotels to rediscover old style standards of service (*The Economist*, 1992).

Perhaps the trend goes back further still. The regional railways which preceded the nationalisation of British Rail were the first to build hotels in England with the opening of the St Pancras hotel in 1838. This was run as a management agreement with the manager gaining 25 per cent of annual profits less a ground rent of £1,000 and ten per cent of operating costs, rates and taxes.

While expanding their joint portfolio to 140 hotels, the joint railways board recognised that the management agreements did not ensure equality of provision. In 1850 they set up their own hotel consortium, employing professional hotel managers from

France and Germany. In 1962 the consortium became a subsidiary company of the nationalised British rail board, of which Charles Forte was a member. Their assets were eventually sold off between 1979 and 1983 due to a decline in profitability brought about by poor management, lack of investment and a decline in railway passenger numbers.

Franchising and branding have also increased in importance within the hospitality sector. Previously, franchising as a growth option was not highly regarded within the industry because of concerns about quality control. However, in recent years franchising has attracted increased attention within the industry. Potential franchisees or investors have more choices than ever. New brands are proliferating as established companies spread their wings, moving into different industry segments or niche marketing. For example, Holiday Inn has expanded rapidly through franchising. The company franchises or operates more than 2,000 hotels and aims to increase that number to 3,000 hotels by the end of 1998. Intercontinental has also franchised some of its three- and four-star brands while Hilton International have recently expressed interest in franchising a new three-star Hilton brand.

Again, parallels exist with the airline industry. Large airline groups concentrate their efforts on their main, often transatlantic routes, whilst franchising out their name and marketing experience to the more local intra-continental routes. An example would be Virgin Airways franchising out their London–Dublin route.

There is also a trend in which hotels are forging closer partnerships with brand name restaurants in an effort to attract customers and improve profits. As Exhibit 2.3 highlights, hoteliers have discovered that operating restaurants has proved too costly with customers preferring to purchase brand name products.

Exhibit 2.3: High Recognition Restaurants

To bring guests closer to a full service hotel experience at limited-service hotel prices, chains are adding brand-name restaurants to their hotels — and the strategy is proving profitable. The idea of co-branding, combining two brand-name properties to maximise the market value of both, has been slow to catch on because hotel general managers were often sure they knew how to run a restaurant.

But research has shown that people are more likely to buy brand-name products. So why re-invent the restaurant when a brand name will do the job even better? Brand names work in that they give the customer an even better value than what they might get at a full-service hotel: the argument being that customers these days want a value proposition, not a status proposition.

Another advantage to co-branding is that hotels and restaurants can work together to open otherwise untapped markets to each other. Choice Hotels has signed a deal with Pizza Hut to make them the sole pizza-delivery company to their limited service hotels. "We're hoping that loyal Pizza Hut customers will come to us when they go on vacation, and vice versa", comments Betsy O'Rourke, vice president of marketing for Choice Hotels International. "Neither of us is dependent on the other, but we can certainly help supplement each other's customer base."

Source: Hotel and Motel Management, 18 September 1995, p. 43.

Another example is that of Principal Hotels, UK, who are now developing their own brands in order to improve their food and beverage trade. Developing brands include the "Copper Face Jack" bar and "Boston Stake Out" restaurant. Principal Hotels believe they will gain 75 per cent of their business from outside the hotel.

Franchising has proved successful because, from the franchiser's point of view, control can be exercised solely through financial rather then managerial means, while the franchisee enjoys market profile by trading under brand names that are well established. They also avoid the risks associated with start-up because of the acquired knowledge of "parent" companies (Goffee and Scase, 1995). The approach also opens the fastest route to growth:

neither of the two major hotel franchise companies — Holiday
Inn and Choice — could have developed to their present size
if they had to finance the construction of their hotels themselves (Quest, 1996: 12).

Substantial marketing benefits also accompany the franchising
approach, as franchisers spend large amounts of money on marketing and advertising their brands. Choice, for example, has an
annual marketing budget of $60 million to help market its brands
as household names in key markets (Quest, 1996).

Impact of Technology

Technological developments have also underlined the importance
of strategic alliances within the industry. Earlier it was noted how
smaller firms were allying with larger concerns in an attempt to
reap the benefits of computerised reservation systems. Technological advances, however, have also increased the amount of
capital required to enter the industry and have in the process created entry barriers for companies hoping to pursue opportunities
in particular markets:

> Technology will become one of the most competitive methods
> that chains will employ to ensure growth. . . . technology will
> shape marketing programs, product design and corporate
> strategies (Olsen, 1993: 63).

The main attraction of investment in technology is the significant
contribution which it makes to lowering overall costs, and providing the quick and reliable response needed to satisfy customers in today's competitive marketplace. In this respect, technology
alters the possibilities for service delivery and assists in the more
effective management of customer expectations (Segal-Horn,
1994). Exhibit 2.4 shows that a strategy that combines the traditional and the interactive will provide for enhanced guest service
and greater overall organisational effectiveness.

Exhibit 2.4: It is Time to Enlarge the Pie

Just as colour television and pay TV first broke through in hotels, the information superhighway will pervade the hotel industry before the residential market. How about using the common infrastructure to enhance the pie for everyone rather than fight over crumbs and pieces?

We've entered an era in which the in-room guest experience is much more than a bed for the night. The combination of conventional movie-based entertainment systems and interactive programming leads to a series of valuable new guest services and programmes such as interactive guest information, multimedia reservation services, interactive shopping, visitor information, even voice mail or fax or TV.

Many of these will become as essential to guest service as room service is today, and will be key to defining and maintaining a brand identity. That's why hotel groups must manage this evolving infrastructure well, in co-operation with infrastructure suppliers and the developers of interactive programmes.

Ultimately, the words "partnership" and "interactive" must become positive additions to the vocabulary of the hotel industry. Implementing those concepts helps everyone enlarge the pie and ends fighting over crumbs.

Source: Lodging Hospitality, December 1995, p. 83.

Particularly, IT has assisted in the development of economies of scale by providing the necessary integration and focus that is required to facilitate the process. As Goffee and Scase (1995: 118) point out, economies of scale have benefited Britain hotel organisations, particularly the large-scale operators, because they

> increase buying power with suppliers, enabling them to centralise administrative activities and providing them with the resources to fund new ventures and products.

For example, global computerised reservation systems (CRS) are receiving increasing attention from the hotel industry. Harrison (1996) argues that in terms of bookings:

automated transactions have shown a phenomenal increase —
from 200,000 in 1981 to 15.5 million bookings in 1993.

This is also borne out by a recent study in *The Economist* (1992)
which argues that computerised on-line reservation systems are
pushing the industry to consolidate

to achieve the necessary scale and muscle to be listed on travel
agents' screens, or tied into airlines' frequent-flyer programmes.

The systems were originally developed by airline organisations
but have now been applied to travel marketing and distribution
systems.

A survey in the *Financial Times* (1995) has also argued that hotels are using technology to provide customers with the flexibility
of service which they demand. In particular, the article pointed
out how technological systems are being used by hotels to assist
with the development of efficient check-in/check-out procedures
and to provide customers, through interactive television services,
with a range of services which they would previously have had to
arrange on the telephone. The author of the article points out that
it is this more effective integration of technology into the service
process which is allowing "companies to improve their range and
quality of services" to existing and prospective guests
(Daneshkhu, 1995). As Exhibit 2.5 points out, hotel organisations
have to tailor their services to meet the needs of the frequent
business traveller. This is in response to the results emanating
from surveys showing that a clear majority of business travellers
are increasingly using their rooms as offices.

Exhibit 2.5: Rooms that Work

Hoteliers are rapidly moving away from perceiving their guest rooms as simply a "home-away-from-home" and instead are steadily seeking to replicate the office environment. Westin Hotels, for example, has plans for rooms where beds, at the touch of a button, are concealed in a wall compartment and replaced by a couch to give the room a more businesslike appearance. Marriott is bringing in the rather curiously named "Room That Works" concept into its major hotels: these feature a large console table and mobile writing-desk, two power outlets and a PC modem jack mounted into the console top, a movable desk light and an ergonomically designed chair. According to Marriott's research of over 1,000 frequent business travellers, some 70 per cent said they used their rooms as an office when on business.

By the turn of the century, hoteliers predict that PCs, perhaps with a videophone facility, will become standard for executive rooms in the top international chains. "We recognise that keeping in touch is the key requirement for business travellers now", says Hyatt's Jim Evans [senior marketing vice president].

Source: Adapted from *Management Today*, October 1995, p. 96.

Internet facilities will assume even greater importance in the future as Internet commerce (or "E-commerce") grows in significance. It is estimated that over 50 per cent of US households have access to the Internet. Although travel bookings over the Internet are still relatively low, interest is growing rapidly. Such bookings allow providers to tailor their services carefully to the needs of their customers.

For example, Forte has equipped the Cumberland Hotel, London with World Wide Web facilities in guestrooms. Working through the television screen using a wireless keyboard, the project manager Mike Allison considered that "business travellers need to have an office wherever they are, including a hotel room". The web would also be available for tourists to use to gain information about London's entertainment, films and restaurants.

If successful, 18 of the Forte hotels in London could have this facility.

The Irish government has been quick to recognise the potential of the Internet, particularly from a tourism perspective. In its recent review of the industry, the Irish Tourist Industry Confederation has established that awareness of IT and a willingness to adapt and apply new innovations in technology will emerge as key issues for efficient working in a wide range of tourism businesses. It recommends that IT should be at the core of identifying and promoting significant segments of Irish tourism world-wide (ITIC, 1998).

Emerging Developments

Drawing together the foregoing observations, it is possible to suggest that three main themes dominate the hotel industry world-wide: increased consolidation; growth in emphasis on franchising and management contracts; and growth in attention given to strategic alliances. These emerging developments suggest that the industry will become less fragmented in the decade ahead as key players strive for ever-increasing market share in a highly competitive marketplace. Porter (1980) argues that the absence of market leaders with power to shape the industry is the most significant competitive feature of fragmented industries. However, the evidence above points to the emergence of a small number of "market leaders" who, through their international presence, have power to influence and shape the British hotel industry. In a recent report, the Economist Intelligence Unit (1996) has argued that if one were to examine the British hotel industry, it would be noted that the industry is heavily influenced by a small number of big participants. The report suggests that companies such as Holiday Inn and Marriott are in the strongest positions to influence the market and present a significant threat to domestic operators.

These key players are increasingly attracted by the potential opportunities for growth and development within the hospitality sector. In particular, operators are influenced by recent industry analyses, such as that generated by *Fortune*, which showed that hoteliers who barely broke even in 1992 made operating profits of $3.3 billion in 1993. The study also shows that such trends have staying power. Specifically, it states:

> With excess capacity built during the eighties finally under control, occupancy rates are climbing. Demand for rooms will increase at four times the rate of new supply in 1996 (*Fortune*, 1996).

For example, Sofitel has embarked on a successful strategy of internationalisation with hotels being constructed and acquired across the globe. The French hotel chain comprises 100 hotels with 20,000 rooms. In Europe, it has 54 hotels in 12 countries. In the Americas, it has 16 hotels in three countries. In Asia and the South Pacific Islands, it has 18 hotels in six countries and five islands.

Segal-Horn (1994) has reached a similar conclusion in her work on the subject. Specifically, she argues that in the various service sectors reviewed,

> the current structure of service industries no longer fits the pattern of "fragmented" industries. They have become significantly concentrated and capital intensive with increased barriers to entry (p. 52).

She also suggests that in the last 20–30 years, service industries have been characterised by a prolonged process of concentration and rationalisation and have witnessed the emergence of very large organisations across the various service sectors. The emergence of these large organisations, which share an interest in establishing identifiable world-wide market presence, carries significant implications for domestic operators. Such developments significantly threaten the positions of currently strong domestic competitors and argues the requirement for organisations to exploit key strengths to "avoid the gradual erosion of domestic markets to new international competition" (Segal-Horn, 1994: 61).

This pattern of consolidated dominance of key markets by a few players is reflected also in the retail tourism industry. Here the large tour operators, such as Thomsons, Airtours and First Choice, have come to dominate the package tour business in Great Britain, having between them a market share of over 50 per cent. They have also integrated other parts of the distribution chain, such that they are now not only tour operators but own the major high street travel agents, charter airlines and even some hotels in the major Mediterranean destinations.

Tourism has always been known as a fragmented market, but within the large, profitable market segments, consolidation and integration create dominance by a few major players. It is the small, regional operations that are not part of a consortium, chain or integrated company that still suffer from the perils of fragmentation and find it hard to break into the profitable market segments.

In this changed environment, there is thus value in analysing the nature of the hospitality industry in greater detail and, in particular, in examining how the exploitation of key strengths, such as quality, can aid the search for customers and competitive advantage. This was one of the main motivating factors behind the introduction of the "Quality Employer Initiative" by the Irish Hotels Federation. The initiative aims to evaluate its members against basic standards on the recruitment and selection of staff, conditions of employment, training, working hours and the provision of pensions. The Federation eventually hopes to make conformance to the Quality Employer standard a condition of membership of the association. The scheme is widely regarded as offering the industry a competitive advantage in the labour market, as no other industry has anything similar in place.

In Britain, a recent study by the National Economic Development Office entitled *UK Tourism: Competing for Growth* (1992), concern was expressed about the poor quality standards in British hotels compared to hotels in Germany and France. One of the seven recommendations offered by the report relates directly to quality improvement:

> Quality — to do consistently what you say you are going to do so that the customer gets what he or she reasonably expects — this is critical to the UK's future success in the competitive world market. The industry must achieve world-class standards; and concentrate on the management of quality (NEDO, 1992: 7).

In a similar vein, reports on the European hotel industry highlight the strategic importance of focusing on quality and service in an increasingly competitive marketplace. The study shows that liberalised rules for the service industry will be accompanied by lower hotel room rates and wider choices of accommodations within Europe. In this changed environment, Fried (1990) states that, "despite the possibilities for greater hotel expansion, the focus on service will remain strong".

Exhibit 2.6 shows how the Four Seasons Hotel Group has effectively applied high standards of quality and service to secure important advantages over competitors in the marketplace. In short, the group has set the standard for luxury hotel customer service.

Exhibit 2.6: Quality and Competitive Advantage at Four Seasons Hotels

Travelers familiar with deluxe hotels are generally aware of the Four Seasons name. Founded in 1961 with the Four Seasons Motor Hotel in Toronto, one of the company's stated objectives is to operate the finest hotel in each destination in which it locates. Its success to date has three principal underpinnings:

- Its commitment to provide its clients with value-added service and problem-free stays.

- Its unrelenting quest for innovation. For example, Four Seasons was the first hotel corporation to employ concierges company-wide in North America. As another example, the company provides overnight repair services for sandals and golf shoes.

- Its controlled expansion. Growth was based on what the company felt it could do. That prevented the company from getting caught in an extended position in the investment frenzy of the 1980s.

Four Seasons has firmly established its niche of operating hotels with 200 to 400 rooms. It expanded to London in 1970 with the opening of the 230-room Inn on the Park, now known as the Four Seasons London, which has been recognised as one of the most successful hotels in the world for quality and consistency. The company entered the US market in 1977 by acquiring the Chicago Ritz-Carlton. Also, the group opened hotels in San Francisco and Washington DC, where it began to compete with such established chains as Hilton, Hyatt, Marriott and Westin.

The company trains its employees for a highly personalised approach to service in all hotels. Developing all aspects of employees' attitudes and job performance is critical to maintaining consistently high-quality performance. Emphasising its long-established principle of being an excellent servant for travelers' needs, the company has gained a reputation for quality service and innovation for both business and leisure travel. Those needs are met with elegant hotel structures and high quality operations. Supported by a group of employees skilled at delivering customer value while keeping costs down.

Source: "Four Seasons-Regent: Building a Global Presence in the Luxury Market", *Cornell Hotel and Restaurant and Administration Quarterly*, August 1996, pp. 58–66.

Research on the Tourism Industry

Given the clear economic importance and the changing competitive nature of the industry reported upon above, one would have expected the hospitality industry to have received significant treatment from researchers. However, relative to other service industries, it is fair to say that the sector has received little attention from mainstream management researchers (Guerrier, 1996a; Harrington and Akehurst, 1996a, 1996b, 1996c; Medlik, 1989).

Part of the reason why hotels have not received adequate attention in the general management literature arises from a perception, particularly from those operating in a hotel management field, that the hotel industry is somewhat different to other service industries. The argument that hotels and hotel-related research be considered a distinctive research field in its own right derives from a view that individuals who were trained in the hotels sector and work within it have a shared interest in generating research specific to this particular industry. However, this view has been questioned by a number of writers. For instance, in a recent article, Jones (1996) questions the sufficiency of such a view, arguing whether uniqueness is more than just espousing "shared values". Specifically, he comments:

> . . . is it enough to have shared values? . . . a paradigm is made up of a body of theory and a distinctive methodology. And it is here that the concept of hospitality as a paradigm falls apart. An extremely high proportion of hospitality research reports on studies that investigate a theory originating outside of hospitality. And the range of methodologies used to investigate hospitality research problems is extremely diverse. . . . the idea of hospitality research exists more in form than in substance (Jones, 1996: 7).

Others writers are also critical of the notion that the hotel industry is in some way unique. In particular, Guerrier (1996a) has argued that since commentators have perceived hotels to be a rather specialist type of business, with emphasis being placed on technical knowledge rather than general management skills, so theorists interested in hotel management have been encouraged to work outside a mainstream management perspective. The writer remarks, however, that hotels have not generated a simultaneous level of interest in the general management literature:

> . . . a feature of hotel management is its insularity. . . . As hotel managers have been developed separately from other manag-

ers, so theorists interested in hotel management have worked outside mainstream management studies, taking the view that the hotel industry is unique. Conversely, the hotel industry has received little attention from mainstream management researchers (Guerrier, 1996a: 16).

This general attitude of insularity carries negative implications for research generated on the hotel industry since it "shields taken-for-granted industry practice from critical analysis by a wider audience" (Price, 1994: 44). Indeed, as Mullins (1993) remarks, the perception of the hospitality industry as being unique or different from other industries will not improve the standard of management. On the contrary, it may account for the lack of progress and change within the industry:

> Today's managers need to be competent to handle new areas of specialism and to process information at a far more sophisticated level than their predecessors (Purcell, 1993: 129).

Consequently, in a recent contribution Edgar and Taylor (1996: 269) argue the need for researchers in the hospitality field "to become more familiar with mainstream research and to move towards more proactive approaches that reflect leading edge practice".

However, Guerrier (1996a) also points out that there is evidence to suggest that that the barriers are beginning to break down and that hotels are beginning to be studied in a wider service industry context. In recent research studies, there is a recognition that hotel-related research needs to widen its focus and locate itself, in comparative terms, with service research emanating from other industry contexts (Lenehan, 1996). This is an encouraging development, especially since hotels share many of the characteristics common to service-based industries such as banking or retailing (Jones, 1989). The service features which are common to these industries may be outlined as follows:

1. More or less intangible

2. Processes or activities rather than things

3. Production and consumption are at least partly simultaneous processes

4. Perishable capacity

5. Consumers normally participate in the production process in one way or another

6. Labour intensive.

Indeed, the nature of service provision fits with the overall definition of services provided by the *Service Industries Journal*:

> Service industries . . . are taken to be those organisations and businesses which (regardless of ownership, profit/non-profit orientation and employee occupations) produce, and are inextricably bound up with the consumption process of, generally intangible products, where the consumer is a central fundamental component of the whole transfer and exchange process (Akehurst, 1985).

This perspective, which views the hotel organisation as sharing common characteristics with other service sectors, provides what Mullins (1993: 10) describes as

> a common point of reference and enables us to take a general approach to the study of hotels, to analyse them and to review the application of general management theory.

The reported study shares the above authors' concerns regarding the insular nature of the industry and concurs with the notion of locating hotel research in a broader general management perspective. In this sense, the authors view the hospitality organisation as a service firm which shares operating characteristics similar to other service organisations.

Importance of Quality

Thus, given that hospitality organisations share characteristics common to most other service organisations, it is fair to say that, in line with developments in other service sectors, quality will assume increased importance within the hospitality industry. Indeed, as a consequence of the changes occurring within the industry, particularly the level and intensity of competition within the domestic market commented upon earlier, it is possible to suggest quality management will warrant serious consideration by researchers in the field. As Martin (1996: 20) argues, although successful international companies have managed to build global brands for products and to some extent for services, they have rarely managed to impose "the same degree of standardised quality on the customer experience, but may increasingly have to do so".

Exhibit 2.7 shows how emphasis is again focusing on full-service strategic approaches. While other US operators have concentrated on developing limited-service hotels, John Q. Hammons Hotels has focused attention on developing full-service alternatives. This focus has been guided by the increased demand for higher quality service in customer circles and also by the precise lack of attention given to this variable by other service providers.

Exhibit 2.7: Comeback for the Full-service Hotel Strategy

After seven years on The Forbes 400, hotel developer John Q. Hammons dropped off in 1994 as new information about the extent of his financial leverage came to light. Since then his Springfield, Mo. based company, which owns or manages 38 hotels, mostly under Holiday Inn and Embassy Suites names, has stumbled. But that may change soon. Hammons has spent the past two years developing full-service hotels while the rest of the industry has built cheaper, limited-service hotels.

Hammons is convinced his full-service strategy will be vindicated. "I'm in a niche where it is hard for the competition to compete," he asserts. The tide may already be shifting. In this year's second quarter, cash flow rose 22 per cent on a 17 per cent increase in revenues. Commentators predict that Hammons' cash flow will continue to grow at a 17 per cent clip for the foreseeable future. And remember this: 77-year-old Hammons didn't become a centimillionaire by following the herd.

Source: *Forbes*, 14 October 1996, p. 20.

The Economist Intelligence Unit Report (1996) also offers support for a greater consideration of quality issues when it states:

> In the hotel market of the 1990s, it is essential to have a very clear strategy, be it to become global or to take a strong position in a region or a specific market segment, and to pursue it ruthlessly. Detailed attention must be paid to branding, quality, capacity management and marketing.

Summary

In line with developments in other service industries, the hospitality industry is undergoing a process of consolidation whereby key players are developing increased international presence through the mediums of franchising, management contracts and the establishment of strategic alliances. With a small number of large companies competing vigorously for increased world-wide market presence, the position of domestic hospitality operators is coming increasingly under threat.

In this environment, academic research on the hospitality sector carries particular significance, especially in the quality domain, where it can be shown that quality management can usefully be exploited to achieve competitive gain. However, research on the industry was noted for its insularity, with writers being slow to develop wider "mainstream" perspectives on management issues in hotels and other hospitality organisations. Additionally, it was discerned that hotels figured less prominently in the research studies carried out in the tourism and hospitality field, and inadequacies were highlighted in the treatment of quality in hospitality settings. Thus, in attempting to account for underlying changes within the industry, the material reported within this textbook will focus attention on quality management and will attempt to address the deficiencies in the treatment of this variable in the research on tourism and hospitality management.

Review Questions

1. Elaborate on key strategic developments emerging within the world-wide hospitality industry.

2. How would you explain the move towards consolidation within the hospitality industry? Can we expect increased consolidation in the coming years?

3. Is there evidence to suggest that globalisation is an important concern within the hospitality industry?

4. In what ways has competition for customers changed over the last number of years?

5. Contrast the hospitality industry to an industry of your choice. What can hospitality organisations learn from other industry sectors?

6. Are the apparently new structural issues of franchising, management contracts and consolidation really that innovative, or is the hospitality industry merely re-inventing past historic practice and borrowing ideas from others sectors?

Chapter 3

Strategic Quality-oriented Tourism Policies

In the previous chapters we have emphasised the growing significance attached to quality management in tourism businesses. In particular we highlighted the strategic importance of quality initiatives within the industry and also discussed the challenges involved in delivering quality services to customers. Much of this work on the importance of service quality focuses on the individual organisation. However, the problem that faces the strategic tourism planner, such as those found in the national tourist offices, and central government and regional agencies, is that they have to deal at a much more conceptual level. Tourism, being an economic sector, is really a collection of disparate industries that both compete with and complement each other. The intangible nature of the tourist's experience is such that all industry segments (e.g. accommodation, catering, entertainment, transport, environmental management, attractions, information provision and marketing) must be of sufficient standard if the tourist is to return to the destination on a repeat visit.

The problem that the strategic tourism planner faces, therefore, is complex: how does one co-ordinate quality standards across industries? How does one ensure that the tourist is made welcome and that staff are friendly when the organisations they encounter range from franchised fast food outlets to five star hotels, and from theme parks to heritage attractions? How does the planner ensure compliance to quality initiatives when they do not control the operational units?

Importance of Quality-Related Policies

Developing a strategy for the development of a national tourism product in a competitive marketplace, where products are increasingly differentiated by quality of provision and experience, is the challenge that Fayos-Sola (1996) considers to be the new paradigm for tourism. Examining the dynamics of competition within the tourism industry, he charts tourism policy development through three "generations":

1. Marketing-led policies of early mass tourism in the 1950s and 1960s

2. Product-led policy of the 1980s based around environmental, social and economic legislation to ameliorate negative impacts

3. Competitiveness-led policies of the 1990s based around quality, a positive role for government in creating the right economic conditions for success, increasing knowledge of market segmentation, new technology, and improving environmental conditions.

Fayos-Sola's proposals are based on an analysis of the changing national and regional policies within Spain following a decline in tourism numbers during the mid-1980s. Ten years later, the British and Irish governments have also begun to address a new set of policies to take account of the growing importance of quality issues in international tourism contexts. These case examples shall be considered in more detail later, following an exploration of the importance and nature of strategic quality-oriented tourism policies.

Quality at the Supra-national Scale

The European Union administers and promotes tourism initiatives through Directorate General XXIII for Enterprise Policy, Distributive Trades, Tourism and Co-operatives, but tends also to use other policy instruments, such as regional development, as delivery mechanisms. However, in the early 1990s DGXXIII identified core challenges that the Community had to address if this sector was to remain competitive. These were (European Commission, 1996):

1. The need to take better account of the requirements of the tourism industry at the appropriate levels [within the EU] to improve its operation and performance and the quality of its services;

2. The need to increase the industry's competitiveness by promoting growth in the medium term whilst respecting the environment and local populations affected;

3. The need to take account of the tourism industry's requirements in other fields of policy directly affecting the sector, particularly those tackled at EU level.

From these challenges, an action plan with a budget of 18 million ECU was elaborated in 1992. In addition to addressing these challenge areas, its additional goals were

> to improve the quality and competitiveness of the tourism sector on offer in the community and to increase awareness of both the level and type of demand for tourism and the extent to which it is satisfied (EC, 1996: 28).

The main driving force would be to achieve this through co-operation and co-ordination between states, to enlist the support of professional bodies and trade representatives and to develop specific guidance measures including those on quality improvements in tourism services.

Therefore, policy initiatives on quality improvements were recognised at the highest level, although implementation has largely been left to member states. The EU document does not, however, really define quality issues at the EU, state or regional level. So what does quality mean in tourism terms? Keller (1997) contrasts the terms "quality of service" and "quality of experience". The former has more to do with the service at the point of delivery of an individual service and the latter with the "total touristic experience", which includes nature, infrastructure, development level, associated products, cultural differences, other customers and timing. The two terms are not, however, exclusive, the latter merely being more broadly defined to include all experiences one is exposed to on vacation.

Quality and Quality Planning at the Destination Level

Others consider quality as dependent on the nature of demand for a destination rather than concentrating on the supply-side requirements of various tourism stakeholders. In this way, quality initiatives are demand-led, rather than supply-driven as was original quality thinking in the manufacturing sector. The management of quality issues at the destination, or larger, level could therefore be "stage managed" and should be sector-specific. This meant that quality could be subjected to policy initiatives that were creative, controlled, and well planned, but the quality of whole destination products could not be assured in the same way as a guarantee on a manufactured product — the destination product is just too complex and fragmented. The way ahead is thus to link customer-oriented marketing (including branding) with destination management techniques and quality programmes within individual operational units.

De Keyser and Vanhove (1997) view this combination of marketing, product development and service standards as crucial. They suggest that the increasing cost of marketing communications tools, in the long term, might not overcome inadequacies of product in a global market that is increasingly innovative and competitive. Also, in line with other contributions in the area, they consider the major issues in quality as bridging the gap between expectations and experience.

Figure 3.1: Outline of Quality in Tourism

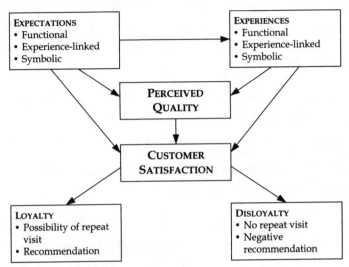

Source: De Keyser and Vanhove (1997)

The commentators suggest that both expectations and perceptions are comprised of three elements:

1. *Functional*: practical aspects

2. *Symbolic*: emotions and status

3. *Experience*: something that enhances the whole value of the
   experience.

It is these elements that affect both perceived quality and satisfaction and, therefore, it is these that need to be researched,
monitored and managed. What the destination should be trying
to achieve is a positive difference between the expectations and
the experience; therefore, quality can only be addressed at the
destination level in a customer-oriented manner. Consequently
quality can occur at all price levels, because expectations occur at
all price levels. As Aguilo (1996: 16–17) asserts when discussing
quality issues in Andalucia, Spain:

> It [quality] is not a question of trying to design a product for very limited groups from a high income bracket (quality tourism is not tourism for millionaires), but to guarantee that the user is satisfied with the type of tourism offer . . . and the ways in which it is marketed.

The planning and delivery of a quality tourism product is, therefore, a complex task. It

> obliges the various participants (tourism service providers and politicians) to learn to work together and enter agreements with each other (De Keyser and Vanhove, 1997: 33).

Internal communication within the tourism sector is as important as the marketing communications with the customer. De Keyser and Vanhove (1997), drawing on the Belgian experience of seaside resorts, outline six steps to the evaluation and analysis of a quality approach to destination planning.

Figure 3.2: Steps of the Quality Evaluation Approach

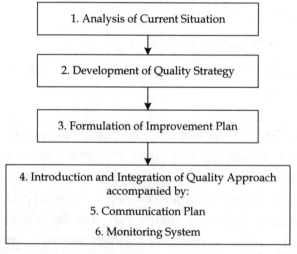

Source: De Keyser and Vanhove (1996)

1. *Analysis of the current situation* with regard to the quality of provision. This includes the opinions not just of managers but also of customers and staff.

2. *Development of a quality strategy* with clear priorities, design criteria, service criteria, reliability of quality controls and implementation, ability to take remedial measures and image creation and reputation.

3. *Continuous improvement plan* for yearly updating, taking into account structural changes and evolving customer needs.

4. *Introduction and integration of quality approach* to all elements of the tourism sector, and associated sectors, in both existing and new initiatives and operations. This is achieved through steps 5 and 6.

5. *A communications plan* to spread the philosophy within the tourism sector, residents of the destination and among its customers and their agents.

6. *A monitoring system* to measure satisfaction levels of all stakeholders, but especially the tourists.

In considering when such a quality plan may be appropriate, Origet du Cluzeau (in Keller, 1997), drawing on French experience, considers that destinations will only address quality issues, and certainly only go so far as formal planning, when it "finds itself having to adapt to uncomfortable situations" (p. 4). Even though experience shows that such plans are relatively easy to prepare and implement, proactive approaches appear rare in mature tourism economies. However, rather alarmingly, in the same report it was suggested that quality plans only really get implemented when finance is forthcoming from outside the destination and the local tourism industry — in other words, only when governments intervene in the market, which tends to be at times of crisis. Opposition to such plans when implemented, however, is usually slight, showing that the industry often seems to recognise their worth but is not proactive in this field. Origet du Cluzeau also remarks that such plans are easier to implement at the subsector level (e.g. for skiing installations, farm holidays, etc.) than industry-wide. These findings suggest that fragmentation of the industry and lack of leadership may be important factors in suppressing quality policy developments, for as Origet du Cluzeau states, the implementation of such polices requires clear management and organisational concepts and forms. In an industry that is characteristically poorly organised, this is a major issue.

Aguilo (1996) summarises the principles of what Fayos-Sola calls third generation policies, as follows:

1. The dominance and pre-eminence of the consumer

2. The authenticity of the product (i.e. its local relevance — was the decision to develop Disneyland, Paris therefore not a third-generation-style policy?)

3. The need for leadership from government bodies

4. An efficient government administration which avoids overlapping responsibilities

5. Specific policies in favour of segments and sub-segments rather than global (national) policies.

Given that quality issues are at the core of the third generation policy initiatives, it can be seen that the development and implementation of quality-oriented policies on a destination scale is a complex task, or what Monfort Mir (1996) calls a "specialised management tool". In this sense, quality as an issue is addressed only by mature tourism economies and even then, this is not necessarily taken up as an issue by all stakeholders. There appears to be a "bi-polarisation" of businesses into those who adopt the quality approach in a proactive manner and those who passively wait for government to intervene. In line with Aguilo's second point above, Monfort Mir (1996) views quality issues not just in terms of service but also in terms of sustainability of resources. The environment (natural and cultural) also require quality management if they are to remain as resources to be exploited for economic gain over the medium to long term.

The above review of strategic quality-oriented destination policy development paints a complex picture of action stimulated by crises, leadership from the outside stimulating a fragmented industry into action, change driven by consumer dissatisfaction, and an ongoing commitment to be driven by the needs of a variety of stakeholders (including residents, tourists, governments and industry) rather than by self-interest. Against this background, we will now discuss approaches used by Spain, Great Britain and the Republic of Ireland in developing quality-oriented policies.

Case Study 3.1: Spain
Quality-Oriented Policies: a Regionalised Approach

Fayos-Sola's proposals of policy generations were based on an analysis of the changing national and regional policies within Spain following a decline in tourism numbers during the mid-1980s.

Spanish tourism developed in the 1960s as a response to the need to break out of a massive balance of payments deficit. Treating tourism as an invisible export, the national government, in the Development Plan 1 (1963), had the aim to "attract the maximum foreign tourism" (Gomez, 1996). This was growth-driven economic development at its most pure. Nobody was to know the long-term effects of such a policy, and in fact Gomez reports that the World Bank believed that tourism was merely a "passing fashion" that was easily side-tracked and was therefore unstable. Spanish economic planners were to be proven correct.

However, the single pursuit of growth meant that quality disasters were inevitable. The environmental and aesthetic appeal of the Costas was seriously damaged, the potential of the interior unrealised and the dead hand of bureaucracy meant that the international market began to take low-cost package tours for granted (Newton, 1996). As tourist tastes changed and competing destinations were able to offer alternatives to Spain, the country's tourism began to suffer. An undiversified product could not cope with such changes, which together with economic crises (from the energy crisis of the early/mid-1970s to exchange rate changes in the 1980s) further hindered the industry's recovery on the international stage.

The long-term reliance on quantity over quality began to show its effects in the mid-1980s (Newton, 1996). A new approach to tourism policy was required. The new goal was to provide value for money and to present a diversified product by promoting the hinterlands of the resorts and major urban areas. This was a major turnaround for a country that had become associated with cheap holidays based around the "sun, sea and sand" product. The switch to a quality-led strategy was indeed as big a turnaround as could be envisaged.

Political changes in Spain in the 1970s and 1980s saw regional governments take a lead in developing their own policies, with support from central government. Vera and Rippin (1996) suggest that the main thrust of territorial (land use) planning at the regional scale was to achieve the objectives of innovation, rationalisation and high quality. To achieve this, they point to certain prerequisites:

1. The administration must be committed to playing a co-ordinator's role, something that could only be done at the regional level

2. Regional planning must include improvements in environmental quality

3. There is a requirement to create new leisure environments

4. Commercial appeal must be added

5. Mono-economies based solely on tourism are not ideal

6. Tourism must be integrated into wider regional development objectives.

Such prerequisites were acknowledged in the national government's *Plan Marco Competitividada* (Plan FUTURES) (1992). Jointly written by the state Ministry and the autonomous regional governments, it addressed new strategies for responding to the changing international markets that required Spain to become more competitive and diversified. Sub-plans such as *Plan de Excelensia Turistica* offered financial support for product diversification and upgrading schemes. Specific regions developed specific plans to meet their own needs; for example, Andalucia, one of the least developed areas of Spain, elaborated *Mejora Global De La Oferta*, a plan specifically aimed at improving the quality of the product. Other plans were also developed to regenerate saturated and environmentally degraded areas.

These types of plans, focusing on product development, were repeated throughout the major resort regions of Spain, with different emphasis on spatial planning, environmental improvement, greening and diversification, as was appropriate to the regions.

However, it would be wrong to think that all of Spain's quality improvement initiatives have been public-sector-led and product-oriented. Aguilo (1996) discussed how leadership had to be established by the public sector, and how joint working relationships between the public and private sectors were required. He also points to how the studies focused on training and personnel development, citing the white paper for the Balearic Islands that states:

> Training courses aimed at the tourist sector are the key to improving the quality of the services offered . . . firstly, it is important to state that a lack of sufficient, suitable training courses designed for the tourist sector had been noted. This is true at all levels of education. It must also be said that, both in

the state and private sectors of education, there has been only a limited, partial response to demands for professional training for the tourist sector. It is also true that in this sector the continuous training courses and activities aimed at bringing people up to date with new ideas and techniques are both few and far between and of substandard quality (Aguilo, 1996: 14).

Arrebola (1995) also points to non-land-use issues that have been addressed in the effort to move Spanish tourism into a new phase of quality-led product and service provision. He discusses the need to show how front office staff can make a significant difference to the quality of experience of the tourist: "People like to be liked, yet some so-called professionals still tend to treat the tourist as an inconvenience." (p. 41). He calls for flexible tourist industry team leaders who can sense the change in demand and taste and who are able to respond. He also points to the programmes instigated by national and regional governments to:

> educate and retrain our tourist-industry personnel, our leaders, to help then develop this vigorous, flexible response and to study the needs of their clientele, not just to satisfy today's market, but to satisfy the much more sophisticated tourist markets of the year 2000 (p. 41).

Arrebola concludes that the Spanish tourism industry must address three key initiatives to survive in the competitive world of late-twentieth-century tourism:

1. *To have a dynamic innovative management response to new demands.* They must make innovation and quality the foundation of their business success; many, he claims, are doing this. Also, resorts must be collectively innovative if they are to satisfy guests' expectations of quality. To achieve this they must show operational excellence, knowledge of their client groups and product leadership.

2. *Continuous assessment of offer (product) in order to update it.* This requires a client-centred approach to strategic planning based around technological improvement to reduce costs and increase job satisfaction for front-line staff, and quality of service. The latter implies that individual establishments become more client-focused rather than managing for internal convenience.

3. *Update the Spanish tourist image and emphasise quality, value for money and client satisfaction.* The lessons of static products must be learnt. He calls for the industry to show appreciation of clients, attend enthusiastically to their needs and ask them if they are satisfied. This requires skills in teamwork, leadership, and staff training. In dealing with destinations, rather than single operating units, general welcoming skills across all sectors of the hospitality industry are important — what Arrebola calls "collective awareness".

To sum up Spain's approach: it has been largely product-diversification-oriented and land-use-based, but supported by training and raising awareness of the needs of a modern tourist economy. The quality initiatives were driven by external events and the consequences of a lack of planning. The way through is a joint effort of the public and private sectors together with the good will of the resident populations.

Case Study 3.2: Great Britain
How Quality Issues Arrived on the Policy Agenda

At the time that Fayos-Sola was proposing the third generation paradigm of policy development, Britain's tourism industry was coming under scrutiny by government and private sector alike. At this point — around the early 1990s — research showed that tourism growth in Britain was lagging behind its main competitors and that the quality of the tourism product and quality of service was one reason for this relatively poor performance.

This case study looks at how Britain identified and addressed quality issues. In doing so, it shows the importance of the private and public sector taking a joint role in identifying and addressing the issues raised. It also shows how the public sector adopted the policies within which the private sector could act to raise its own quality standards.

The British government has stated that its role within the tourism sector is based around four main tasks (Department of National Heritage, 1996a: 1):

1. Seeking to ensure that the impact of government policies on the industry is, as far as possible, positive

2. Helping to overcome weaknesses in the functioning of the market caused by fragmentation of the industry

3. Acting as a catalyst for action

4. Acting as a clearinghouse for information and good practice.

The identification of these tasks emerged out of a wide-ranging analysis of the state of the British tourism industry. This analysis has been ongoing since a report by the Confederation of British Industry (CBI, 1994) showed that Britain was losing its market share to other destinations around the world.

Identifying the Problem

Pressure began to build on the British government to develop a positive and coherent policy for tourism following the setting up of the Department of National Heritage in the late 1980s. However, with a high turnover of Tourism Ministers and Secretaries of State within the Department, tourism's priority within overall government economic policy seemed low. At this time, the CBI set up, for the first time, panels of experts to identify problems and the way ahead for certain sectors of the economy. One of the first of these was the panel for the tourism sector (Tourism Action Group).

In his introduction to their first report, "A Wealth of Attractions: a new agenda to boost Britain's tourism potential" (CBI, 1994), Howard Davies, then Director General, CBI, noted that "our growth rate has been slipping, and our balance of payments has deteriorated". He called for a three-pronged attack of:

- Better representation by the industry of its own interests

- Government's need to acknowledge tourism in all its policy-making

- Tourism's need to be accepted as a vital mainstream industry which contributes as much to the wealth of the nation as any other.

By calling for tourism to be taken seriously by itself, by government and by the public, Davies launched a debate that would see a fragmented industry trying to unite itself — an industry perceived by many as having all the substance of "candy floss" being given serious policy consideration, and a re-orientation of focus from being product-dominated to being service- and quality-driven.

In trying to boost the industry's image, the CBI (1994) presented clear, well-sourced information showing that tourism generated 5.6 per cent of Britain's GDP in 1991 (equivalent to £27.7 billion) and six per cent of all jobs in 1992 (1.48 million) with a growth rate of 31 per cent between 1983 and 1993. Highlighting the competitive pressures from other destinations, it pointed out the "formidable competition from countries dedicated to achieving fundamental improvements in their products to meet the needs of the next century" (p. 13) (e.g. France, Spain and Turkey). Specifically, the CBI considered the importance of product and infrastructure improvements and investment in "the quality of employees" (p. 13). The CBI demonstrated how these pressures arise in diagrammatic form, as shown in Figure 3.3 below.

Figure 3.3: Competitive Pressures in Tourism

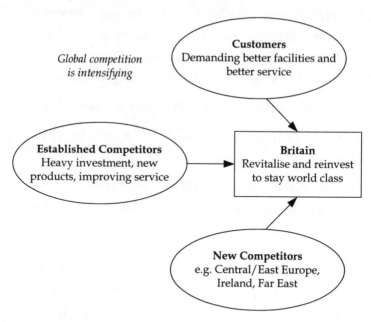

Source: CBI (1994)

The CBI called for strong leadership from and within government to heighten the profile of the industry and a need to focus on the work of the tourism careers and training agencies, in particular to increase the value that the government's Training and Enterprise Councils add to the service industries. The CBI itself pledged to lobby and research on behalf of the industry. Specifically, it would "promote a greater focus in education and training on the needs of the service sector" whilst it advocated the industry to "improve Britain's international and domestic reputation for value for money — particularly by developing the product and raising the quality and service standards" (p. 22).

Swiftly following the "Wealth of Attractions" report, the CBI produced a benchmarking report "World Hosts: International Benchmarking in the Hospitality Industry" (undated, circa 1996a). The report showed that whilst British three and four star hotels compared reasonably well with those in France and Germany in relation to achieved room rates, average occupancy, and profitability, significant weaknesses remained. Staff turnover was high, leading to much remedial training and the awarding of often unrecognised or even no qualifications.

Reinvestment in the hotel product was also reported as being low, with refurbishment as a percentage of turnover at eight per cent compared to 14 per cent in France and 16 per cent in Germany.

The report also highlighted particular issues concerning the delivery of a quality tourism experience. The product itself was being over-exploited, little was being put back into it by means of reinvestment and there was a lot of wastage of human capital and effort.

It is not surprising, therefore, that the CBI called for a programme of action from the industry itself that focused on both product and staff development, the two main elements that must be right for the tourist to gain a quality experience. In relation to staff, it considered that improvements in quality would only occur as the image of the industry improved, as staff became qualified and staff turnover was reduced. Hence they recommended the implementation of industry-wide schemes, such as a Welcome Host programme, closer working relationships between business and education (especially in relation to craft practices), a commitment from industry to invest in its staff, and more overt and transferable skills generated by the general education system.

In relation to image, this could, it was reported, only be improved by realising higher wages through more highly productive, varied and dynamic occupations and a well-defined career structure — something the tourism industry has not historically cultivated. In product development terms, new buildings, refurbishment and reinvestment were seen as the key. However, these problems were largely seen to concern relationships between key players in the investment sector such as town planners, builders and contractors and financiers. Town planners could potentially present obstacles and onerous conditions, making investors shy away from a product whose return on investment at the mid-market level is on average only six per cent, compared with 15 per cent at the budget end. Builders' and contractors' tortuous contracts and on-site management could raise the costs and time for completions. Financiers can often gain better returns from other economic sectors. Therefore, general improvements in communications and mutual understanding were called for between tourism and other economic sectors.

We have spent some time going over the history of the topic, especially the CBI's involvement, as it often takes someone from the outside with the knowledge of how to "get the ear" of government to make things happen. Much of what the CBI had said was already acknowledged, but little action taken. However, these authoritative reports themselves acted as catalysts for government action.

From 1995, the Secretary of State for National Heritage, Stephen Dorrell, began to get to grips with issues relating to the tourism industry. Writing in the first of the "Competing with the Best" series (DNH, 1995a), he clearly set out the role of government with regard to tourism. He had, as Secretary of State, a responsibility for many cultural and historic attractions, particularly to make them accessible to visitors. However, he made it clear that he also wanted "to see industry providing all the *other* elements of the tourism experience — to the standards that tourists demand" (p. 4, original emphasis). Improving the tourist experience was, therefore, a joint government and industry venture.

"Competing with the Best" (to which we will allude again in later chapters) covered much the same ground as the CBI's "A Wealth of Attractions", highlighting key performance figures, emphasising the fall in world market share, the role of government in relation to tourism and weaknesses in the functioning of the market, and provided a review of the way ahead. In relation to quality issues, "Competing with the Best" was important, as it put tourism higher on the political agenda than at any time since the passing of the Development of Tourism Act (1969). It also highlighted the needs of a modern service-oriented industry, that needed to become market- rather than product-oriented.

Although it said little about quality issues, other than stating that "tourism is all about service" (DNH, 1995a: 12), it clearly stated the respective roles of the government — as sponsor — and the industry — as investor in people, and product, and as operator. This division of responsibility was to run through all the ensuing documentation produced not only by the DNH but also by other bodies such as the English Tourist Board and in further CBI reports.

Indeed, the "Competing with the Best" series generated three further publications:

1. *Hotels: the Consumer's View (DNH, 1995b)*. This report was important for identifying what customers considered as quality. It highlighted the attitude of staff, the feeling of being cared for, methods of handling complaints, comfort, ambience and atmosphere. From the customer's point of view, quality standards are clearly based around product and service, and both need to be targeted at specific audiences. The report goes on to detail these different needs, although it is not necessary to relate them here.

2. *Benchmarking for Smaller Hotels (DNH, 1996b)*. This report concerned the benchmarking of 70 small hotels, bed-and-breakfast establishments and guesthouses. The exercise considered elements under three headings: guest-facing processes; business processes; and outputs. In keeping with the government's role as catalyst for product and service quality improvement it produced as part of the report a self-completion benchmarking questionnaire that all small hoteliers may use to assess their own operation.

3. *People Working in Tourism and Hospitality (DNH, 1996c).* The report identified a "self-perpetuating vicious circle" of:

> recruitment difficulties, shortages of skilled qualified staff, relatively low pay, high staff turnover, and a relatively unattractive image as an employment sector.

It considered that the fragmentation of the industry helps to reinforce this, as the dissemination of good practice and control is difficult. The DNH, it reported, hoped to create a "virtuous circle" that would help improve the bottom line through:

> staff retention, service excellence, favourable customer expectations, favourable staff and potential employee perceptions, good management practice, staff recognition and reward.

The DNH (1996c: 7) considered that "excellent service at a competitive price can only be provided by competent, well-managed and well motivated people". This means:

- Recruiting the right people in the first place

- Equipping them with the skills they need

- Managing staff well to create motivation, job satisfaction and high productivity.

This clearly linked quality improvement to strategic management programmes, and shifted the debate from merely training front-line staff in the "have-a-nice-day" approach to quality service to incorporating quality issues into management practice.

One of the most worrying findings, however, was the low level of management training. Reporting on the Hospitality Training Foundation's (HTC) 1995 Labour Force Survey, the DNH showed that only 28.8 per cent of hotel managers had a degree and 22.8 per cent A-levels or equivalent. Perhaps more importantly, 24.1

per cent had no qualifications at all. Further, the report found that two-thirds of employees were not required to have any qualifications.

To overcome this situation, the DNH proposed an industry-wide programme of awareness through industry representatives on the DNH's own Tourism Advisory Forum, to disseminate good practice, hold local workshops, promote key training schemes, promote local training partnerships and develop an awareness-raising campaign for those considering entry into the industry.

The final 1996 report of interest here was the CBI's "Visitors Welcome: Tourism in the Third Millennium". The reports by this time were following a similar pattern, expressing the need to improve product quality, service quality, marketing and investment. Each played its part in raising awareness of the tourism sector's problems and challenges, and added more evidence to the mounting pile. This report, as far as quality was concerned, added a further call for a single hotel classification scheme to help consumer confidence, called for an extension of benchmarking, for the creation of a career structure, investment culture and investment-friendly environment, especially at the local level, and for improvements in training.

In relation to the latter, CBI echoed the DNH's "vicious circle" analysis and highlighted the shortage of labour within all layers of the hospitality industry in Britain. Business reported up to a 45 per cent shortage of managers, 50 per cent of food preparation staff, 30 per cent reception staff, and similar gaps for marketing, accommodation operations and other customer contact staff.

The CBI called for a "learning passport" where training was a continuous process, equipping staff with transferable skills that would allow flexibility across the industry. They also considered that training and educational establishments and industry should work closer together to develop appropriate training for the industry, rather that be trainer-led; that Training and Enterprise

Councils should become more involved in the sector; and that trade associations should promote benchmarking and Investors in People programmes.

To conclude this review of major reports, we can see that the British tourism industry was found wanting through a lack of product awareness and customer orientation, just like Spain ten years before. Many heavyweight reports were produced to raise awareness of the subject and promote a programme of product and service improvement, marketing and investment, which were to work through (often unspecified) partnerships and a myriad of agencies, trade and advisory groups.

In responding to the industry's call for a lead, the British government produced the "Competing with the Best" series, but called for the industry itself to "talk with one voice" so that government departments knew who to listen to. The industry responded by forming key trade associations and congresses, to which the government responded by setting up a Tourism Advisory Forum to advise the Department of National Heritage on policy matters, and to form a conduit for information flows between the Department and industry. From this government/industry collaboration came, in early 1997, a single national tourism strategy called "Success through Partnership: a Strategy for Tourism — Competing with the Best" (DNH, 1997).

This strategy document brought together the various "Competing with the Best" reports and the work to date of the Tourism Advisory Forum. The report's Mission Statement is as follows:

> To develop tourism as a high-quality profitable and sustainable activity, through a partnership of industry, government and the tourist boards, so as to realise the growth potential of the industry and the associated social and cultural benefits for the nation (DNH, 1997: 1).

Quality, therefore, is identified as a fundamental issue in the improvement of the competitiveness of the industry. The strategy's action plan particularly addresses the quality issues in product development and investment, especially through the need to respond to changes in the market. As part of this, continuing communication within the industry is seen as a major requirement, and investment in service quality (and therefore staff training and retention) is a particular target. These and other areas for attention (marketing, information provision and distribution, and impact management) are to be forwarded through sub-groups of the Tourism Advisory Forum, and due to report in mid-1998.

Quality has also been incorporated as a major issue in the English Tourist Board's (ETB) consultative documents, Agenda 2000, and emerging corporate planning exercise, Action 2000. In this, the Board put together a major consultation process asking industry for its views on how to:

- Ensure that domestic and overseas consumers receive the products, quality of service and support they demand;

- Ensure that the industry, Regional Tourist Boards (RTBs) and local authorities have a better understanding of the domestic market and that they work together to develop effective information channels and coherent marketing strategies;

- Establish clear responsibilities for the ETB and other tourism bodies that take into account changes in the industry and the commercial realities of the current public sector environment (ETB, 1997).

Quality was one of the five areas that the ETB identified as being key to shaping the future of the industry, in particular highlighting training, benchmarking, accommodation rating schemes and dealing with complaints.

Another key area was product development. After consultation with the industry, the ETB decided to develop its product development recommendations in relation to tourist demand (ETB, 1998). In other words, even product development is consumer- rather than product-led. Sector-by-sector studies (e.g. the caravan industry, cycling holidays, farm holidays) highlight elements of good practice, market trends, and outcomes of focus group discussions. In this way, the tourism product would be sensitive to customer needs and requirements, which when linked to service quality programmes such as Welcome Host should help to improve the quality, attractiveness and competitiveness of the English tourism product.

Case Study 3.3: Republic of Ireland
Quality Initiatives within the Tourism Sector

The Irish tourism industry encompasses Government and state bodies and private sector SME providers and is a significant contributor to both economic and employment growth. Within the Irish tourism sector, strategic government intervention has paid enormous dividends. In the 1980s, the development of the Irish economy was very much driven by the location of multinational companies in Ireland, which forged relatively weak links with indigenous industry and therefore provided a poor platform for native development.

Two sectors were, however, identified as having national competitive advantage; that is, as providing opportunities for the development of innovative indigenous industry: agriculture/ food and hospitality/tourism. With regard to the hospitality industry, on the positive side it was argued that the Irish people were naturally hospitable, the environment was clean and there was a good range of cultural and natural attractions. However, there was concern about the quality of accommodation and food available, about cost competitiveness and about the marketing of Ireland as a destination.

The development of Irish tourism has progressed within two Operational Plans, from 1989–93 and 1994–99, facilitated by European Regional Development Funds (ERDF) and Social Funds (ESF). The plans have provided ambitious targets and a continuity of approach, even with changes of government. Tourism has full ministry status: the Minister for Tourism, Recreation and Sport is a member of the cabinet. The success of the strategy can be seen in the growth of overseas visits or numbers. Between 1992 and 1997, the number of tourists visiting Ireland from overseas increased from three million to five million, an increase of 60 per cent. A recent survey commissioned by the Bank of Ireland in association with Horwath Bastow Charleton found that hotel occupancy levels in the Republic grew from 66 per cent in 1996 to 70 per cent in 1997. Tourism-related jobs accounted for about 50 per cent of the net increase in employment over the 1988–93 period and the industry's share of GNP has increased from 5.8 per cent in 1988 to over 7 per cent in 1993. This growth has occurred at a time when tourism has been growing relatively slowly in Europe. The objective of Ireland's tourism strategy has been to maximise tourism potential through investment in marketing, infrastructure development, training and education.

Specifically, the strategy pursued under the Operational Programme for Tourism has concentrated on the following:

- A large expansion in marketing activities;

- Further product development to meet specific market deficiencies;

- Major improvements in the conference, angling and cultural tourism products; and

- An expansion in the range and scale of training to cater for anticipated employment growth.

Investment in education and training has been a key issue of concern within the Operational Programme. Specifically, tourism training strategies have aimed to:

- Boost human capital in Ireland by enhancing education and skills levels; and

- Improve employment prospects for unemployed people and persons excluded from the labour market.

Training programmes have been designed to cater for anticipated employment growth within the tourism sector, as well as catering for new tourism products and higher service standards. The intention, from a strategic perspective, is that a quality culture will prevail within the tourism sector in Ireland. The main vehicle for this is CERT, a state-sponsored body responsible to the Minister of Tourism, which co-ordinates the implementation of all aspects of government policy in the areas of education and training for tourism. CERT provides research on the industry's education and training needs, organises recruitment and selection of students for professional craft courses, designs training programmes, funds training schools and colleges and provides in-company training. In addition, the National Tourism Certification Board (NTCB) provides a system of programme development, assessment and certification, recognised nationally and internationally. CERT's role is both comprehensive and cohesive and thus ensures close affinity between the development of national tourism policy and the strategies which meet its human resource objectives.

A variety of programmes have also been implemented to equip unemployed people and early school leavers with the technical, communications and other skills necessary to take up employment opportunities within the tourism sector. All these initiatives, which seek to broaden the range of skills that individual employees possess, will be crucial to the future development of the tourism industry in Ireland. It is recognised that the industry will only prove attractive to high quality employees if training is perceived as modern and encompassing; otherwise, current levels of staff turnover will persist into the future.

Marketing has also been important in boosting tourism revenue in Ireland. Under the Programme, visitor satisfaction with the Irish tourism product is now monitored every two years using a

"Visitors Attitude Survey" which will aim to measure satisfaction ratings in the key areas of price, quality and customer service. Specific marketing activities have focused on the overseas marketing of Ireland as a holiday destination. In this regard, support has been made available for the following:

- Expanding sea and air access

- Developing new markets

- Developing product and niche markets

- Attracting more high-yield business.

Priority has been given to increasing market share in established markets and to achieving successful entry into new markets. Large amounts of funding have been made available to the private sector so as to encourage industry to take on an increasing role in securing the future success of Irish tourism. Advertising, publicity and public relations, trade and consumer promotions and direct consumer servicing will all operate to achieve key objectives identified within the programme. Priority has been given to supporting new or extended marketing programmes which seek to generate high-yield business. For example, local LEADER projects, funded by the EU for rural development, have proved helpful in identifying product gaps and in providing seed funding for new projects. The existence of CERT, with a remit of education and training across all sectors of tourism, has meant that these initiatives have been supported by a comprehensive range of training programmes and advisory services.

In addition, new and existing product suppliers have been encouraged to participate in trade and consumer promotions and brochure production, and to identify target and niche markets for their products. Programmes that market abroad attractive packages of visitor facilities on a regional basis have also been considered for assistance.

In terms of infrastructural development, substantial investments have been made in air and sea port facilities and in the purchase of new aircraft and passenger ferries. These have significantly improved access. Convenient access is a key determinant of increases in visitor traffic and is recognised as a critical element in achieving season extension and greater regional spread. Progress in this area will need to continue if negative impacts on tourist sites are to be minimised. In this regard, marketing and other incentives will need to be given to support the development of new air routes and ferry capacity will need to be further developed to increase tourist traffic within the regions. Membership of the EU has provided a number of benefits to Ireland through the provision of funding and employment training incentives, the opening up of markets and the promotion of environmental best practice.

Other factors have also influenced Ireland's tourism industry performance positively in recent years. Initiatives such as the social partnerships, the stabilising of Ireland's currency in the programme to take an early and full part in EMU and the subsequent business growth and economic development emerging from this strategy. Also influencing growth in tourism revenue is the image of Ireland as a fashionable destination. International achievements in the arts, coupled with strong economic performance, have given Ireland this reputation. Clearly, the expansion of Irish tourism has been affected by violence in Northern Ireland. Continued progress in this area will impact positively on the industry in both parts of the island. Research suggests that the impact of a permanent cease-fire on tourism performance is significant. For example, peace in Northern Ireland will open up new markets which would be expected to increase potential market size by 20 per cent. It would also provide greater opportunity for North/ South marketing initiatives between commercial sectors.

Ireland has a very distinct image in most international markets and, as in the other case studies, quality needs to be highlighted as a key fundamental issue in the further development of the industry. Although successful in positioning itself as a "value-for-money" location, continued development of access is critical for the future development of the Irish tourism industry. Government should therefore continue to provide incentives for investment in developing tourist areas and finance destination marketing and market research activities. Such government intervention at the local, regional and national levels should continue to provide the impetus for innovation and enterprise amongst small and medium-sized organisations.

Summary

This chapter has shown, in some detail, how quality issues have been addressed at the strategic level in Spain, Britain and the Republic of Ireland. It has also reviewed some of the work on the subject of destination quality. That these cases are used is of little relevance, other than showing real-life examples. Similar key issues and processes will have to be addressed by any other mature or emerging tourism destinations that wish to remain competitive in the new global tourism market. Quality issues will increasingly become a differentiating factor in the destination selection process of tourists, as consumers become more aware of the wider choice of destinations and products available.

In order to stay ahead of the competition, destinations at the national or regional scale will have to address such policy arenas. Leaving quality issues to the unit or single organisational level alone will not suffice, because of the fragmented nature of the tourism industry and complex nature of the product. Neither will emerging destinations have the luxury of moving through the sequential policy generations outlined by Fayos-Sola. Quality is now an international issue that all destinations must address, regardless of their position in the product lifecycle.

As Fayos-Sola suggests, co-operation between the private and public sectors has proven to be crucial to the whole process of quality and competitiveness in Great Britain, Spain and the Republic of Ireland. Other key factors that are equally applicable to these destinations, and probably to most others addressing quality issues, include:

- A professional and competent workforce

- The importance of quality-awareness-raising research by respected agents and bodies

- Improved ongoing communications between government and industry

- Improved communications between various segments of the tourism industry and between the tourism industry and other sectors

- Practical measures being developed alongside policies

- Market-led product and service quality improvements

- Implementation to be mainly private-sector-led.

For quality to be addressed on a truly sector-wide basis requires major strategic shifts in emphasis at the national and/or regional level. This chapter has presented both a theoretical background and practical examples of how this can be achieved.

Review Questions

1. Why has it become necessary for destinations to develop third generation tourism policies?

2. Who are likely to be the main players in promoting the need to address service quality issues? What roles will they play?

3. Why is internal tourism industry communication considered such an important prerequisite to quality improvements?

4. Industries and organisations can be product-led or marketing-led. What orientation is the most appropriate for promoting service quality in the tourism industry and why?

Chapter 4

Quality and Competitive Advantage

Introduction

The changes reported in previous chapters have presented hospitality businesses with growing challenges. Customers have become more discerning and are shifting their loyalties between companies in the anticipation of continuing improvements in product and service quality. As a consequence, the management of quality has emerged as a fundamental component of an organisation's overall strategic efforts. Managers are continuously examining current processes against the demands of customers in the marketplace and are increasingly updating their operations in line with customer demands. As Chapter 3 points out, this is an issue across the whole of the tourism sector, which can eventually challenge the competitive position of destinations and whole countries within the world-wide tourism marketplace.

In an article highlighting important areas in need of further research, Guerrier (1996c) asks:

> how do organisations achieve service quality? And how does
> . . . total quality management operate in practice?

These issues are of major concern to individuals working in the hospitality field and will be the focus of concern in the present chapter. Again, through an analysis of theory and practice, we hope to assess the current state of play and examine the extent to which quality has been incorporated as a strategic concern within businesses operating in the hospitality sector.

Dynamics of Managing Quality

In the opening chapter of this text, quality management practices were introduced as strategic initiatives designed to encourage employee flexibility and improve overall organisational performance. It was shown that involvement of staff at all levels is crucial if standards and service are to be improved on a continual basis. In short, it was argued that the quality phenomenon has matured and grown out of its original roots in "Total Quality Control" and has embraced wider issues such as change, involvement and commitment:

> The problem of defining a total approach to quality stems from the development of TQM as a more general philosophy of change which, whilst having its roots in many of the principles of Total Quality Control, now encompasses a broader and more strategically oriented change management model aimed at revising existing organisational attitudes and beliefs systems (Dawson, 1994).

However, although the evidence suggests that quality management in the 1990s is centred around a focus on involvement, communications and teams, studies show that the management of quality in contemporary hospitality organisations is lacking in precisely these dimensions. Recent work by the authors suggests that quality programmes in hotel organisations in Ireland and Britain exhibit a strong emphasis on procedures and standards and show a lack of concern for addressing the wider strategic implications associated with quality management.

This suggests problems with the management of the quality dynamic. While most companies are embracing quality initiatives of one type or another, this is often in a piecemeal and ad hoc way. Management issues such as the restructuring of traditional work relationships and the rethinking of human resource practices, which necessarily accompany the introduction of quality into the organisation, have not been fully thought through

(Monks et al., 1996). These issues are worthy of consideration and will be explored here and in later chapters.

Some suggest, for example, that

> . . . for quality management gurus, quality does not necessarily mean the attainment of exceptionally high standards with regards to employees' terms and conditions of work. Instead, it means the development of uniform and dependable work practices that are congruent with delivering products or services at low cost with a quality suited to the market (Wilkinson and Willmott, 1995: 3).

There has also been a lack of concern for understanding the role and importance of middle-level managers in the management of quality programmes. There is a growing consensus that middle-level managers have an important influence on the success or otherwise of implementation initiatives. It is well established that the commitment of middle managers is essential if quality initiatives are to be implemented effectively. Olian and Rynes (1991: 324–5) make the point forcefully when they claim that the

> . . . characteristic of successful quality implementations is that the support of middle managers is gained. Because of their critical role as channelers of information both to and from work teams and those who can choose to share or, alternatively, to jealously guard power, middle managers can make or break a quality effort.

An example of where such middle management issues have been taken into account in improving customer care and the delivery of a quality product and service is Radisson Edwardian hotels. Facing increased interest rates and a market suffering the effects of the Gulf War, the company needed the support of all in the company and realised that they had lost touch with their people. As a response, the group introduced a flat management structure where general managers were given responsibility for different aspects of the business, such as food and beverage and front of house, across the group. General management duties at individual hotels were carried out on a rota basis by heads of department. There were some traditional managers who didn't like it because they lost their fiefdom, but the changes have helped the company to remain successful in a competitive marketplace.

Elsewhere, however, it has been shown that middle-level managers may be obstructing the process of introducing quality to an organisation. Quality initiatives typically imply a sharing of expertise and power which middle managers have an interest in preserving. Thus, it is not surprising that they feel threatened when faced with implementing procedures designed to give lower-level employees more discretion in areas which traditionally were the preserve of middle managers. In recent years, the middle managerial role in facilitating quality implementation has been affected by the emphasis being placed in recent years on new forms of strategic initiatives: "downsizing", "re-engineering" and "de-layering". These have served to intensify managerial anxieties and complicate the process of developing a quality ethos. Indeed, it has been shown that although middle-level managers account for only five to eight per cent of the labour force in the US, they made up 17 per cent of all dismissals between 1989 and 1991.

Consequently, there is growing scepticism about the nature and extent of middle-level managerial support and commitment to quality initiatives. In particular, Monks et al. (1996) assert that middle managers may be reluctant participants in the quality implementation process and may demonstrate attitudes of compliance rather than commitment when faced with implementing key quality initiatives. This suggests possible tensions in the practical application of the quality concept, especially at the middle managerial level. However, these issues have generally been overlooked in strategic quality programmes.

Strategic Nature of Quality Initiatives

There is an abundance of material offering simplistic approaches to the management of quality. These prescriptive, albeit quick-fix, approaches have encouraged ineffective practices in organisations. Only recently have writers begun to question the quality dynamic and consider its strategic ramifications. There is now a consensus for undertaking quality management using a total management or holistic approach, embracing internal as well as external operating practices. In this regard, an attempt is being made to bring critical account to bear on the philosophy and illuminate the complexities involved in implementation.

Further, there is a concern for understanding the strategic nature of quality programmes and the ways in which well-managed quality initiatives contribute to long-term competitive success. As Dawson and Patrickson (1992) point out, quality issues are no longer restricted to production departments or manufacturing companies, but are the concern of the whole gamut of public and private enterprises who wish to enhance their system of employee relations, reduce operational efficiencies and increase their competitive position.

Consider Holiday Inns Inc. below (Exhibit 4.1), where as part of a major revitalisation of the company, executives were encouraged to visit hotels within the group to share details and strategy behind quality, operations and customer service enhancements. The strategy has brought a new level of consistency and customer service to their hotels. Holiday Inns have launched a campaign whereby 200 executives embarked on a month-long trip to the company's 1,800 hotels in the US and Canada. The effort, which was launched in February 1996, is aimed at enhancing the quality, consistency and service of the hotels and is part of the company's modernisation strategy.

Exhibit 4.1: Holiday Execs Hit the Road Promoting Service

Over 200 Holiday Inns Inc. executives went on a 32-day road trip to visit the company's 1,800 hotels in the US and Canada. The first instalment of the programme required all franchisees that had joined the Holiday Inn system before 1 January, 1989 and had not upgraded the guest-rooms, public areas and exterior of their hotels since that time to either modernise and upgrade their properties, or leave the Holiday Inn system.

More than 90 per cent of property owners chose to participate and have invested more than $1 billion thus far to upgrade their hotels. The second wave of the modernisation programme is now under way. The goal behind their efforts is to make every Holiday Inn hotel as good as the best Holiday Inn hotel and provide a consistent, guest-friendly lodging experience system-wide.

Source: *Hotel & Motel Management*, 3 March 1997, p. 28.

Recently, therefore, quality management has been viewed as an important means by which organisations can achieve differential advantage over the competition. This chapter will also seek to examine the importance of service quality in achieving the strategic goals of the organisation. Through an examination of theory and practice, it is hoped to establish whether quality strategy can be positioned as a way in which to differentiate the firm's offerings.

A useful starting point to the discussion of the wider strategic implications of adopting a quality orientation is to examine the nature of strategy and to understand the ways in which quality may be viewed as an aspect of organisational strategy. The concept of organisational strategy has attracted much attention from organisational researchers and there have been numerous attempts to define the concept. Early contributors in the strategy domain viewed the design of strategy as deliberate, conscious and articulated (Chandler, 1962; Andrews, 1980).

Later writers on strategic management, however, disputed this view of strategy. Quin (1980) defined strategy as a pattern or plan that integrates an organisation's major goals, policies and action sequences into a cohesive whole and the writer proposes that the integration of the plan into "a cohesive whole" constitutes strategy. This view of strategy he terms "logical incrementalism":

> . . . its incremental character goes without saying . . . he believes it to be logical because it proceeds flexibly and experimentally from broad concept to particular commitment, using delay to acquire more information and thus reduce risks (Moore, 1992: 60).

Mintzberg (1992) also disputes the "rational, articulated" view of strategy. He defines strategy as more than just planning. He considers strategy to be a pattern of activities over time which include observations of what actually occurred. Mintzberg (1992) does not imply that plans are irrelevant, rather that actions speak louder than intentions and subsume these.

Indeed, the debate between some of the early thinkers and their more contemporary colleagues culminated in a series of articles which attempt to "rethink the strategic management process" (Mintzberg, 1994; Ansoff, 1994). However, these debates, while illuminating to scholars of strategic management,

> are simply too adversarial. We break up whole systems into shards and then point these at opponents (Hampden-Turner, 1990: 69).

For example, within the wider tourism industry, the major integrated multiples, such as Thomsons and Air Tours, followed a discounting strategy driven by the immediate need to sell contracted hotel bedrooms and aircraft seats. Like hotel rooms, if a holiday is not sold, then it contributes to a loss of notional profit and, indeed, is a cost to the operator. Late sales, therefore, became a strategy of the major tour operators in the early 1990s. Offering holidays at greatly discounted prices, it was possible to get a week's half-board in Greece for around £70. However, this did backfire in several ways. The expectations of the holidaymaker did not decrease as the price fell, and since many discounted holidays were in the lower quality resorts and hotels, customer satisfaction declined. Nor was it a sustainable strategy. The over-supply of holidays at a time of economic recession in the genera-tor areas was the main factor in the need to discount. Tour op-erators had to change strategy; losses could not be sustained at this rate when the profit margin per holiday is only about three per cent on brochure price. The new strategy was to contract less hotel rooms and aircraft seats, thus limiting supply and keeping prices up.

It is clear that the strategies followed by the major tour opera-tors were not planned in advance in full knowledge of the eco-nomic and market conditions. They had to react to changes in cir-cumstances and alter their strategy accordingly. If the main influ-encing factors are outside one's control, an incremental approach is almost inevitable.

Whether this incremental approach is widespread among tourism businesses is, however, unclear, as there is a lack of re-search in strategic planning in tourism and hospitality businesses. In discussing the findings of a literature review of strategic plan-ning in tourism, Athiyaman (1995) concludes that gaps exist in almost all areas of strategy research in tourism. Little or no com-prehensive work is found on any aspect of tourism strategy re-search. Similarly, Gilbert and Kapur conclude in a 1990 review:

> . . . strategic planning is rarely discussed in journals applied to the hospitality (tourism) industry. It is difficult to know whether hospitality (tourism) companies are managed strate-gically and indeed, whether a formalised process of develop-ing, implementing and evaluating strategy is operated.

It has been suggested that this may be because tourism compa-nies are unwilling to disclose sensitive information or that they do not much care about research and/or planning.

Notwithstanding the aforementioned important contributions, critical evaluation of the strategic management literature is, perhaps, best understood by studying Porter (1980; 1985), whose work has been the most influential in the strategy field. The present chapter, although informed by other contributions, draws primarily from Porter's (1980; 1985) work in understanding the ways in which quality may be viewed as an aspect of organisational strategy. Specifically, Porter (1980) identifies three types of strategy, which form the basis by which an organisation can achieve and sustain competitive advantage:

- Overall cost leadership

- Differentiation

- Focus strategy where the firm directs attention on a well-defined market niche and deploys either a cost leadership or differentiation approach.

This chapter is primarily concerned with the differentiation approach to achieving and sustaining competitive advantage. In relation to differentiation, Porter (1985) wrote:

> In a differentiation strategy, a firm seeks to be unique in its industry along some dimensions that are widely valued by buyers.

Differentiation can be achieved through a range of features such as better quality, lower (or indeed, higher) price customer service, reputation, awareness. As outlined above, this chapter is concerned with differentiation as it relates to providing quality service for the customer, and ultimately advantage for the organisation. Kerfoot and Knights (1995: 234) lend credibility to the requirement for adopting such an approach, claiming:

> The pursuit of quality in recent years . . . could be seen essentially as a search for competitive advantage through differentiation strategies. This has occurred largely as a result of a

concern among companies to differentiate themselves from
competitors ...

As outlined in earlier chapters, the customer base which organisations now serve has become increasingly sophisticated and discerning, and guests demand significantly more of tourism operators than was the case a decade ago.

> The public is increasingly becoming more sophisticated in re-
> spect of standards which are expected, and more vocal about
> products and services which do not meet requirements in
> terms of choice and quality (O'Neill and Black, 1996: 15).

A recent report prepared by the management consultancy KPMG
(1995) suggests that the hospitality industry is entering a major
period of change wherein hospitality operators will need to address the multiple challenges of:

- Fast-changing technology creating greater demands from
  guests for enhanced service

- Increasing levels of investment needed to maintain and improve the product

- Demographic squeeze on 16–24 year olds, intensifying competition for competent, young staff

- Relatedly, achieving high quality service levels given the
  above difficulties in recruiting and retaining staff.

The report suggests that advantage will increasingly accrue to
those organisations that differentiate their offerings on the basis
of high quality service. The review also highlights that training
should become a key concern for tourism companies, given the
importance of staff input in delivering a quality offering. Because
of the labour-intensive nature of service operations and the fact
that direct contact between employees and customers forms an
important part of the service experience, then the question pres-

ents itself: how do hospitality organisations, particularly me-dium-large operators provide on a mass scale, high-quality, but affordable personal services?

In the past, training has largely been aimed at the middle and upper management levels. However, the focus is now shifting onto the operative levels — the people that are more likely to meet the public. For instance, David Batts, the chairman of the London Tourist Board (1997), is so convinced that this is the way forward that his own Radisson Edwardian hotels and other op-erators, together with Westminster City Council, have helped to fund London's first hotel and catering training centre, aimed at those who work at jobs below management level. He believes that there are plenty of places where you can learn to be a hotel man-ager but there is nowhere to learn the more basic skills. He carries on to state his belief in quality and training by predicting that there could be 25–30 of these centres in Great Britain training 25,000 people per year.

Exhibit 4.2 illustrates precisely the value of the differentiation approach, especially within the luxury sector. Luxury hotels have to measure the benefits of increased occupancy rates obtained through aggressive volume discounting against the possibility that their image of exclusivity might be tarnished.

However, although writers have been suggestive of the differ-entiating capacity of service quality,

> . . . this dimension of positioning the quality component in strategic terms does not seem to have been widely addressed — the word quality is generally used to imply seeking some improvement on the current situation (Gamble and Jones, 1991: 80).

Exhibit 4.2: Sweet Hospitality

Running a hotel is an expensive business with high fixed costs — 80 per cent at the top end of the market — and perishable products. Each room standing empty as the sun goes down represents an irre-coverable loss of revenue to the hotelier, who will nevertheless shell out for maintenance, heating and staffing. Each meal unsold eats into the notional profits of the catering division. Success depends on yield management achieving a good balance between sales volume and profitability.

This means that in tough times, even the fanciest hotels learn humility. After more than a year of hardship — the falling off in travel during the Gulf crisis simply masked the severity of the eco-nomic downturn — hotels are hungry for custom and ready to bend their rules to get it. The recession has forced many luxury hotels to resort to volume discounting and operational cost-cutting. The strat-egy is not without its risks. Luxury hotels have to weigh higher oc-cupancy rates against loss of image. Their unique selling point is ex-clusivity, not value for money. Reckless discounting also causes problems for all types of hotels by establishing unrealistic price ex-pectations that cannot be met in the longer term. "If you send out messages that you're willing to trade at marginal profitability, you spoil the market," says Michael Prager, vice president of ITT Shera-ton's Europe, Africa and Middle East division.

Nor does fierce competition among operators always ensure that staff try harder. Cost-cutting can undermine employee morale, while a rapid increase of hotel capacity in one city often over-stretches the local supply of well-trained staff. Novotel, the three-star French chain, always markets its properties as value for money, setting rates at about 15 per cent below its nearest competitors'. "In the long term, customers benefit from our approach," says Robert Tether, Novotel's UK sales and marketing director. "They won't get a good deal today and be ripped off tomorrow".

Source: International Management, February 1992, Vol. 47, No. 2, p. 54.

There has been a suggestion that service quality and strategy is-sues have been addressed separately within the literature. The strategy literature has not been concerned with service quality, while the service quality contributions lack a strategic dimension. As Powell (1995: 16) remarks:

TQM's impact on strategic management research and practice remains unclear and underexamined, and the existing empirical studies of TQM performance . . . lack rigor and theoretical support.

Strategic Quality

Thus, only recently have attempts been made to address the strategic nature of quality initiatives. Writing from the context of his own work on competitiveness, Porter (1985) argued that improvements in quality are meaningless without an understanding of their competitive implications. Others have also lent credibility to Porter's views emphasising the key differentiating abilities of strategies based on service quality (Lewis, 1989). In their review, Edgett and Parkinson (1993: 19) emphasise the point when they write that "attention is . . . increasingly being focused on strategies for organisational design to deliver services effectively".

This echoes the quality perspective provided by the Malcolm Baldrige National Quality Award (1994) which states that customer-driven quality is a key strategic business issue which needs to be an integral part of overall business planning. The emphasis on strategic considerations reflects a broader organisational concern for understanding and responding to the requirements of a transient and value-conscious consumer and calls for greater strategic awareness to achieve consistency in the provision of services.

An early study of quality management conducted in the US claimed that quality had become a major strategic variable in the battle for market share and emphasised the emergence of service quality as one of the most potent means of reducing costs and improving overall organisational effectiveness (Leonard and Sasser, 1982). Firms who work to provide customers with more value through services will inevitably improve (internal and external) standards of quality and performance. The possibility of gaining better business results from the achievement of sustainable customer satisfaction through service quality and close trading relationships have become strategic concerns. This reinforces the suggestion that competitive service strategies should embrace the notion of service quality and provide organisations with an opportunity to monitor quality standards over time.

This has certainly been the case for hospitality operators in many Asian countries. In Singapore, for example, the tourism industry has developed a reputation for providing high quality services and products. These have been initiated by the leadership of key organisations such as Singapore International Airlines and some of the major hotel organisations including the Mandarin and Shangri-la. Government, in collaboration with private sector companies, work together to achieve a continuously improving culture of quality. Agencies such as the Service Quality Institute also work hard to promote the strategic benefits of adhering to the quality philosophy. In consequence, companies are developing an international reputation for quality based on service provision and as such are held up as models of excellence by western operators (JHIC, 1998).

The perspective on quality has progressed from an initial operations focus on methodical improvement to a strategic based one concerned with ways in which quality can be used to effect strategic advantage (see Table 4.1).

Table 4.1: Development of Strategic Approach to Quality

Approach	Message	Perspective on Quality
Production	Processes to accomplish purpose can be improved	Quality can be pursued through methodical improvement
Marketing	Quality is in the eye of the beholder	Quality is the purpose of serving others well
Strategy	Quality needs to be pursued strategically	Quality can be used to gain strategic advantage

Source: Adapted from Pruett and Thomas, 1996

This strategic view of quality can be seen as all-encompassing and takes account of both production and marketing perspectives in the pursuit of organisational advantage. Exhibit 4.3 below illustrates the growing emphasis placed on quality and service in hospitality markets. Specifically, the example concerns the changing nature of the pub business in Great Britain, where stiffer competition from the rest of the leisure industry is forcing a competitive reassessment of the traditional pub.

Exhibit 4.3: End of the Traditional Pub Era

The pub in the year 2000 will almost certainly centre around adding value by offering more than just alcoholic drinks. As customers become more discriminating, their expectations about service and quality will increase. Amenities and food will be an increasingly important factor in differentiating among competing outlets. A strong brand or theme will also be a way of adding value. Bass, for example, is focusing on leisure-related outlets and plans in the next few years to build about 150 new pubs, many of which will have a leisure focus. Whitbread . . . plans to extend its hotshots pub concept, which offers pool and pub games to a young market.

The trend toward themes and concept pubs reflects an effort to differentiate oneself from the competition, particularly those targeting the young market. The 18-to-25 market has moved away from traditional pubs toward cafés and trendy bars, many of which are based around a club culture and are more fashionable meeting places. The traditional pub is being replaced by multifaceted leisure outlets, diners, and child-friendly, continental-style cafés. Jarvis, Whitbread's chief executive officer, is not the least embarrassed to say that one of his big new pubs "is more like Disney World than a 'boozer'" or to talk of a pub visit as a "leisure occasion". The word "pub" itself may eventually become a misnomer.

Source: "The British Pub — An Industry in Transition", *Cornell Hotel and Restaurant Administration Quarterly*, December 1996, pp. 62–73.

Nevertheless, comparatively less attention has been given to this aspect of quality management and there is a need to examine the integrative nature of service quality and in particular its links

with strategic management. This is significant if hospitality organisations are to compete effectively in the changed marketplace
of the 1990s.

Quality as Competitive Advantage

One of the ways in which the link between quality and organisational strategy has been emphasised has been to view quality as a
source of competitive advantage. Building on the notion introduced earlier that quality may constitute an important instrument
of differentiation for service organisations, commentators stress
that the achievement of such differentiation can lead to competitive advantage for the organisation.

It is suggested that superior skills in the form of the distinctive
capabilities of an organisation's staff help distinguish it from
competing organisations, and superior resources allow a firm to
utilise its capabilities effectively. These sources enable the firm to
carry out its activities in ways which lead to either lower cost or
differentiation. Skills and resources that are specific to a particular
firm are also understood as "drivers" of cost and/or differentiation advantages. Both resource- and skills-based drivers are important sources of organisational advantage. However, these
"drivers" do not confer competitive advantage automatically on
an organisation; they need to be properly exploited if they are to
result in organisational advantage. As Oster (1994: 115) points
out:

> Much has been written about the kinds of attributes that dis-
> tinguish one firm from a seemingly similar neighbour. At
> times a firm earns rents not because of its unique individual
> resources, but because of its distinctive competence in using
> those resources.

Thus, it is essential that the organisation identify those skills and
resources that have the greatest potential of providing it with a
source of sustainable competitive advantage. This is the way in

which we view the relationship between quality and strategy. It is held that in a strategic sense, service quality can contribute significantly to the achievement of competitive advantage: properly exploited, it can be utilised to attain competitive differentiation advantages for the firm.

In a review of quality practices in British hotels, respondents claimed that the competitive advantages they had over rivals in the industry were related to "functional" quality dimensions. Functional elements such as trained and motivated staff, consistency of service and competency of management all figured highly as sources of competitive advantage. "Technical-related" elements such as size and location featured less significantly as instruments of differentiation (Harrington and Akehurst, 1996b).

Other work also reinforces this view. Oberoi and Hales (1990) in their study of quality in conference hotels showed that functional quality elements were more important in assessments of overall service quality. Specifically, they pointed out that

> . . . the functional attributes are major contributors to the overall quality as perceived by consumers. In addition, it would appear that the technical attributes do not significantly influence perceived overall quality. Rather, in some cases they are a participant in the overall quality provided (p. 719).

The notion of developing competitive advantage around service quality may be illustrated by the emergence of the Four Seasons Hotel Group as a key player in the international hospitality market. As outlined in Exhibit 4.4, through its purchase of the Hong Kong-based Regent International in 1992, the company has been in a position to expand its operations in Asia as well as further enhance its competitive advantage in luxury operations.

Exhibit 4.4: When 99 Per Cent Isn't Enough

"Four Seasons is probably the premier luxury hotel chain", echoes Daniel Daniele, director of hospitality consulting for Ernst & Young in Chicago. "They've lived up to that reputation, and other hotel companies try to emulate them".

The fact that to many industry analysts, the chain has become synonymous with top quality customer service has given the chain the edge in its most important market: the travel agents, meeting planners and incentive trip planners who book most luxury hotel business — and who have long memories when it comes to customer complaints. That ability to please even the toughest customers will be even more important in the wake of the chain's acquisition last August of Hong Kong-based Regent International Hotels Ltd. . .

Operating a business in Japan is never easy for a Western company, but for Four Seasons may prove to be something of a natural: corporate culture at Four Seasons includes many qualities typically associated with Japanese corporate culture. . . . "What's really required is to build into employees over time the ability to distinguish between different guests' needs and to adjust their behaviour accordingly" says John Young [senior vice president of Human Resources]. "We need to help people to understand, and allow them to improvise, the way North Americans typically behave. That is where good service comes from: clarity of role, confidence and competence".

Source: Adapted from *Management Review*, March 1993, p. 49.

Hence we argue that quality, when applied to the method of organising work, helps create organisational advantage for the firm. Location, market access, technology procurement and access to capital are no longer sustainable sources of advantage since they are readily available to most global companies. On the other hand, quality, with its focus on participative decision-making, teamwork and collective responsibility, is much more difficult to copy and hence represents the "ultimate" source of competitive advantage for global organisations. This aspect of quality has been much alluded to in the literature; however, as noted earlier, only relatively recently are contributors beginning to address the lack of clarity about the implications of quality for the process of strategic management.

Benchmarking for Competitive Success

An approach to considering the strategic significance of quality management initiatives has been to benchmark organisational practices and activities against best practice in a particular industry. The approach is closely linked with TQM in that it is concerned with improving existing processes and behaviour and achieving continuous improvement. First, we must consider its origins and then examine its practical application and significance.

The notion of benchmarking originated in Japan and was introduced to the western world by the Xerox corporation in the late 1980s. It was utilised extensively by Japanese companies in their attempts to emulate "best practice" and achieve superior performance standards across different industry sectors. The practice of benchmarking has an external focus and helps the organisation evaluate its competitive position.

Benchmarking is linked to quality initiatives in that it assists in making an organisation "market-focused", it provides the impetus for organisations continually to improve internal processes and the motivation continually to review the approaches in place for delivering products or services to customers. One prominent writer in the field places this issue in context when he writes:

> . . . benchmarking is an integral component of TQM where there is a high visibility of tools utilisation, systems, working through multidisciplinary teams and using a problem-solving approach. It also means that the entire organisational commitment is to satisfy customer requirements. In this case, the goal of benchmarking is to extend the internal standard of effectiveness to be highly competitive (Zairi, 1994).

Thus, benchmarking motivates managers to question environmental conditions, customer experiences, market trends and other important factors that impact overall organisational effectiveness. The tool emphasises the strategic significance of continually monitoring and emulating standards of performance. However, this technique has received only limited attention from writers in the hospitality domain. This is a situation that must change, especially given the importance attached to raising performance standards in a recent survey of senior executives within the industry. Specifically, the report "Tourism: Competing with the Best" (Department of National Heritage, 1996b), commissioned by the British Department of National Heritage, suggests that the key characteristic which successful employers within the industry share is their commitment to excellence and customer satisfaction:

> They believe that if they can deliver these consistently, and keep raising standards, their distinctive reputation in the marketplace will ensure their competitive success. They recognise that this means taking a long-term view, investing in the product and their people rather than trying to maximise the short-term returns.

The Irish Tourist Industry Confederation (ITIC) has also placed importance on benchmarking in its most recent report, "Strategy for Growth Beyond 2000", on the future of the tourism industry. It is suggested that, to compete effectively, all hospitality businesses will need to compare their offerings with best practice in the rest of the world. Increasingly, well-travelled customers, especially in the context of EMU, will wish to compare service offerings with those provided in other parts of the globe. Benchmarking will thus assume greater importance in this regard (ITIC, 1998).

Benchmarking: A Practical Perspective

To encourage a greater uptake of interest in benchmarking within the hospitality sector, we now outline an approach propounded by one of the leading thinkers in the area. In achieving a greater focus on roles, processes and strategic issues, Zairi (1994: 6) proposes the following approach:

1. Effectiveness Stage

Firstly, the effectiveness stage should be concerned to examine the effectiveness with which internal processes are controlled and managed. The following steps are suggested:

- *Understand internal processes*: using charting techniques, what has to take place must be established.

- *Appraise current processes*: if processes are to be effectively managed, then they must be quantified.

- *Identify areas for improvement*: through evaluation, limitations can be identified and solutions devised.

- *Improve processes*: implemented solutions must lead to improvements.

- *Measure and evaluate*: improvements must be assessed through measurement. Efforts towards improvement must be evaluated for further action.

- *Establish internal standards*: performance can be optimised through a process of continuous assessment. This is the point where standards can be considered as acceptable.

- *Control and manage processes*: all processes that can be controlled must be managed proactively. Control helps to eradicate complacency amongst managers and provides for consistency in the effective management of key organisational processes.

2. Competitiveness Stage

Secondly, the competitiveness stage represents the conversion of an internal standard of effectiveness into a competitive one, through benchmarking exercises. In this regard, the following steps are proposed:

- *Identify suitable partners*: organisations need to select their partners carefully if the exercise is to prove worthwhile and is to have an enduring effect.

- *Agree on a measurement strategy*: there has to be an agreed methodology and issues of confidentiality must be ironed out between partner companies.

- *Compare standards*: data collection analysis should lead to comparisons.

- *Carefully examine differences in performance*: assess the nature of any differences and try to explain why they occur.

- *Consider relevant practices for improving performance*: this represents the action stage of the exercise and is a measure of the extent of management commitment.

- *Repeat exercise* with same/new partner organisations on a regular basis.

It is proposed that, through the application of the above approach, the management of quality initiatives can be kept in check. This can be achieved through a process of continuous evaluation of internal processes against "best practice" in the industry.

The Confederation of British Industry (CBI) set up a tourism action group to help "make Britain the global pacesetter in heritage, cultural and hospitality tourism". As part of this process, it undertook a benchmarking exercise of three- and four-star hotels in France and Germany — the purpose of the exercise being to "use benchmarking to identify potential improvements in business practices and performance" (CBI, undated).

The exercise found three areas of concern for the hotel industry to focus upon:

1. British hotels have a higher staff turnover and a lower percentage of qualified staff than their counterparts on the continent, leading to reliance on remedial training and a skills gap.

2. British hotels have a lower level of reinvestment of profits on refurbishment (eight per cent of turnover compared to 14 per cent in France and 16 per cent in Germany).

3. Performance varies markedly between hotels. "This is a further source of competitive weakness and there is a need to bring more businesses closer to the level of the best." (CBI, undated).

The study concluded that there were five main areas of action to concentrate effort upon:

- Further use of industry-wide programmes such as "Welcome Host" (basic customer care training) especially in smaller firms

- Need to "deepen" the relationship between business and education and have more business-specific courses

- The "Investors in People" (training and staff development) culture must permeate through the industry

- Core skills and qualifications must become an outcome of all learning

- Every school and college should be linked to a tourism business and the industry must adopt professional career development practices as the norm.

For the first time, challenges were set for the hospitality industry, and an agenda for action was established. This report, amongst others, was influential in helping to shape government thinking about the way ahead for a globally competitive hospitality and tourism industry in Britain.

Performance Measurement

A further means by which hospitality organisations might achieve integration between their strategic goals and quality practices is through performance measurement. It is well established that the effective management of quality relies on the extent to which the organisation evaluates its quality specifications on a continuous basis. Krishnan et al (1993: 7) make this point when they argue that:

> . . . attaining quality through a process of continuous improvement over time depends critically upon a firm's ability to define in specific performance terms what it means by quality and then to measure these performance variables objectively.

However, the specification of quality procedures is a complicated process, particularly given the intangible nature of services. The specific characteristics of services mean that quality needs to be built into the offering; it cannot be inspected into the offering at a later stage. Gamble and Jones (1991: 75) refer to this aspect as "design quality" and emphasise the requirement for specifications to take account of this element of the quality process:

> Design quality refers to the standard to which management resources and monitors a product. It is probably the most critical element of the quality strategy.

Oakland (1993) suggests that performance measurement is significant in that it helps to:

- Ensure that customer requirements have been met

- Provide standards for establishing comparisons

- Provide visibility and a "score-board" for individuals to monitor their own performance levels

- Identify quality problems and determine areas requiring attention.

Similarly, others have claimed that ineffective performance measurement impedes successful quality implementation, as measurement provides the link between strategy and action. Inappropriate measures lead to actions incongruent with strategies, however well formulated and communicated. Appropriate measures should provide and strengthen this link, and both lead to attainment of strategic goals and impact on the goals and strategies needed to achieve them. Thus, the evaluation of service quality initiatives forms an important part of service quality management. The evaluation process allows the communication channel to function effectively by soliciting customer feedback as well as providing employees with up-to-date information on the organisation's quality initiatives.

These are in line with benefits emphasised by managers in a report of quality management practices within the British hotel industry (Harrington and Akehurst, 1996a). As well as stressing the importance of measurement in achieving timeless consistency and uniformity in service provision, managers emphasised benefits such as ability to plan better for future requirements and to focus on customer requirements as important products of the measurement process. Indeed, an overwhelming number of respondents supported the measurement of organisational service quality. The respondents indicated that a number of techniques were currently being used to monitor service quality procedures in their organisations and it was encouraging to note that alternative techniques for monitoring service quality were growing in importance at respondent hotels.

However, there were indications of a divergence between exhortation and reality. This was evidenced by the fact that the guest questionnaire remains the most predominant means of measuring quality at the hotel unit level, with almost a third (28 per cent) of those who responded indicating that their hotels used "guest questionnaires" to measure quality. This approach was favoured by respondents because of its ease of development and administration. Other measurement approaches were used to support the guest questionnaire technique including, among others, management observation and employee feedback.

The popularity of the questionnaire technique is a cause for concern, since it is for the most part unrepresentative. Participants tend to be categorised in terms of satisfaction: either extremely satisfied or highly dissatisfied. Also, such measures have poor construct validity: survey questions are not based on any established concepts or theories. Finally, there are problems with poor statistical validity: survey participants are usually solicited by a non-random self-selection process. Such measurement techniques carry negative implications for quality measurement in hotels, supplying incomplete or inaccurate information which does not assist hotel managers in decision-making. Interestingly, only seven per cent of managers had ever used group interviews with customers as a means of measuring quality, which lends credibility to the claim that service organisations measure that which is easy to measure.

Significant findings were also recorded from the open-ended responses provided by managers. It was noted that extensions to the popular comment card/guest questionnaire techniques have limited appeal and use in practice. Although respondents outlined that their organisations had used alternative methods to evaluate quality, they emphasised that the actual application of such techniques proved problematic and was constrained by the lack of organisational resource committed to their effective operation. As one respondent commented: "We have tried other ways to evaluate quality, such as group interviews with guests, but these are difficult to arrange because senior managers won't allocate the necessary resources" (Harrington and Akehurst, 1996a). Other managers also emphasised the overall commitment which was necessary to support multi-method approaches to evaluating quality. In particular, they were concerned about the lack of top level commitment shown in their organisations towards quality evaluation and were conscious of the effects which this might have for the performances of front-line staff.

Some companies have recognised the limitations of the comment-card approach and have designed more innovative means of tracking customer satisfaction. For example the Hilton International have adopted a "Guest Satisfaction Index" that takes account of the limitations of the comment-card approach. In consequence of the limitations associated with the traditional approaches to evaluating customer satisfaction, the British Hospitality Association has established an innovative benchmark system to monitor satisfaction. It has the support of fourteen major hotel groups and hopes to achieve major improvements in both service delivery and recovery (JHIC, 1998). Similarly, in Ireland, both the Hotels Federation and the Restaurants Association have introduced codes of best practice that members should adhere to. They aim to raise standards within the tourism sector and improve levels of customer satisfaction. They also wish to rid the industry of unprofessional operators whose practices do damage to the rest of the sector.

A requirement therefore exists to encourage management and staff to play a more active part in the evaluation process. Currently, as outlined above, the predominant approach to assessing quality standards in hospitality organisations is to monitor customers' service perceptions. However, simultaneous attention needs to be given to evaluating staff and managerial feedback when monitoring quality. Berry et al. (1994: 42) comment that the evaluation of employee feedback

> . . . is as important to service improvement as customer re-
> search . . . employees offer insight into conditions that reduce
> service quality in the organisation . . . and because of employ-
> ees' more intensive exposure to the service delivery system,
> they often see the system breaking down before customers do.

Although the measurement methods quoted by managers encompass a concern for facilitating organisational opinion on delivery effectiveness, the open-ended responses show that the input was most often concerned with reported customer
(dis)satisfaction. Such feedback should be broadened to allow for
greater organisational involvement in the development and
evaluation of quality procedures.

Exhibit 4.5 below sets out the most common methods of obtaining customer feedback across a number of industries. Also,
common methods of "listening to the customer" are outlined.
These are drawn from research carried out in US and Japanese
hotels.

Exhibit 4.5: Customer Feedback Methods

Among all industries, the most common methods of obtaining customer feedback and other information include:

- Comment cards
- Mail, phone, and in-person questionnaires
- "Free-phone" numbers
- Focus groups
- Employee feedback
- Management observation and
- Sales data.

The following approaches, in order of popularity, were identified as
methods of "listening to the customer":

- Guest comment cards
- Management–guest interaction
- Employee feedback
- Formal customer interviews — mail, phone, in-person
- Spotters ("mystery guests")
- Role playing ("confederates")
- Focus groups
- Guest-survey programs and
- Guest-preference research.

Source: W.A. Band (1992), "Listening to the Customer", *Sales and Marketing Management*, October, pp. 15–16, 36.

Indeed, the importance of performance measurement is also underscored in another study, "Tourism: Competing with the Best", commissioned by the British Department of National Heritage (1996c). In this report, it was shown that the returns to companies operating performance measurement systems was substantial:

> One company found that an initiative combining training, performance measurement and recognition for achievement led to 50 per cent reduction in complaints, and a 400 per cent increase in compliments. Another company has managed to achieve a repeat customer rate of 60 per cent.

Further, the requirement for organisations to initiate performance measurement procedures as part of their overall strategic quality implementation process is highlighted by a recent world-wide study which showed that customer-related issues will be the most crucial for business success in the decades ahead (JHIC, 1998). As Zairi and Youseff (1995: 3) comment:

> . . . customer satisfaction is more often based on gut feelings than data collection and organised intelligence systems. . . .

most companies do not assess competitor performance in a systematic way. It is not a process but a part-time activity.

These issues will loom large for hospitality businesses in the years ahead.

Summary

In this chapter we have attempted to address the strategic nature of quality management programmes. Although much alluded to within the business press, there are shortcomings in the attention given to this dimension of quality management in the literature. As quality has assumed increased importance in a variety of markets, both its management and strategic significance have become central concerns for researchers and practitioners. These issues pose particular problems for managers in the hospitality field given the nature of the product provided and the skills and capabilities of those involved in delivering services to customers.

In consequence, we considered ways in which we might achieve greater integration between quality programmes and the organisation's overall strategic initiatives. Firstly, the importance of viewing service quality as a source of competitive advantage was emphasised. Secondly, the value of achieving greater competitiveness through benchmarking was outlined and finally, performance measurement was discussed so as to provide readers with a detailed overview of the approaches through which strategic quality could be understood and applied. In doing so, it is hoped that readers will take a strategic approach to developing and managing quality programmes and that the material discussed will stimulate greater consideration of these issues in practitioner contexts.

Review Questions

1. Does quality need to be managed? Assume that you have been appointed quality manager at a hospitality organisation

of your choice. How would you want to initiate relevant quality initiatives?

2. In your view, has quality assumed greater strategic significance within the hospitality sector? What evidence would you proffer to support your argument?

3. What do understand by the term competitive advantage? How might it be illustrated in a hospitality organisation of your choice?

4. You have been asked to undertake a benchmarking exercise at a large local restaurant group. How would you manage the benchmarking process? What are the key issues involved?

5. Outline how you might persuade a hotel manager to initiate a performance measurement system. What benefits would you expect from introducing such a system?

Chapter 5

Hard and Soft Quality Management

Introduction

In previous chapters an attempt was made to examine the strategic importance of the quality concept, particularly its role in helping to reduce costs and promote greater commitment to continuous improvement. For the most part, organisations have been focusing their efforts on two main aspects of quality management, namely, quality certification and Total Quality Management (TQM). Quality certification examines the procedures and documentation that make up a quality system while TQM takes a wider perspective and focuses on issues such as employee development and customer responsiveness. Although the emphasis of the text is on the latter, it is important also to be aware of the nature and implications of quality standards within the hospitality industry. In particular, there is a requirement to appraise the current strong level of interest in quality certification and, at the same time, to examine the growing criticisms of quality standards within the business press.

In this chapter, we examine such issues. In particular, we distinguish between certification and continuous improvement and evaluate the benefits of both approaches. The notion of "soft" quality management is defined and the competitive importance of this aspect of quality management is examined. Finally, we discuss the implications of the increasing focus on soft quality management and propose an integrated approach to the management of service delivery in hospitality organisations. First we turn attention to quality standards.

Quality Standards in Tourism Organisations

ISO 9000 represents a set of standards, laid down by the International Organisation for Standardisation, that outline best practice for quality management. There are three main parts to the ISO 9000 award: ISO 9001 (design, development, production, installation, and servicing) ISO 9002 (model for Quality Assurance in production and installation alone) and ISO 9003 (assesses Quality Assurance in production and installation).

The achievement of the award requires management to produce a quality manual documenting the company's objectives, organisation and an overview of the quality assurance system. The quality manual may be produced internally, developed with the assistance of a team of consultants or produced from an easily adaptable off-the-shelf package. The ISO 9000 system covers all the activities of the company from training through administrative systems and management reviews. Developing and implementing the quality system typically takes between six and nine months, and should the quality manual be deemed satisfactory, an on-site inspection of the business is carried out before the award of certification is made. Once awarded the standard, a company may include the ISO 9000 standard in all its advertising. However, the organisation will be subject to unannounced surveillance audits two or three times per year. These audits are focused on specific activities within the quality manual but cover all clauses of the standard over a one-year period.

ISO 9000 standards have become the most important international standards ever produced. To date, over 40 countries have adopted them as national standards. In a recent survey of member countries, 43 of the 47 countries that replied indicated that they had a national standard identical to ISO 9000. In the majority of cases, certification systems to that standard were already in place and the number of certified companies in their countries was growing. The world-wide acceptance of the standard demonstrates that a quality system certified to ISO 9000 is essential for success in the international marketplace.

Quality Standards — Help or Hindrance?

Successful implementation of quality systems can bring substantial benefits to the organisation. Certification is now almost mandatory in some sectors and is a critical factor in winning contracts and custom. Customers are demanding greater value and the focus on quality is much sharper. The framework guiding the design and implementation of quality standards serves as an important driving force behind more effective management practices. It signals the abandonment of many familiar and in some cases inefficient work practices and provides dependability and good value in products and services sold. More specifically, achievement of ISO 9000 certification can provide the following:

- ISO 9000 is emerging as a minimum guarantee of quality for customers and it is anticipated that the standard will be increasingly sought in the future. Standards are now set by those who buy services, not by those who supply them.

- ISO 9000 can ease considerably the search for new markets and customers. The world of business is becoming more competitive and quality has become a byword for success. Certification will mean that companies will have less difficulty selling their products into new markets.

- ISO 9000 should bring both cost and time savings to an organisation. It will assist in avoiding costly mistakes and in eliminating the need for corrective action at a later stage.

- ISO 9000 forces managers to examine and deal with problems facing their businesses. Instead of assigning blame on individuals, managers are faced with addressing the underlying problems.

- The successful introduction of a quality improvement process requires more than administrative structures. Ways must be found to encourage the participation of front-line employees in managerial decision-making and to gain their commitment to quality implementation efforts. In this respect, the standard should act as a foundation for further quality improvement in the form of Total Quality Management (TQM).

However, quality certification has not been free of criticism and recent contributions have questioned the effectiveness of the standard in helping organisations achieve business excellence. Seddon (1997) has been most vocal in his criticism of ISO 9000. At the heart of his criticism lie a number of key issues that warrant exploration and discussion. First, certification, he argues, adds to costs, demoralises staff and prevents the organisation from taking opportunities to improve performance. Seddon also claims that the standard imposes a traditional command-and-control ethos and a rigid set of written rules. It assumes that people cannot be trusted to improve and control their own work, a process which would invariably result in less errors. In short, he writes that ISO 9000 gives people a second job: they do their work and then they write about it.

Companies have also been concerned about the costs of implementation. Smaller companies often cannot justify the expenditure required to invest in the standard. This is significant, especially when we consider the problems smaller organisations encounter when building their customer base. Also, firms who are already active in their pursuit of quality principles may find the standard of little value. Where a strong commitment to quality management already exists in a company, improvement resulting from implementation of the standard is likely to be small.

In this case, achievement of the standard adds significantly to costs without actually leading to significant improvements in customer satisfaction. However, the official recognition that being able to advertise the fact that one has met a recognised standard, even if below an in-house standard, gives confidence to customers when they are considering purchasing one product over another. The rush for hospitality and tourism firms to be accredited with "Investor in People" certification in Great Britain suggests that this outward focus is as important as the inward quality improvement focus.

Thus, ISO 9000 is traditional in its focus and application. While it seeks to ensure conformity of a product or service, it does not guarantee high levels of customer satisfaction for a company. Instead of adhering to the standard, Seddon (1997) advocates a return to the question: what is important to the customer? What matters in the marketplace? Quality certification aims to "prevent non-conformity" but is this necessarily what the customer wants? He recommends that firms should focus on their capabilities and in particular understand the ways in which they design and deliver products or services to customers. He points out:

> Keep challenging the "have to" [mentality]. The most common reason for registration is that customers are demanding it. If you can show your customers that you understand what matters to them and you have translated their needs into the way you manage your business, why should you need the Standard? There is not a customer in the world who would not be persuaded by data showing evidence of your performance against what matters to them (p. 188).

Exhibit 5.1 emphasises the significance of Seddon's (1997) contribution regarding the importance of customer input in shaping the quality process. Specifically, it shows how Piccadilly Cafeterias recently returned to profitability by refocusing its operations and offerings around customer expectations. The company reintro-

duced quality recipes and pleasant interiors instituted by Piccadilly founder Tandy Hamilton and saw its sales and profits improve dramatically.

Exhibit 5.1: Lumpy Mashed Potatoes — Yuck!

In the late 1980s, Piccadilly's CEO announced major cost-saving
measures which were to have disastrous consequences for the company. Where it was possible to cut costs . . . Piccadilly did it. It
worked for a while. Between 1987 and 1989, profits increased 24 per
cent, to $11.3 million. But customers noted the difference: "Them
mashed potatoes got lumpy and didn't taste fresh" commented one
customer, and "those pie crusts weren't flaky but got mushy". Customers who had grown up on Piccadilly's meals began staying
away, and in 1990, sales per cafeteria began to suffer. In 1991, after
48 consecutive years of profits, the company posted its first quarterly loss.

Decisive action was called for and in early 1992 the board of directors appointed a new chief executive, Charles Bennett. Out went
the "heat-and-eat" philosophy of his predecessor; back in came
good old-fashioned recipes. The contrast couldn't have been greater
and it showed on the bottom line. Though the 137-store chain does
virtually no advertising, customer counts at the refurbished cafeterias are up 15 per cent and its share price has doubled to a recent
$14. Yet Bennett did nothing remarkable: just improved the quality
of the product a bit and fixed the places up. Which goes to show that
no matter how smart your bean counters are, you can't run a business on a spreadsheet alone.

Source: *Forbes*, 28 March 1994, pp. 63–65.

"Manufactured" Quality and Continuous Improvement

From the above discussion, we may liken ISO 9000 standards to a
form of "manufactured" quality. While certification focuses on
the procedures that make up a quality system, TQM takes a
broader view and emphasises employee involvement and continuous improvement. This is an important point that is often lost
on managers charged with introducing quality into the organisation. Over the last number of years, there has been a consensus

that the application of quality standards in an organisation was sufficient to ensure lower costs, greater employee morale and customer responsiveness. However, that has not been the case. As Seddon (1997) and others have pointed out, certification is one of a wide range of activities needed to achieve overall business excellence. This position needs to be made stronger by those engaged in research and consultancy. Zairi (1996: 109) makes the point when he remarks:

> There has however been far too much emphasis in the past on accreditation and achieving successful registration to quality standards such as ISO 9000. . . . many companies do not fully realise the implications of managing quality systems such as ISO 9000, the level of commitment required and the resources needed to ensure high quality standards are maintained.

He claims that the challenge for organisations is to drive the process from a "strategic corporate perspective". Certification in itself is not enough to ensure high levels of quality improvement within hospitality organisations. While TQM strives to improve all the operations of the business, ISO 9000 takes a narrower view and focuses only around the products or services of an organisation. Quality certification is positive in that it ensures conformance to requirements and encourages greater commitment to achieving high standards of quality. However, TQM encourages greater stimulation of individual employees and overall greater anticipation of customer requirements in the marketplace. By focusing on training as opposed to education, communication and involvement as TQM does, certification does not emphasise enough the need for continuous improvement of quality. In this regard, ISO 9000 should be viewed as a basis from which continuous improvement will follow.

One organisation which accepted the need to embrace a TQM approach to managing its business was English Lake Hotels. Two events convinced the management of the organisation that it was time to transform the attitudes and culture of its employees. The first was the discovery that the staff in one of its hotels, which was converted into a top-class facility, were unable to cope with greater responsibilities. The other was the appointment of the company's chairman as a board member of a training and enterprise council, which gave him an appreciation of training. Exhibit 5.2 below outlines the approach used by the company to transform it into a high quality operation.

Exhibit 5.2: Lake District Gets TQM Treatment

English Lake Hotels is a 43-year-old business which consists of five hotels — four around Lake Windermere and one in Lancaster — two leisure clubs and a water sports and activity centre. It has a turnover of more than seven million pounds and a full-time staff of around 270. Just five years ago, there was no company-wide recruitment or training policy. However, all that changed when staff started to complain about increasing pressures and responsibilities at work and when the chairman and managing director, Michael Berry, was appointed to a training and enterprise council in Cumbria.

On Berry's advice, the company decided to introduce the Investors in People (IIP) programme in all eight businesses. This brought a systematic approach to training and staff evaluation. The chairman also wanted to evolve a teamwork culture to replace the "us and them"-type attitudes which prevailed within the group. In doing this, he decided to consult the Disney University in Orlando, Florida where he stated: "They had developed something which did exactly what we wanted to do, that really motivated and empowered their staff to provide this quality of service".

On returning from the US, he and other directors used mixed-media presentations to teach staff about the importance of providing a "quality service experience" measured against four key standards: safety, courtesy, presentation and efficiency. Employees were also encouraged to think about how to improve the quality of service they were offering, by considering better methods of delivery and more efficient use of resources. Formal performance reviews were introduced and individuals were encouraged to keep their own personal action plans.

> The hotel's culture has now been turned on its head, with all departments putting pressure on the managers to make improvements and in some cases, tackling problems and taking decisions that the management would previously have taken. As a consequence of introducing these changes, the company will see considerable improvement in its profit position in the coming years. This will be a direct result of greater productivity and improved guest satisfaction. As one employee points out: "You can go and ask for things and you get them as long as you are trying to improve the situation. Before it might have been a bit harder."

Source: *People Management*, 8 February 1996, p. 38.

Research from a team of consultants at the London Business School supports our view of ISO 9000. The researchers examined the effectiveness of both certification and TQM in a wide-scale empirical study of quality management in Europe. They conducted interviews at 641 sites in four countries, Finland, Germany, Netherlands and Britain. They concluded the following:

- There was a significant relationship between certification and quality, customer satisfaction and productivity. This was found to be supportive of quality certification, particularly in terms of the impact on quality.

- Further examination revealed that apart from a direct impact on quality, the impact of certification was relatively low compared with that of TQM.

- Companies with certification such as ISO 9000 reported significantly higher quality than those without. However, quality certification in an already poor company will not necessarily change quality performance in the short term. It is only one of a number of activities needed to ensure high quality performance.

- Quality management requires management action and will to realise downstream benefits (Voss and Blackmon, 1995).

In assessing a case study on the introduction of ISO 9000 to the Cardiff Copthorne Hotel, Baker and Cave (1995) found that to achieve accreditation took over a year and cost some £30,000, plus another £5,000 to implement. Further ongoing costs of £550 for the British Standard Institute's fee and £1,200 per year for two inspections mean that ISO 9000 is expensive to achieve and run. This cost has to be justified on the bottom line.

The process of accreditation and inspection proved difficult early on because of the lack of knowledge of the BSI inspectors of the hospitality industry, although these issues have since been addressed. Perceived benefits of ISO 9000 have been improvements in staff turnover and the belief by senior managers that it makes their tasks easier, as set procedures have to be followed. However, ISO 9000 itself does not improve quality. It is the implementation of the procedures that does this and, therefore, the quality of the management and staff are key success factors.

Despite the investment and perceived benefits, the Copthorne group has no intention of introducing the standard into its other hotels, but local management, in the face of a lack of evidence to suggest ISO 9000 has improved turnover, retain the standard as an "act of faith". Simon Reed, the hotel's general manager, "doubts . . . that the Copthorne group, or indeed the industry as a whole, will ever wholeheartedly embrace ISO 9000" (Baker and Cave, 1995) because of the costs associated with setting up and implementing it and also the inability to attribute improved turnover or gross margins to the implementation of the scheme.

The lesson here may be that "manufactured quality" does not necessarily bring tangible results, especially when it is not tailored to the industry in question.

Additionally, the following important point needs to be made: achieving results from investment in quality does not come automatically. Time is required for the impact to work its way through the organisation and many of the downstream results in operating performance require further actions on the part of the management team.

Thus, we may distinguish between "manufactured quality" or a focus on quality certification and continuous improvement as follows: certification to the ISO 9000 standard refers to quality management systems or structures that assist in achieving or sustaining the gains of TQM. TQM is, however, concerned with the continuous enhancement of customer satisfaction through quality-driven company-wide management. This goes beyond the mere application of quality principles, becoming a business philosophy concerned with changing attitudes, beliefs, values and the culture of the organisation (Rajagopal et al., 1995). However, to date the importance of viewing TQM in this way has been overlooked by both researchers and practitioners alike. There has been an overemphasis on the technical or "hard" side of TQM and too little attention given to the "softer", human dimension. This is critical since the

> . . . assumption that employees and managers will welcome TQM is fallacious because there is often a great deal of resistance to its implementation at all levels in the organisation. People are a key resource for all companies but senior management often misunderstands and mismanages them (Rajagopal et al., 1995).

Indeed, the need for a greater consideration of the "softer" side of TQM also has been underscored by the growth and relevance of the service sector and its importance to world economies.

Competitive Importance of "Soft" Quality

Traditionally, definitions of quality management were oriented towards manufacturing industries. This is to be expected, especially given that a concern for quality improvement evolved from within manufacturing sectors. However, quality management needs to extend its focus further to embrace the concerns of the service sector. This is a recurrent theme within the text; however, the point cannot be overstated. Consider the following statistics.

In 1929, 55 per cent of the working population was employed in the service sector in the United States, and approximately 54 per cent of the gross domestic national product was generated by services in 1948. By the early 1990s, however, services represented over 70 per cent of GDP and 80 per cent of employment (Zeithaml and Bitner, 1997). The authors argue that marketing strategies and concepts have developed in response to the tremendous growth of service industries resulting in their increased importance to world economies. In relation to the tourism industry they comment:

> International tourism is the largest services export in the US and the third largest export overall. Spending by foreign visitors on such services as hotel rooms, restaurant meals, and airfares generated one-third of the US international services trade surplus in 1992.

Similarly, the World Travel and Tourism Council (WTTC, 1994) suggests that tourism, of which hospitality is an important sector:

- Is the world's largest industry

- Is the world's largest employer and creator of jobs

- Accounts for ten per cent of global wages

- Accounts for 11 per cent of non-food consumer retailing, and

- Is responsible for ten per cent of world GDP.

Burns and Holden (1995: 4) remark that "such claims emphasise the sheer scale of the phenomenon . . . and the effect it can have on the external socio-political environment".

However, although the service sector's size has grown over the last number of decades, its productivity growth has declined. In the US, for example, improvements in productivity growth are continuing at low levels despite large increases in expenditure on information technology. In a recent report, van Biema and Greenwald (1997: 890) suggest that productivity performance lies predominantly with managers. Although a detailed discussion of this problem is outside the remit of this text, some points made by the writers are noteworthy and carry significance for the management of quality in hospitality organisations.

First, it is suggested that efforts at improving organisational performance should attend to what workers actually do and how their activities might be streamlined. Second, best practice analysis within an organisation can be a good start for managers because efficient units can provide useful information, management techniques and performance targets. Simultaneously, comparisons across organisations can help companies avoid repeating past mistakes. Such activities should form a part of any quality management approach to improving performance. Central to the current discussion, van Biema and Greenwald (1997: 93) comment that the proper implementation of quality management tools can yield enormous performance gains in services as they have in manufacturing. Hence the growing importance of recent discussions on "soft" quality management within the services sector.

Contemporary Perspectives on TQM

In particular, the distinction between traditional manufacturing and service approaches to defining quality have been viewed as a difference in emphasis between "hard" and "soft" aspects of quality management (Wilkinson et al., 1991; 1992; Rees, 1995). This distinction has been alluded to in earlier chapters; however, in this section we need to discuss in detail the nature of "hard" and "soft" quality management and the implications which each carries for the management of quality in organisations.

The traditional approach to managing quality programmes focused on product quality. Initiatives centred around ways in which products could be made to conform to specifications and to date there has been a strong manufacturing dimension to the management of quality in organisations. Common techniques which are referred to in discussions of quality strategy include:

- Statistical process control (SPC)

- Quality function deployment (QFD)

- Quality costing

- Checklists

- Flowcharts

- Quality control tools.

Certain questions present themselves. Will procedures and practices that have been developed in manufacturing contexts find application in service operations? How might the "softer" dimensions to quality management be used to underpin quality strategy in hospitality organisations?

Wilkinson et al. (1992: 2) review "quality" in a similar manner. Specifically, he sets out the following approaches to reviewing the concept. First, he identifies the "soft" qualitative aspects which place emphasis on customer responsiveness and competitiveness secured through employee empowerment. Second, he focuses on the "hard" production characteristics of quality development and "conformance to requirements". In particular, this relates to statistical techniques used to assess quality and other standardised approaches applied to control performance. However, it is the practices of the manufacturing sector that have dominated much of the debate and discussion on quality management, to the neglect of services. Recent reports point to major problems with the philosophy. These relate to problems concerning the notion of "total" and the lack of concern given to the human dimension in quality programmes. It is suggested that, when conceived in a partial fashion as a set of tools and techniques without consideration of the human factor, quality programmes can fail to achieve their desired outcomes. As Wilkinson (1994: 274) points out:

> A failure to change attitudes and culture has meant a narrow vision of quality has been transmitted, and this can be at least partially attributed to the neglect of human resource policies in the organisation and a failure to align human resources policies with TQM to ensure integration.

Evidence suggests that organisations operating within the service sector, who by their nature have a high degree of staff/customer interaction, focus attention on the more qualitative and softer aspects of quality (Rees, 1995). Thus, it would be expected that hospitality firms, who are the main focus of this textbook, would develop their specification and quality evaluation efforts around "softer" aspects of quality management. Why should this be the case? As outlined above and in Chapter 1, services differ from products in significant ways. The intangible nature of services means that it is necessary to rethink the traditional approaches to managing quality. The key differences have been outlined; these relate to the fact that service attributes are difficult to demonstrate, are produced and consumed at the same time and are better viewed as a process rather than an outcome (Legge, 1995). In consequence, in hospitality companies it is generally more appropriate to take a "softer" perspective on quality and view the concept as "meeting and/or exceeding customers' expectations". Exhibit 5.3 shows how top restaurants in London are taking a more professional approach to recruitment and training of waiting staff. This is in recognition of the importance which customers are attaching to "softer" HRM aspects of quality management.

Exhibit 5.3: Service Delivery in the Restaurant Business

Waiting in a restaurant is more than a matter of moving meals from kitchen to table. It tells you much about the character of the people carrying the tray, of the restaurant in which they work, and more contentiously, of the society in which they live.

Service is revealing of a society, but it is essentially a personal experience. There is genuine pleasure in the courtesy of an attentive, intelligent waiter or waitress who anticipates. Bad service in Britain, now less obviously class-ridden, tells of a country still struggling to put "professional help" in perspective.

Technology is helping the hospitality business. Many waiters carry portable electronic order pads which, with enough keys for all possible menu permutations, eliminates the unseemly dash into he kitchen with barely legible, handwritten orders. But technology alone will not turn around a restaurant's waiting staff.

Competition is forcing restaurateurs at last to offer proper terms and conditions — recent advertisements from top London restaurants promise recognition, reward, paid holiday and free life assurance — to attract the best staff. Training companies and industrial psychologists are being deployed to improve standards. In the UK, Scher Associates carries out manager and waiter training, mystery dining programmes and guest questionnaires for 75 companies ranging from Forte and Sheraton Hotels to Caprice Holdings. It measures customer responses against the hotel's anticipated service standards. Consumers also should appreciate the skills a good waiter possesses. Most importantly, we all must appreciate the basic humanity of those who stand and wait — before they are swept away by a tide of fast food and self-service restaurants.

Source: "They also Serve who only Stand and Wait", *Financial Times*, 11/12 January 1997.

However, from case study work in a British hotel firm, Rees (1995) showed that contrary to the argument outlining the desirability for hotel service organisations of developing "soft" approaches to quality, in practice, the case analysis suggested that managers were increasingly interested in the quantitative aspects of quality. Rees concluded from his research that quality practices have different emphases depending on the organisation under examination. Thus, for some organisations it will be important that emphasis is placed on the hard quantifiable manufacturing aspects, while for others the quality effort is focused on the softer techniques, with only limited account being taken of the quantitative issues.

In an attempt to take a wider perspective on quality management, the Hotel and Catering International Management Association (HCIMA) in Great Britain has recently launched a major quality initiative that it hopes will become the definitive standard in Great Britain. The association's new standard ("Professional Service Standard") involves self-assessment for hospitality organisations, with uniform measures for evaluating standards of service; a national benchmarking database of all subscribing companies; and an accreditation scheme that will allow participants to display a "hospitality assured" logo. The initiative is based on ISO 9002 and "investors in people" and has been developed specifically to take account of the industry requirements. The scheme has been welcomed by a wide range of organisations who view it as an important means by which to improve standards through effective training and development of staff (*Caterer and Hotelkeeper*, 9 October 1997, pp. 10–11).

To date, less attention has been given to this aspect of quality management. Only recently, for example, have attempts been made to address HRM issues in quality management research (Kerfoot and Knights, 1995; Wilkinson and Willmott, 1995) and in particular the ways in which HRM policy can be developed to support the organisation's quality objectives.

Mirage Resorts is a company that recognises that a highly competent workforce is the key to success in an intensely competitive marketplace. To achieve this, it spends a considerable amount of money in hiring and training the most qualified and friendliest employees it can find. Exhibit 5.4 provides an outline of some of the approaches the company takes and shows the benefits these initiatives have in creating and nurturing customer goodwill.

Exhibit 5.4: Las Vegas Resort Bets on Training and Wins

Mirage Resorts, a 3,000-guestroom hotel and gaming casino holds a winning hand in service in competitive Las Vegas. The company spends large sums of money in recruiting and training the best people possible for the positions on offer at the company. Stephen Wynn, CEO, states: "Our people are the mortar that holds together the bricks; they breathe life into mere buildings". The strategy is working, for although a large number of people who visit Las Vegas do so just once a year, approximately 50 per cent of the people who stay at the Mirage once stay again.

Fun is emphasised at Mirage Resorts. Certainly, the company looks out for its workers in terms of offering several different medical plans; multiple life and disability insurance programmes; paid time off and bonuses for perfect attendance. But even more than that, Mirage Resorts offers a fun work environment. The VP for Human Resources, Arthur Nathan, admits that keeping managers focused on making the workplace fun is probably the greatest challenge that he faces: "Managers tend to be get-the-tasks-done types of people. My job is to change them to have a greater people orientation, to better deal with the full range of issues that come up when managing people." Of course, the jobs that need to be performed for a business to run — even if that business is providing entertainment — can't be all fun and games. Providing quality service is serious business at Mirage. The company spent approximately $3.5 million on pre-opening training for The Mirage and $8 million per year corporate-wide on training.

The emphasis on people as a basis for delivering high quality service to the customer is paying dividends. In 1994, Mirage Resorts had gross revenues of close to $1.4 billion and according to *Forbes* magazine, has the highest productivity of large casino and hotel companies. The company reported $7,500 dollars in profits for each of its 15,700 employees in 1994 and ranked highest in sales in the travel, hotel and gaming sector in the US. As one employee commented: "It gives you a good feeling to be part of something that you know is going to be the very best out there, the best it can be."

Source: Personnel Journal, September 1995, pp. 79–85.

Implications for Service Delivery

In attempting to address the softer aspects of quality management, hospitality organisations need to examine carefully the ways in which service is currently delivered to customers. Broadly, we view the process of delivering service to the customer as falling into two main approaches. First, there is the important human dimension to service delivery. This aspect of service delivery is introduced here but is expanded upon in Chapter 6. Second, and of growing significance in today's organisation, is the technological dimension. In the sections which follow we review the importance of both approaches and examine the value of applying an integrated approach to service delivery.

Human Dimension to Service Delivery

The human dimension to service delivery places great emphasis on the ways in which organisational employees can positively influence the service given to customers. Attention has been focused on the role of employees as "part-time marketeers" (Gummesson, 1991) and more specifically, on the contribution which they bring to the service quality implementation process. Gummesson (1991) describes employee contributions in terms of their influence on customer relations, customer-perceived quality and overall customer satisfaction. This emphasis placed on employee contributions is an important consideration, particularly when it has been shown that customers attach more importance to people-related quality determinants than to those of a tangible nature. In fact, the results of a study by Schneider and Bowen (1985) offers support for directing attention towards the human element. In a retail banking context, they established that a relationship existed between well-managed service encounters, improved customer satisfaction and employee satisfaction, supporting the notion that employee-managed service encounters can deliver high levels of personal service for the customer. Others also found that three of five dimensions of service quality — responsiveness,

assurance and empathy — related directly to the quality of employee performance in the service delivery process (Parasuraman,
Zeithaml and Berry, 1988).

Consequently, comment has been made on the benefits of empowering front-line service employees by authorising them to use
their discretion to deliver better quality service for the customer.
Bowen and Lawler (1992) have pointed out that there are four
empowerment criteria which encompass a requirement for involving employees. The front-end employee should receive:

- Information about the organisation's performance

- Rewards based on the organisation's performance

- Knowledge that enables them to understand and contribute to
  organisational performance, and

- Power to make decisions that influence organisational direction and performance.

They claim that the benefits of empowerment centre around its
ability to facilitate faster and more flexible response to customers'
needs, and the improvements it makes on levels of employee motivation and satisfaction.

For example, surveys regularly show that the attitude of the
Irish people and those working in tourism is of a high quality.
This is again supported by findings from a recent research project
commissioned by the board of the Overseas Tourism Marketing
Initiative (OTMI). The study, entitled "Consumer Journeys" was
co-ordinated across the US, Germany, France and Britain, revealed that Ireland's unique selling proposition (USP) is people
and spontaneity (Bord Fáilte, 1998).

The natural ability to "bring people out of themselves and a
genuine interest in people spanning all generations" were shown
as key factors in this regard. The research identifies interaction
with Irish people and their way of life as a key manifestation of

people and spontaneity. One of the most important challenges emerging from the research concerns ways in which this USP — people and spontaneity — can be delivered in the future. An examination of approaches which may be used to support industry-led training initiatives will form an important part of future work in this area. In line with the arguments presented above, it is suggested that a trained and empowered workforce is more motivated, particularly if actively involved and given discretion in decisions regarding the customer and, consequently, delivers a higher quality service to customers (Hackman and Oldman, 1980). Moreover, in situations where problems do occur, a trained and empowered staff is more likely to be in a better position to take the necessary corrective action and retrieve the situation for the company. In fact, it has been shown that satisfactorily resolved situations can serve to enhance the customers' perceptions of quality (Hart, Heskitt and Sasser, 1990).

Internal Marketing

The concern for issues of involvement and empowerment has been legitimised by the developing focus on internal marketing (IM). The internal marketing philosophy emphasises the requirement to market to staff their role in providing service for the customer within a supportive organisational environment (Collins and Payne, 1991). Thus, non-customer contact support staff are encouraged to view their colleagues who manage the service encounter as customers in an overall company effort to establish and sustain a culture which supports the notion of providing high quality service for the customer. Gronroos (1990) describes internal marketing's role as encompassing that of assisting employees to understand the significance of their positions and promoting a culture of service quality both inside and outside the organisation. As Hales and Mecrate-Butcher (1994: 313) point out:

> . . . only employees with a good level of knowledge of prod-
> ucts and services available, a degree of initiative to seize mar-
> keting opportunities, the autonomy to pursue opportunities
> and the commitment to do so, will be willing or able to take
> advantage of service encounters with customers.

In a tour operator organisation, the idea of internal marketing
could be of great benefit. The front-line staff dealing with the
holidaymakers are the tour reps located in the resort. The reps are
the first point of call for any holidaymaker who wishes to enquire
about services offered by the company at the destination (e.g. day
trip excursions) and for those who wish to complain.

Tour operators use customer services departments in the generating areas to deal with the complaints that the reps cannot
handle, or that are made when the holidaymaker returns home.
To investigate the complaint, the customer services staff often
have to enquire of resort offices and reps the details of the situation in the resort. If the customer services staff view the reps as a
client, treating them with courtesy and efficiency, valuing their
input and feeding back information, they could make the reps'
already hectic lives easier. Customer services officers who view
reps as merely information sources provide little positive value to
the tour operator's organisation — they do not help to improve
the situation in the resort and therefore the overall product. In
fact, a negative approach to dealing with complaints and resort
staff could help make the situation at the resort worse by affecting
staff morale.

The process of providing quality for the customer is critically
influenced by the skills and attitudes of employees; therefore staff
are viewed as customers in their own right to whom the organisation's quality philosophy must be marketed. There is nothing
entirely new about the notion of IM, since internal programmes to
encourage commitment to organisational goals have always existed. However, what is new is the active, market-oriented approach as suggested by the IM concept:

> Some marketing activities from traditional external marketing
> may be used together with training and other traditional per-
> sonnel development activities . . . internal marketing offers an
> umbrella for all these and other activities which make the de-
> velopment of personnel a strategic issue (Gronroos, 1994: 14).

The most common application of IM is that which relates to an
overall organisational concern for attracting, selecting and retaining quality employees who appreciate their role in the delivery of excellent service quality to external customers. However, as
Foreman and Money (1995) point out, IM has application beyond
this particular focus. These writers also see an important role for
IM in the implementation of strategic initiatives:

> . . . the IM program parallels the conventional external mar-
> keting program directly, and the "external" marketing strat-
> egy is marketed to all the organisational constituents in order
> to get the support so necessary to the success of its imple-
> mentation (p. 762).

Others have also alluded to this aspect of IM (Filipo, 1986; Piercy
and Morgan, 1991). The suggestion is that IM can help facilitate
the implementation of marketing strategy by encouraging a process whereby "external" marketing strategy is marketed internally
so as to get the support necessary for its implementation (Piercy
and Morgan, 1991). This also has relevance within a hospitality
context. In a wide-ranging study of quality practices within the
British hotel industry (Harrington and Akehurst, 1996a), the important human dimension to quality implementation was highlighted. Emphasis was placed on the requirement to direct attention to the ways in which a concern for quality can be marketed
internally, so as to facilitate the successful implementation of the
organisation's quality strategy. Specifically, the study emphasised
two important components of quality implementation: employee
resourcefulness and senior managerial commitment (Harrington,
1997). In particular, the employee resourcefulness component was

seen to encompass a concern for the promotion of quality implementation issues and lends credibility to advocates of IM in the
strategy implementation process.

Quality implementation in this case represents a "product" to
be marketed in the sense of convincing employees to "accept" or
"buy" into the implementation process (Hales, 1995). In other
words:

> The notion that customer focus is not simply an orientation
> towards the needs of a final customer, but also governs the re-
> sponsibilities of employees and departments in their internal
> transactions, is a powerful mechanism for shifting power re-
> lations and communication patterns within the organisation
> (Krishnan et al., 1993: 14).

Nonetheless, it should be pointed out that the practical application
of systems based on empowerment, involvement and internal marketing has proved problematic for organisations operating in the
services sector. Initiatives to introduce programmes of involvement
and empowerment are often obstructed by middle managers who
see them as threatening to their existence. Moreover, there is a
built-in assumption that employees will universally welcome an
extension of their roles and responsibilities where, in many cases,
they are content with existing arrangements, particularly in the
British hotel industry where poor levels of pay and benefits do not
aid the creation of a loyal workforce. For such empowerment to be
effective, Herzberg's hygiene factors have to be addressed first. It is
not surprising, therefore, that both the CBI and the Department of
National Heritage in England both called for a career structure and
appropriate reward structure as part of the improvements in the
competitiveness of the tourism industry in Britain.

In particular, it has been shown that, within British hotels,
managers are not placing emphasis on resource provision and
employee incentives, issues on which the effective operation of
IM is dependent. Also, the extent to which employees can be re-

garded as customers needs to be questioned. While the "pivotal roles of the various specific types of employees (contact staff, back-room staff, etc.) are recognised", there exists a requirement for a closer examination of "how best they can be motivated to facilitate implementation of various strategy implementation programs" (Rafiq and Ahmed, 1993: 230). Further, in this light the notion of "coercion" needs to be examined,

> where the internal "product" may be unwanted, yet employees may feel compelled as a customer by the contractual nature of the employment particularly as . . . marketing exchanges consist of "non-coercive" activities (Foreman and Money, 1995: 758).

Thus, although the significance of IM as a strategy for facilitating the effective application of quality is acknowledged, there is evidence to suggest that the adversarial, low trust pattern of industrial relations in some British businesses makes commitment to quality difficult to secure. As Snape et al. (1995) suggest, this conflict is in clear contrast to the "commitment vision of quality" (p. 48). Thus, in emphasising the requirement for closer attention to be accorded to "soft" factors, there is also a need to address the issue of conflict and the implications it carries for service delivery.

Trust between managers and workers is crucial for effective work relationships, especially under conditions of uncertainty. Delayered organisations in particular depend on trust and empowerment as bureaucracies are dismantled and fewer managers remain to monitor employee behaviour. With weakening hierarchies, employees are increasingly faced with situations where procedures do not exist and where trust becomes essential for co-ordinated action. As the command-and-control model of leadership is relinquished, the challenge is to get individuals to follow voluntarily. Such an objective is dauntingly difficult to achieve. Yet tapping the emotional energies of employees is becoming increasingly important in an environment of change and uncertainty.

The behaviour and knowledge of front-line staff is extremely important from a customer's perspective and is a significant factor in the service delivery process. Exhibit 5.5 shows how one hotel group, Hotel Sofitel North America, has introduced new training initiatives to give its employees the responsibility and tools to improve customer satisfaction continually.

Exhibit 5.5: Managing Employees for Service Delivery at Sofitel

Sofitel began by selecting "ambassadors" at each hotel to lead a customer satisfaction team. The teams organised customer focus groups, in which customers helped develop a survey of ideal attributes. As well as focus groups, the company introduced comprehensive training programmes. These were introduced initially at a regional level and rolled out company-wide shortly afterwards. The briefing sessions encouraged participants to develop a shared vision for achieving excellence and to introduce new approaches for collecting customer feedback using quality surveys. After the training the teams began developing and administering surveys, with the goal of achieving nearly 100 per cent response from a representative sample of customers. To ensure continued progress, Sofitel's management:

- Created a newsletter to update employees on their achievements

- Established an internal 800-number telephone support service for employees

- Scheduled regular executive visits for team presentations and dialogue

- Linked compensation and performance reviews to customer-satisfaction achievements

- Created reward and recognition programs, and

- Re-designed the employee orientation program to highlight the importance of customer satisfaction.

The above steps helped Sofitel North America improve the quality of its services through an intense focus on customer satisfaction and achieve world-class service performance standards.

Source: Barsky, J.D. (1996), "Building a Program for World-Class Service", *Cornell Hotel and Restaurant and Administration Quarterly*, February, pp. 17–27.

Information Technology Dimension

A contrasting approach through which commentators have sought to examine the service delivery process has been to focus on the methods by which information technology can influence delivery of service to the customer. The conflict between technological efficiency, as represented by Levitt's "industrialisation of services" and "softer" personal service elements, has been well documented. However the actual practicality of delivering service around both of these elements merits closer inspection.

As argued, the key to increased customer satisfaction, and hence greater competitive advantage, is derived from the quality of service delivered by the human resource (Levitt, 1972). The paramount importance of service delivery therefore merits, according to Levitt, an adoption of a manufacturing approach reducing the error inherent in humanistic inefficiency. The "industrialisation of services" as advocated by Levitt (1972, 1976, 1981), representing a conflicting view to employee empowerment, aims to eliminate the unpredictable humanistic discretionary elements of service through a systematic design, effecting a higher standardisation of service quality. Such an approach advocates the adoption of new technology so that inefficient and unpredictable elements of traditional humanistic, or "soft" delivery attributes are de-emphasised. Its replacement could be an automated, capital-intensive system technocratically oriented in what Levitt describes as a "production line approach to service delivery". This Tayloristic view of service delivery argues:

> Manufacturing thinks technocratically, and that explains its success . . . by contrast, service looks for solutions in the performer of the task. This is the paralysing legacy of our inherited attitudes: the solution to improved service is viewed as being dependent on improvements in the skills and attitudes of the performers of that service. . . . While it may pain and offend us to say so, thinking in humanistic rather than technocratic terms

ensures that the service sector will be forever inefficient and
that our satisfactions will be forever marginal (Levitt, 1972).

Such a view may well be out of date. As the service industries now
dominate economies in post-industrial nations such as Great Britain, the US and Canada, trying to negate the human element is to
try to turn the clock back to times long past. Service industries rely
on people, and for many there is no alternative sector of employment. Creating a satisfied workforce is key to quality and product
delivery in the service industries. Where technology has replaced
human effort in service industries there is still a human interface
between company and client that cannot be ignored.

Such a system reduces the need for training and negates the
need for worker motivation. The efficiencies it creates coupled with
low-cost gains make it immediately attractive to management,
maintaining their prerogative to manage. However, the de-skilling
of front-line service staff effectively reduces the flexibility of service
delivery to a mechanistic and rigid process. It undermines any personal qualities attributable to service delivery which the customer
may desire. Hence, indications that perceived service quality is
proportionally biased towards personal "soft" elements fly in the
face of widespread automation in the service sector. Reduced personal contact and a resulting dilution of guest satisfaction are the
end products of a technology-driven service delivery. Even its
lauded short-term benefits, such as cost reduction, are questionable
when compared to incurred maintenance costs.

Yet the rigidities of the system have not prevented its application and widespread adoption in many organisations, including
those operating within the hospitality sector. Evidence of industrialised service delivery can be seen in the application of IT as
utilised in the automation of front- and back-office manual systems. Consider Exhibit 5.6, where hotels are expending large
sums upgrading their systems to keep pace with changes in the
marketplace. It is now not uncommon for customers to expect

and/or demand high-tech facilitates when making travel arrangements.

Exhibit 5.6: Room Service with a Difference

In recent months, the Airport Hyatt in San Jose, California, has undergone a complete rewiring of the hotel costing $1 million that transforms it into what the owners claim is the most high-tech place to stay on the planet. Every room has its own Pentium computer, complete with fax modem, printer and CD-ROM. A LAN-Based intranet lets you hook up to server installations of popular packages such as Microsoft Word and Excel and a high speed corporate T1 line is fed to every hotel desktop to allow fast Internet access for business travellers. Fourth Network, the US company which wired the San Jose Hyatt, now has contracts to put some 200,000 rooms online around the world over the coming year.

Holiday Inn, Embassy Suites and Hilton are among the US chains experimenting with in-room access. Marriott, which led the field with rooms designed for the notebook traveller, is now trying out a private workstation area, complete with PC and the Net online. At the Century Plaza in Los Angeles you can even rent a $1,500 a night "cybersuite".

The drive to establish some form of Net access will be commonplace in rooms in the future. There are growing security issues with notebook computers, and business travellers are finding them inconvenient on business trips, particularly when all they might wish to do is read their e-mail. Future possible options for hotels include TVs equipped with Web-access boxes and plans are underway to introduce a Web site that will let you retrieve and despatch e-mail without a conventional client. This will make it possible to do everything you do with e-mail now from any PC or Net terminal in the world, just through a simple password system. All these latest developments assist the process of delivering continually high standards of quality to the customer and ensure a greater degree of responsiveness to changing market expectations.

Source: "Room Service with a Difference", *The Sunday Times*, 22 June 1997.

This cost-driven approach aims to increase the efficiency of operations through reduced labour overheads, quicker performance times, closer productivity monitoring and performance related pay. Central reservation systems, as utilised by the airline industry, received increasing attention from a revenue-driven hotel industry utilising yield management techniques in an attempt to survive recessionary competition. Central Reservation Systems (CROs) and property management systems (PMS) represent modern applications of both of these principles, the latter being more cost-driven, the former guided by the maximisation of yield. It can be argued that, in isolation, neither represents customer-driven achievements in enhancing service quality and as such their ultimate contributions to organisational profitability are constrained.

As IT advances continue, such as developments in PMS, CRO and Global Distribution Systems (GDS), converging towards single system integration, there is evidence that IT companies are beginning to focus on the needs of their customers' customers. For example, the development of the Sabre reservations system by American Airlines and the Galileo system by a European airlines consortium have formed the basis for what is now known as the Global Distribution System (GDS). This system links travel agents and other channel intermediaries with airline, hotel and other travel-related services. Using the system, travel agents can interconnect with the reservation systems of airlines, hotels, car rental companies and entertainment services.

However, many of the problems inherent in IT's application to service delivery in the hospitality industry are due to the piece-meal method by which the systems were adopted. The capacity for hotels to increase efficiency in service delivery from guest booking to guest check-in has never been greater and will continue to increase. Yet unless IT development ceases to be technology-driven and becomes customer-guided, then investment in such advances will carry an inherent caveat: that in the quest for efficiency the perceived quality of service will be increasingly sacrificed (Harrington and Stearn, 1996). Consider Exhibit 5.7 below, where it is argued that effective service delivery is strongly related to the attitudes of front-line employees. Technological advancement alone will not guarantee successful management of the service encounter with the customer.

Sometimes technology helps. Ritz-Carlton has built up a detailed database of customers' past visits to its hotels, so that its front-desk staff can anticipate a client's idiosyncrasies, even if they have never stayed in that city before. Citibank has installed a system that alerts managers when a call is not answered by the third ring — though this may not suit sleepier climates: one British firm told its employees to stop picking up the phone at the first ring because it unnerved customers.

Exhibit 5.7: Service with a Smile

When forging their opinions about a company, nothing seems to stir people's passions more than their dealings with its employees. Whether it is a selfless flight attendant or a clueless switchboard operator, the calibre of firm's front-line personnel can have a huge impact on its image. In service industries, almost by definition, helpful employees are the key to success. Britain's Marks & Spencer and Hong Kong's Giordano, which regularly top surveys of customer attitudes in their respective markets, generally make higher returns than their peers. Companies, squeezed by global competition and with precious little in the way of new technology to distinguish one widget from another, are making service a priority.

But high tech tricks are rare. In most cases, good customer service comes down to managing people — with those people often being dispersed across hundreds of different operations. Forum, a Boston consultancy, points to the success of Asia's luxury hotels. They are often less high-tech than their western equivalents and their incentive systems are often minimal. But everything the hotel does — from whisking a guest's bags up to his room as he checks in to ensuring swift departure to catch a plane — is designed to ease a business traveller's life.

The culture of their employees has a lot to do with the success of Asia's hotels. This plays into the idea that some gurus now say is even more important than providing front-line employees with customer databases: choosing the right people in the first place.

Source: The Economist, 12 July 1997, p. 63; R. Whiteley and D. Hessan (1996), *Customer-Centred Growth*, London: Century Business Press.

Personal Service and Technological Efficiency: An Integrated Approach

Given the issues reported in Exhibit 5.7, there is a need to take a more integrated perspective on the ways in which the service delivery process might be managed. We view service and technological efficiency as being mutually supportive. The delivery of quality service for the customer can only be facilitated by greater appreciation of how these variables work together. Information technology will only deliver efficiency for the organisation if service personnel use it effectively and are adequately trained to do so. Similarly, the provision of personal service for the customer is often highly dependent on the existence of user-friendly information technology systems. An appreciation of how service personnel and information technology support each other is particularly important in today's competitive marketplace where increasingly customers are demanding flexible services from hotel organisations. A recent survey in the *Financial Times* (Daneshkhu, 1995) emphasised the significance of achieving integration between these two aspects of the service delivery process when it was shown how hotels were using technology to provide customers with the flexibility of service which they were demanding. In particular, technological systems were used by hotels to assist with the development of efficient check-in/check-out procedures and to provide customers, through interactive television services, with a range of services which they would previously have had to arrange on the telephone. Daneshkhu points out that this more effective integration of technology into the service process is allowing companies to improve their range and quality of services to existing and prospective guests (Daneshkhu, 1995).

Indeed, it has been argued elsewhere that customers increasingly are expecting organisations to provide them with an integrated solution to their requirements (Barnes and Glynn, 1993). In the 1990s, customers are more discerning and knowledgeable about the quality and range of services available to them and are willing to switch their loyalties between organisations to achieve satisfaction. Hence, there is a taken-for-granted assumption that the service which should be provided to customers is an integrated one, facilitated by the effective integration of service personnel and technological capability. It is no longer enough to focus attention on one or other of these capabilities to achieve competitive advantage in the marketplace; instead, organisations must blend these dimensions of service together to achieve competitive success. As Barnes and Glynn (1993: 43) point out:

> It is no longer enough to maximise production efficiency and product quality within a single organisation or industry. Continuous improvement in these areas in now accepted. . . . Those seeking to achieve competitive advantage must look beyond technology to find success.

Indeed such an approach necessitates a high level of flexibility that can only be derived through greater integration of "soft" and "hard" service delivery attributes. There is an increasing awareness by hospitality companies that IT needs to make a greater contribution to enhancing service as opposed to exclusively increasing efficiency of operations:

> . . . hoteliers need to view technology in the light of whether it actually advances guest service because it is only in this way that a property can expect to make money (Vlitos-Rowe, 1995).

It is important, therefore, that managers do not lose sight of the need to be governed by customer needs and expectations. Consumers are increasingly quality conscious; hence delivery of a quality service as perceived by the customer should be the overriding goal of the organisation and is essential to the long-term survival of the modern hospitality business. How organisational systems contribute to that service should therefore be the expressed concern of management.

Applying the Integrated Approach

The effective integration of the human and technological dimensions in the service delivery process holds out some important challenges for hospitality organisations in the 1990s. It is argued that the integrated approach is challenged by organisational contextual issues which differ between organisations and, indeed, across industries. Previously, there has been a tendency to view organisations as mechanistic institutions whose progress could be monitored by an examination of departmental inputs and outputs and where implementation of service programmes was assumed to conform to a structured, prescribed approach. Such approaches to understanding organisations, and implementing service strategy, are no longer appropriate. There is a requirement to understand organisations as collections of people and the delivery of service strategy as a non-rational process. Hence, the integration of human and technological resources in the service delivery process is necessarily a complicated issue, requiring greater attention from managers.

Specifically, the integration to which we refer requires open systems of communication between departments and individuals to facilitate quality service for the customer. IT advances such as the Internet are increasingly being applied to such requirements. Many organisations are finding large-scale benefits in communication through internal use of what is now being dubbed the "Intranet". Such a system facilitates a higher degree and better quality of internal marketing. However, the task of breaking down functional barriers is a complex process for organisations concerned to evolve structures based on inter-functional cooperation. This problem is particularly relevant for hotel organisations where there is a tendency to departmentalise operations and a reliance on specialists to effect decision-making. Hence, the obvious question presents itself: how do hotel companies approach the task of building bridges between technology specialists and those charged with managing the service encounter with customers?

Integration also necessitates involvement and commitment from employees if it is to operate effectively. However, securing commitment from employees is a particularly challenging activity for management, especially in hotel companies where rates of employee turnover are high and where reward structures are only beginning to be institutionalised. Moreover, as stated earlier, there is an assumption with regard to employee involvement that employees are somewhat desirous of increased responsibility, where in reality many employees might not want to take an active line on managerial matters. Consequently, in terms of examining the integration issue, it is necessary to examine how employees can be encouraged to identify more closely with the firm's service delivery objectives.

Application of IT to the service delivery process necessitates greater emphasis on employee training, not, as Levitt argues, less. The ability to operate new systems and to utilise them effectively cannot be achieved without a comprehensively trained staff. This issue is explored in greater detail in Chapter 6. The efficiency of IT systems is contingent on the human element operating them. The extent to which technological change impacts the organisation is also largely dependent on the flexibility of a skilled workforce. Effective relationship marketing relies on quality of information. Anything less than the complete understanding of a system by staff can result in missed opportunity, through incorrect data entry by operational staff or misapplication of information by marketing management. The advent of direct marketing raises the stakes in service-delivery-based competition. By attempting to solidify a relationship with customers, firms must accept the accompanying responsibilities of maintaining the quality of that relationship. The experience begins prior to service purchase and continues into the future. Service quality should be seen therefore as a process, not merely an event. As expectations of customers are increased, the ramifications of not meeting such expectations also increase:

> Expectations ignored or unmet can seriously hamper the ultimate result which customers get, and leave the turf wide open for niche service providers to step in and take over (Vandermerwe, 1994: 46).

The integration of IT and customer service is perhaps best seen in the retail travel trade. The major high street travel agencies are, in fact, agents of the large tour operator companies, often owned by them (e.g. Thomson owns Lunn Poly and Air Tours owns Going Places). The travel agents rely wholly on the reservation system technology located on their desk to identify holiday packages, car hire, flights and other holiday services. The failure of the operator to use this technology smoothly does not instil confidence in the purchaser, who is buying what is perhaps their biggest single yearly purchase sight-unseen and largely on a company's reputation. Poor use of technology, linked to poor customer skills, will be a big "turn-off", because it is these two things, together with the brochure, that are the only visible signs that a holiday experience exists and can be relied upon to be delivered. The purchaser is unlikely to buy from an agent that demonstrates incompetence in either of these key aspects, but will go to one of the many other agencies located on the high street.

It is vital, therefore, for the travel agents to train their staff in both IT and customer service skills. For travel agents, "the sale is the thing"; if they do not deliver to the customer they do not make their commission.

Customer loyalty, it can be argued, is skin deep. With increasing sophistication of both "perceptions of quality" and IT, the concomitant need for a flexible and equally sophisticated workforce becomes more apparent. The integration of such approaches is driven by a need to maintain focus on the objectives of the organisation. We argue that strategy should be customer-driven; as such, approaches to the service delivery process should be governed by customer expectations. The challenge for management in the hospitality industry, and indeed in all service sectors, is to develop the organisational capacity to monitor customer expectations and the processes to deliver effectively on those demands.

As outlined earlier in this chapter, standardised service delivery, which through "conformance" is often easy to implement and easy to replicate, cannot offer differentiation in the long term (Vandermerwe, 1994). The human element in quality service delivery is often more difficult to implement effectively. Accordingly, it is a better condition for sustainable competitive advantage as intangible assets are less prone to imitation. The dilemma for management lies in its ability to integrate the "hard" and "soft" systems of the organisation in such a fashion so as to deliver a higher quality of service than the competition. In doing so, we argue for a greater organisational understanding of what service quality means to the customer, as "only the customer can assess the quality of service, for quality, like beauty is in the eye of the beholder" (Berry et al., 1989).

Summary

Efforts to improve quality service in hospitality organisations can focus on approaches based on certification and TQM. Each of these aspects of quality management has received increased attention in recent years and successful accounts of practice have been reported by organisations who have applied comprehensive approaches to the management of quality. These initiatives have helped such organisations achieve differentiation and, ultimately, competitive advantage in a crowded marketplace.

However, in many cases organisations have pursued quality standards to the neglect of continuous improvement and have been made to suffer as a consequence. In this chapter we reported the problems of adhering to such a view of quality management and we suggest the importance of taking account of what has come to be labelled "soft" quality management. To encourage greater discussion of this aspect of quality management within the hospitality industry, we have proposed an integrated approach to service delivery showing how human resources and technology can interact to deliver quality for the customer.

We argue that service personnel and technological systems should support each other in the delivery of service to the customer. Hospitality organisations must understand how to achieve effective integration between these elements, especially given the customer demands for greater flexibility of service. In particular, the following questions must be asked:

- How can hospitality organisations facilitate quality management?

- What are the infrastructural requirements necessary for the introduction of TQM to the organisation?

These issues will be considered further in Chapters 6 and 7.

Review Questions

1. Evaluate the role of quality standards in hospitality organisations. What is your view on the growing criticism of certification within the business press? Use examples to illustrate your answer.

2. Do you think it is fair to distinguish between quality standards and continuous improvement? Do these initiatives support each other or are there cases where the application of one programme hinders the development of the other?

3. What do you understand by the concept of "soft" quality? Why has this aspect of quality management received greater attention in recent years? Does it warrant discussion or is it another way of representing the TQM philosophy?

4. Elaborate on the challenges involved in delivering services effectively to customers. Have technological advancements enhanced or obstructed the delivery process? What do you see as the challenges for hospitality providers in the decade ahead?

5. What potential would you see for internal marketing in a hospitality context? Is the concept a "fad" or has it practical application within hospitality organisations? Use examples to support your views.

Chapter 6

Infrastructure for Quality Management

Introduction

Achieving business excellence and successfully implementing quality management programmes requires a supportive hierarchical infrastructure. Consistent with our arguments in Chapter 5, we would like to pursue the integration theme further in the present chapter and consider the infrastructural or enabling conditions that facilitate the quality management process. This will involve a number of issues. First, it will require an initial discussion of the strategic significance of human resource development in modern hospitality organisations and an evaluation of current practices. Second, it will involve a consideration of the specific issues which impact the development of TQM; and third, it will address some of the difficulties inherent in applying quality management in hospitality operations.

In the past, highly efficient organisations have often been the least flexible. However, innovation, technology and flexibility within the workplace have now emerged as key factors as companies struggle to lower costs and improve services. Yet industries such as the tourism industry, based as it is around high value-added goods and services, can only develop as quickly as the skills and capabilities of its people and as quickly as individual organisations within the industry develop the capacity to maximise the effectiveness of these skills. The requirement for increased adaptability, flexibility, innovation and customer orientation impact upon all employees in an organisation.

What is Human Resource Development?

Initial attempts to reconsider the focus of training in organisations can be traced to the US in the early 1980s. Specifically, commentators understood human resource development (HRD) to encompass organised learning experiences in a definite time period designed to increase the possibility of improving job performance or growth. In defining learning experiences, emphasis is placed on three activities: training; education and development (Nadler and Wigge, 1986). This view is shared by others who see HRD as *the* strategic management of the training and development function so as to improve employee performance and achieve the objectives of the organisation. Throughout, emphasis should be placed on ensuring the full utilisation of the knowledge and skills of the individual employee and proper management of employee learning for strategies being pursued (Garavan, 1991).

Similarly, Guest (1987) suggests the importance of achieving integration between human resource strategy and the organisation's overall strategic plan. If human resource policies cohere, if line managers have internalised the importance of human resources and this is reflected in their behaviour, and if employees identify with the organisation, he comments, then strategic plans are more likely to be implemented. The practice of HRD is therefore based on the theories of change. Circumstances may dictate that individuals, groups or the entire organisation may have to change. The concept of HRD relates to the ways in which the behaviour of individuals may be changed to provide for improved job performance.

It is thus important to distinguish between traditional training and development and the strategic connotations associated with HRD. The notion of strategic HRD can be viewed as a proactive, system-wide intervention, with emphasis on fit, linking HRD with strategic planning and cultural change, as against the old assumptions which were that training and development were reactive, piecemeal interventions in response to specific problems (Beer and Spector, 1985). However, HRD can only be regarded as strategic if it is effectively incorporated into the overall corporate business strategy. In this way it can achieve and sustain the status it needs to influence overall business performance and help the organisation strengthen its competitive position. Exhibit 6.1 tracks the evolution of the personnel function and suggests that, as "know-how" and learning have increased in importance, so the human resource function has assumed increased strategic significance in business organisations.

Exhibit 6.1: People Power Rises in Quality

Personnel was once a corporate backwater, where those lacking the "right stuff" for high office were sent until retirement. The job was mostly administrative, and included some subsidy hunting. Then came the Human Resources revolution. HR was still personnel, with a college education. The function and the status were the same, but everything was more complicated and sophisticated and white-collar workers were expected to have qualifications and know-how to operate the new computer software. However, with automation of the administrative side, the HR function was revealed to be so important that the traditional HR department is verging on the superfluous.

First, the recruitment decision has become saturated in strategic significance. When know-how, an ability to learn and quick reflexes are the crucial components of competitive advantage, the skills and other qualities of the next person a company hires define the organisation's strategy. Second, people management has been shown to be more complicated than previously thought. It is partly to do with pay, but it is also to do with regular promotion, fair treatment, security and training expectations. There is a strong emotional component to the relationship which must be understood and managed. And, third, the rise of the HR manager as a plausible challenger for leadership is being hastened by the intensity of modern competition and the need for companies to keep reinventing themselves.

> The ultimate constraint on the rate at which a company can change is the psychological robustness and learning ability of its people, the nurturing of which is the responsibility of the personnel function.

Source: *The European*, 1–7 April 1994, p. 21.

Strategic HRD and the Tourism Sector

Training initiatives have increased in importance in recent years within the tourism industry and there has been a general uptake of interest in the management of human resources. As explained in earlier chapters, the greater emphasis being placed on wider training and development issues reflects the evolutionary shift from standards-based quality schemes, such as the Investors in People award and certification, to the concept of continuous quality improvement (Teare, 1995: 66). In this text, we distinguish between static and dynamic quality: static quality is more in line with a standards-based approach to defining the concept, while dynamic quality is concerned with "delighting" the customer and is more encompassing. The latter aspect of quality management — that of responding to customer requirements — is seen as driving the focus on training and development within hospitality operations (Day and Peters, 1994).

However, despite the growing emphasis on the strategic aspects of human resource management, there has been only a small number of studies into human resource practices and management in hospitality firms. The reports to date have shown:

- Poor development of personnel policies

- Narrowly defined personnel roles, and

- Poor professional preparation in terms of training and experience.

In particular, Purcell (1993: 128) views the lack of investment in training and career development and the general low qualification levels as the major obstacles to competitiveness within the British hospitality sector. Others comment that the industry is dominated by the spirit of "amateur management" and its ability to respond to the challenges of the 1990s will be dependent on attracting high quality employees into positions of management within the industry (Parsons and Cave, 1991). These features are not specific to the British hospitality industry.

A comprehensive study of managerial competencies conducted by one of the authors (Lenehan, 1996) also reports concerns about the nature of human resource management and strategy in the Irish hospitality industry. The evidence from the study highlights the requirement to redirect the role of the general manager in hospitality and tourism industries from an operational focus to a more business management role. Executive development and training institutions need to provide more training in marketing and human resource development. Specifically, it was recommended that such institutions need to promote learning as a cherished organisational value and seek to link management training and development to company and business strategy. Equally, institutions should adopt a broad view of what constitutes strategic decision-making in the hospitality industry, by reflecting on the structure of tourism and hospitality firms in Ireland and the realities and limits within which managers in small businesses have to operate (Lenehan, 1996).

In the Republic of Ireland, CERT, the State Tourism Training Agency, has introduced a grant-aided employment scheme for personnel and training managers. The scheme aims to provide companies with an opportunity to avail of grant assistance and training support for the development of human resource structures. The Industry Training Support Scheme (ITSS) provides tourism businesses who lack personnel systems or training structures grant aid and training support to employ an experienced specialist to establish a human resource structure within the company.

In support of the programme, CERT provides intensive pre-employment training programmes for candidates. Subjects that facilitate the implementation of human resource structures and systems form an integral part of the programme. These include the "Trainers in Industry" programme, principles and practices of human resource management, planning and documenting training, modern systems for staff recruitment and retention, and employment legislation. The programme concludes with an "action plan" outlining strategies for the application of training and personnel systems throughout the company. Such plans allow for detailed assessment of the progress of the work by CERT and provide opportunities to review effectiveness and performance. Thus far, the response from industry to the programme has been encouraging and increasingly it is being viewed as a means for companies to identify organisational and training needs and establish procedures for professional practices in human resource management.

This scheme has worked very effectively in Ireland. However, introducing such initiatives implies significant challenges for the hospitality sector. An international study of quality practices across four countries found that quality practices are more likely to be successful if adopted as part of an effort to expand front-line employee responsibilities from a focus on a particular task to a focus on broader service processes. Achieving and sustaining these changes

> requires the commitment of organisational stakeholders, to incorporate the interests of employees into strategic-level decision-making (Kochan et al., 1995: 220).

Nevertheless, the general consensus is that many employers within the industry place a heavy reliance on

> cheap, disadvantaged labour (typically women and ethnic minorities) from the secondary labour market to fill operative level posts (Price, 1994: 47).

This approach carries with it a range of personnel practices aimed at keeping labour costs low and minimising the employers' commitment to employees. The research which has been carried out tends to support this view of human resource practices within the industry.

In a detailed study of quality practices within the British hotel sector (Harrington, 1997), concern was expressed regarding the actual support provided for the development of a strategic approach to managing human resources. Exhibit 6.2 below outlines some of the study's key findings.

Exhibit 6.2: Quality Management and HR Practices in British Hotels

In a recent report of quality practices within the UK hotel industry (Harrington, 1997), it was shown that over three-quarters (85 per cent) of managers indicated that operating staff were "very important" to the organisation's quality endeavours and invested resources to train employees in service quality related issues on a weekly basis. The finding would not have been unsurprising in that it reflects the changed market conditions within which hotel managers now operate. The greater emphasis on responsiveness, which is a characteristic of the environment within which hotel companies operate, has placed greater emphasis on internal contributions from employees. Staff are taking on increasing responsibilities for managing the quality dynamic both inside and outside the organisation. Therefore, it would be expected that a simultaneous concern for developing effective training procedures would accompany the introduction of quality in hotel organisational contexts.

Organisations are increasingly turning to their staff to provide the quality service which will help to achieve differentiation in a complex and competitive marketplace. A feature of the past decade has been the emergence of knowledge as a primary organisational resource: organisations are at last recognising the decisive influence which employees have on the way the organisation is perceived by customers. Hence, the increase in commitment to training in many hotel organisations. These results reinforce the fundamental basis of the organisation's quality ethos: the quality of service delivery is influenced by a chain of customers, both within and outside the organisation.

At the same time, it was disconcerting to note that almost half of respondents (44 per cent) reported problems with staff turnover. The finding sits uneasily alongside the principled commitment which managers showed to the development of their employees, and questions the success with which hotel organisations are generating organisational conformance to the requirements of both internal and external customers. These results are not, however, in line with other findings showing respondents reporting problems with staff turnover. Clearly, one cannot argue that there is a direct linkage between the high levels of staff turnover and quality developments, especially given intervening variables such as antisocial work hours, etc. However, the findings do reveal that hotel organisations are finding it difficult to accommodate the changes associated with the introduction of quality initiatives. Although an uptake of interest is clearly apparent from the results of the study, evidence also suggests problems in the area of implementation.

Source: Harrington, D. (1997), "Empirical Study of Quality Practices within the UK Hotel Industry", South Bank University, unpublished PhD Thesis.

These findings suggest problems with the notion of incorporating human resource management as a strategic concern in hospitality organisations. This is an issue of serious concern for those charged with managing hospitality operations. The linkage between the effective delivery of high quality service to the customer and the development of human resource management practices needs to be reinforced within the hospitality industry. We hope to contribute to the debate in this textbook by elaborating and discussing key issues of relevance for modern hospitality managers.

The debate presented so far in the chapter assumes that the hospitality organisations in question have a human resource department or at least a human resource development policy; also that they have a management strategy. This is fine for the well-organised large hotel, but the tourism and hospitality industry is dominated by small operations: 87 per cent of British hospitality businesses employ less than ten people, typically in guest houses, pubs, small specialist attractions or restaurants. How can these organisations address quality through strategic HRD?

Quality issues are important for these organisations. With low marketing budgets, and limited management capacity, quality issues are important, as word of mouth recommendation becomes a key marketing tool. A new solution has been sought by Hugh Becker, the chief executive of Teesdale Traditonal Taverns who spotted the need for training in all operative and management skills, including quality and customer care issues. The project, called "micro-millions", is aimed at those organisations employing five people or less. The torch has been taken up by the Hospitality Training Foundation (HTF) and County Durham and Darlington training and enterprise council. Reporting on the initial pilot scheme, Williams (1998) sets out the aims as being:

> to raise standards of professionalism, quality and profitability among micro-operators. Long term it seeks to promote best practice and therefore help to strengthen the economy.

The specific objectives of the project are to:

- Develop standards that are relevant to micro-operators and can be used as support materials — i.e. to outline the correct procedures for specific tasks, to develop job descriptions, standards of excellence and more

- Develop a business tool that can signpost the micro-operator to training and support

- Develop suitable training materials to fill any gaps in existing provision of support for micro-operators (Williams, 1998: 14).

The project was based on a needs analysis of the micro-operators who required practical-based occupational qualifications, local delivery, flexibility to fit the diverse range of organisations and diversity of training, as the job of the micro-operator is necessarily one of multitasking.

The pilot project also revealed that the benefits of training and development had to be promoted as awareness was low among the target audience. A set of standards of operation and associated training materials are due by the end of 1998.

Given the collective size of the micro-operator sector within hospitality — there are 3.5 million such operations in England — Williams suggests that:

> we fail to nurture and cultivate them at our peril. Far from training resources being wasted on them, a more studied, focused and deliberate application of resources in this area would deliver a substantial and necessary return on investment.

It is clear that the infrastructure needed by the micro-operator is vastly different from the in-house training and HRD policies of the large employers. The public sector must play a catalytic role, just as it does in helping small tourism businesses to market themselves through the regional tourist boards in England. A cooperative and partnership approach between micro-operators, training organisations and the public authorities is the only clear route to success in this field.

Such infrastructural issues form an important part of the discussion reported upon in this chapter. Thus far we have emphasised the importance of treating quality management as a strategic issue in hospitality organisations. As we and others have made clear, quality management cannot be improved without a fundamental change in attitude and approach amongst hospitality employers:

> Developments in both these areas depend on personnel practices which show long-term commitment to employees; they call for greater autonomy; improved terms and conditions; greater expenditure on training and development and better qualified and trained managers and proprietors (Purcell, 1994: 56).

These issues deserve wider coverage and more detailed treatment than has previously been the case. In the sections which follow, we elaborate on some of the factors that influence the development of the above practices. In particular, we examine the *infrastructure* that facilitates the introduction of quality management in an organisation. Some of the difficulties inherent in applying a strategic approach to managing human resources in hospitality organisations are also outlined.

Quality Management Infrastructure: Challenges and Obstacles

Senior Management

While the commitment of staff to developing and sustaining a quality culture is critical, managers have a major responsibility for facilitating quality improvement. The following comments are illustrative in this respect:

> Without the energising vision of leadership, without the direction, inspiration and support, the direct investments in service improvement — in technology, systems, training, and research, for example — do not produce full benefit (Berry et al., 1994).

> In any country or organisation, total quality activity can begin only if top management is conscious of the critical need for company-wide commitment to quality and its own responsibility for introducing such activity (Kano, 1994).

> Without personal example and the reinforcement of ideas from top management, quality standards are unlikely in the long run to be accepted and maintained (Gilbert and Joshi, 1992).

In a study of quality management in British hotels, it was shown how top managers play a key role in the effective provision of resources for quality improvement and influence considerably the nature and operation of inter-departmental co-operation. Together, these commitments from senior managers have assisted in satisfying the "rising expectations of customers and staff plus the need for increased profitability in a complex and competitive marketplace" (Stewart and Johns, 1996: 7). Others similarly highlight the importance of securing senior managerial commitment to the quality process. For example, it has been shown that the strong commitment from senior management to provide necessary resource support underpinned the evolution of a quality culture at Scotts Hotels (Lockwood et al., 1992).

Senior management plays a key role because quality management is a strategic issue. Quality is viewed as a key mechanism through which uniqueness can be lost or gained and, hence, it is recognised as a critical consideration for management. Initiatives can only be made to work if senior executives show commitment and conviction to the quality philosophy. Although everybody within the organisation has a part to play, their efforts and involvement will count for little unless senior management make the case for quality very clearly. There needs to be consistent reinforcement by senior management of the benefits of providing service quality for the customer and active support for the implementation process. Consider the following results of work conducted by a leading group of management consultants.

McKinsey and Company, management consultants, reported the following key requirements for success in a survey of CEOs in 500 European organisations (quoted in KPMG, 1995):

- Top management attention — 95 per cent agreement

- People development — 85 per cent agreement

- Corporate team spirit — 82 per cent agreement

- Quality performance information — 73 per cent agreement

- Top management capability building — 70 per cent agreement

- Sense of urgency — 60 per cent agreement.

Clearly, the study shows the significance of senior management attention to the quality process. It emphasises that senior managerial commitment is essential if quality initiatives are to be implemented effectively. This is a consistent theme in the published material on service quality. A clear concern for top managers when faced with operationalising quality initiatives is how they achieve consistency between development and implementation in their respective organisations. Senior managerial commitment addresses such an implementation gap and places emphasis on a commitment-based approach to the implementation of quality procedures. The commitment-based approach is facilitated by ongoing dialogue and is informed by members at all levels within the organisation. This approach was applied to great effect by Hampton Inn in the late 1980s. Exhibit 6.3 shows how a 100 per cent Satisfaction Guarantee Programme employed by the company allows empowered staff to do anything to make sure that guests are fully satisfied with each hotel's customer service. The programme resulted in a more productive and challenged workforce that is more satisfied than ever, mainly because the approach was based on consent and commitment rather than control and command.

Exhibit 6.3: Commitment-Based Quality Management at Hampton Inn

---

In October 1989, Hampton Inn became the first national hotel chain to create a formal, ongoing policy of "guaranteed" customer satisfaction. The company's 100 per cent Satisfaction Guarantee simply states that if guests are not completely satisfied with their stay at a Hampton Inn hotel, they are not expected to pay.

The effectiveness of the guarantee is based on a strong programme of employee empowerment. Employees at every level of hotel operations — from housekeeping staff to front-desk personnel — are empowered to use the guarantee as a tool to deliver total guest satisfaction without asking the general manager for permission in advance. All employees receive extensive training to help them achieve the objectives set out within the guarantee and to implement it in specific situations.

Since its introduction, the guarantee has become the cornerstone of the Hampton Inn corporate culture, as well as a source of pride and motivation for hotel employees. Research undertaken by the company suggests that the guarantee strongly influences customer satisfaction and loyalty and that guests that have experienced the guarantee are more likely to stay with Hampton Inn again in the future. For the company's 7,000 employees, Hampton Inn's empowerment programme has increased job satisfaction levels and the feeling of "ownership" throughout all levels of the organisation.

Source: Thompson, R. (1993) "An Employee's View of Empowerment", *HR Focus*, July, pp. 14–16.

Resistance to implementing customer quality strategies is most often encountered at the senior managerial level where managerial values, ingrained over the years, are opposed to introducing changes. The introduction of systems based on ongoing dialogue is, therefore, a difficult exercise for many organisations. It is argued, however, that commitment is an important first step in encouraging openness and consensus in quality implementation.

Through dialogue and effective feedback, managers can shape cultural rituals, communications and reward systems, areas which directly influence the introduction of quality initiatives. Inconsistent behaviours can be identified and senior executives can engage debate on quality issues at all levels within the organisation. Moreover, information can be collected from both customers and employees which helps shape future quality endeavours. Hence, as emphasised in earlier chapters, in recognition of the need to evolve systems based on open communication and commitment, and in an attempt to broaden its application to non-manufacturing activities, quality management has developed a "soft side", in which there is a need for increased employee involvement, commitment and group problem-solving.

However, such organisational configurations based on openness and cross-functionality can prove difficult to manage during, and even after, implementation. This point is particularly relevant for hospitality organisations, who for the most part departmentalise work procedures and rely on specialists to effect decision-making. Crossing lines between departments in hotel firms is a problematic exercise for specialist operators who encounter difficulties placing customer queries in context. Formal structural arrangements, in these instances, impede successful process integration between functions. Senior managers therefore have to encourage cross-functionality from the top and support its implementation through the mediums of regular staff meetings, internal newsletters, informal discussions and electronic communications.

Findings from previous studies are also consistent with the above argument in favour of increased commitment from senior management towards quality implementation. In their pioneering work on service quality, Zeithaml, Parasuraman and Berry (1991: 137) make the case very clearly for top managerial commitment to the implementation of service quality when they write:

> Only senior management can build the cultural foundation for quality service in the organisation . . . top management must provide a strong internal service to unleash a company's true capacity for service excellence.

There is a consensus that implementation of service quality procedures does not conform to a top-down, imposed approach. Decisions regarding quality implementation need to be shared between managers and employees.

The problem, however, is that managers often regard TQM as an exclusively managerial initiative and, as a consequence, are reluctant to encourage the involvement of employees in quality improvement decisions. Moreover, there are possible contradictions between employee involvement and managerial control. While the language of quality management is about autonomy and involvement, very often its introduction in an organisation is accompanied by tighter surveillance of staff and monitoring of performance. Managerially designed control systems are often a major cause of quality failure. It is important to be mindful of Legge (1995: 244) who claims that:

> . . . the language of the customer and enterprise serves to co-opt organisational stakeholders who have a vested interest in the changes that are encompassed by the quality umbrella.

In some cases, quality initiatives have

> been used as a bandwagon by which line management can assert its centrality and authority, and the accompanying administrative controls from the centre . . . can be re-represented as management through customer responsiveness.

This raises questions regarding the nature and practical application of quality procedures.

Senior executives are often reluctant to relinquish control and responsibility for decision-making from the top of the organisation and show a willingness to pursue organisational objectives through rigid hierarchical procedures. This is a particular problem for hotel companies where, through policies and procedures which unintentionally place limits on operational efficiency, employee productivity, and potential guest satisfaction, most such organisations have substantial de facto barriers to improving the system (Sternberg, 1992).

"Top–Bottom" Integration

Thus, while accepting the importance of top management commitment, we caution against an exclusive emphasis on the concerns of top managers. In line with our arguments above for the need for closer integration between management and employees in quality initiatives, there is a requirement for a greater understanding of how strategic understanding and commitment may be shared by individuals at all levels within the organisation.

The delivery of service quality is in the end dependent on the abilities and skills of employees in effectively managing the interface with customers. Their competencies and skills in effecting quality for the customer is in turn strongly related to the quality of training provision and to the extent to which power and authority for decision-making are distributed within the organisation. There has been a growing consensus that leaders should reinvent the workplace to move more control to employees. The more control people have over an activity, the more they will enjoy it. They must be given the opportunity to prove their competence as part of their own agenda. This requires a "totally different paradigm about employees than most leaders hold today" (Steininger, 1994: 610).

An integrated, "top–bottom" approach is thus needed when introducing quality initiatives. Often, the disappointing results associated with the introduction of quality management initiatives may be explained by the lack of integration between these initiatives and the existing hierarchy/management systems: the drive for quality needs to be fully integrated within the organisation from top to bottom. Responsibility needs to be distributed from the top of the organisation to those who operate with customers at the front-end. As Kaplan (1991: 9) remarks:

> If today's organisations want commitment and creativity from their people then it is vital to give employees their own heads. The senior manager's job is not so much to make decisions as it is to preside over an effective decision-making process. The manager's job is not to lead in any highly directive sense but "to lead others to lead themselves".

However, related studies point to the need for bottom-up involvement from employees to ensure that commitment is translated into actionable policy at the front-end with customers. The process needs to be informed by those who operate closest to the customer so that the approach adopted by the organisation can be assessed on a continual basis. The requirement for quality management to take account of both "top" and "bottom" organisational interests challenge the "top-downist" emphasis in much of the prescriptive literature on quality management. Exhibit 6.4 shows how approaches based on consent have increased in importance in recent years. The challenge for hospitality providers is how to achieve a suitable balance between control on the one hand and consent on the other.

Exhibit 6.4: Quality for the 1990s

Total Quality Management (TQM) is an idea whose time has come but seems likely to prevail after most other management fads and fashions have been consigned to the dustbin. Companies are turning to quality to help them cope with and survive the competitive challenges facing industry. Deregulation, the onward march of globalisation and the advance of technology have redefined industrial success. Only those companies who are able to develop services quickly and who can supply them at a consistently high level of quality — and on time — will command positions of leadership in the 1990s.

In order to compete at this level, European and US companies are seeking to improve their business performance by changing organisational structures and work practices. Management layers are being cut out — to save costs and to bring top decision-makers closer to front-line employees — and responsibility for quality is being defused throughout the company.

Change is the leitmotif of this trend and the desire of companies to achieve change is forcing them to confront the most fundamental managerial task: striking a new balance between control on the one hand and consent on the other. If "control" was the dominant mode of management in the past, "consent" — or at least a more consensual approach — is beginning to supersede it and might even become the dominant mode in the 1990s.

The emphasis on "consent" is not possible to impose but if it is to work properly, it is important that the entire workforce is carried along and that they are receptive to the idea of continually monitoring all practices (especially self-monitoring) and are willing to change. Thus, nothing can stand still and everything is up for improvement. It must be a bottom-up as well as a top-down process. If expectations among the workforce are raised, they must be satisfied.

Source: *Financial Times*, 10 September 1990.

The top-down and bottom-up approaches outlined above have been discussed mostly in relation to the hotel, a large productive unit. However, many tourism organisations have a very dispersed set of operations. Tour operators, for example, tend to have small head offices but many hundreds of tour representatives posted in overseas resorts. The management of these reps, who may never meet the top managers, is vital for the operators. The rep is the company's face, the main link between head office and customer. The behaviour, attitude and approach to customer care by the reps is important to help secure repeat purchases of holidays. Yet these representatives may be out of the country for months at a time. The training and commitment, therefore, must take place before the rep begins their work in the resort. Induction programmes, rather than on-going training, are vital. Manuals and systems are important in the resort, as is a supportive team environment between the tour reps and the resort manager. Feedback up the management chain is also important to ensure that issues raised in the resort reach the ears of those in head office.

In pursuing service quality, senior executives within the organisation thus need to be supportive of a participative style of managing where they openly engage with employees to identify any obstacles that might obstruct the implementation process. In a recent study on quality management in the US, a similar conclusion was reached. Specifically, success with quality appeared to depend critically on executive commitment, open organisation and employee empowerment (Powell, 1995).

Quality Culture

This process implies significant change, both cultural and structural, within the organisation and in turn requires a management approach which is sensitive to the requirement to identify with different employee groups at the various stages of introducing quality to the organisation. The extent to which employees perceive the organisation as putting a premium on quality management significantly influences the nature of their interactions with customers. If employees perceive the organisation as having a high quality customer-oriented culture, then they are more likely to manage the customer interface effectively. The provision of sufficient training and suitable responsibility for decision-making are thus considered to be important contributors to the development of long-term beneficial relationships with customers.

As Goffee and Scase (1995: 128) correctly point out:

> Employees with low levels of corporate commitment and limited attachment to operating standards are unlikely to provide good service delivery. It is precisely for these shortcomings — highlighted by competitors who have been able to provide and reward demonstrably better service with more highly motivated employees — that a number of established service enterprises have suffered a significant loss of market share during the 1990s.

The development of a quality ethos therefore requires a shift from management strategies of "direct control" to "responsible autonomy" centred around ideas of self-control and high levels of commitment. Emphasis on employee commitment within the organisation must work beyond the exhortation approach of many programmes by changing the context within which work is carried out. Studies of quality management have shown that essential management style and leadership characteristics in developing a quality-oriented culture include (Cravens, 1997):

- Attention to detail

- Careful planning

- Problem monitoring

- High personal standards

- Ongoing commitment to quality improvement

- Responsive and participative management style

- Trustworthiness.

Exhibit 6.5 below outlines the human resource practices which underpin quality improvement in US hotel organisations. In particular, it is suggested that a culture based on human resource management can be used to encourage greater employee involvement and commitment.

Exhibit 6.5: Human Resources and the Quality Culture in US Hotels

---

The human resource strategies which support a quality culture in US hotels includes the following:

i. Senior management's vision of total quality culture should be communicated throughout the organisation.

ii. Systems are in place to allow employees to express their ideas and concerns regarding quality initiatives.

iii. Jobs are designed to empower employees, working either individually or in teams, to solve quality-related problems.

iv. TQM training, supported by top management, is provided to all employees.

v. Performance-review systems focus not only on past performance, but on what management can do to assist employees in their future job-related quality efforts.

vi. Variety of symbolic and material rewards are provided to individuals and teams for quality achievements.

vii. Health and safety programmes are proactive.

viii. Recruitment, selection and career development reflect the changing realities of a TQM environment.

ix. Measurement procedures are in place to track job performance, employee satisfaction and customer satisfaction.

Source: *Cornell Hotel & Restaurant Administration Quarterly*, October 1996, pp. 67–78.

These practices hold out important challenges for hospitality organisations. They need to understand that people are more than
cogs; they are individuals with thoughts, feelings and insights
that need to be addressed. In this sense, we feel that service quality is an attitude of mind as much as anything else and engen-
dering support for organisational initiatives involving service
quality requires organisational cultures based on openness and
participation. Commentators have correctly pointed out that
management doesn't have the monopoly on brains or judgement:
they need to utilise all the strengths that reside within the organisation. Hence, as emphasised elsewhere, staff must be allowed
the opportunity to analyse organisational/departmental problems either individually or as part of a team, and test out proposed courses of action. They need to develop a sense of "ownership" over company problems and an understanding of how
these issues relate to the broader internal and external environ-
ment(s). Only by sharing in employee concerns, and showing appreciation for their contributions, can managers earn the internal
respect that allows them to drive quality initiatives forward.

Our arguments in this regard concur with those of the Irish
Tourist Industry Confederation (ITIC), who in a recent report on
Irish tourism, "Strategy for Growth Beyond 2000", recommended
the following:

- Increased provision of training in general business skills for
  employees;

- Increased provision by industry for the continuing training and
  development of professional craft and middle management
  personnel;

- The encouragement of management which empowers people to
  make their own decisions and take ownership of their areas of
  responsibility;

- Acceleration of the transfer between staff of competences and skills using techniques such as mentoring;

- A study of innovative management techniques being developed in other markets to determine whether these might have application in Irish tourism firms.

However, the process of institutionalising such changes aimed at building trust and commitment is a considerable task for management. Changing employees' behaviour and attitudes requires enormous political and diplomatic skills on the part of management. Relinquishing control does not happen fast. It takes time and resources to get people to take responsibility, to learn and change on a constant basis. The problem is that in relinquishing control, managers are charged with the task of getting people to follow them voluntarily. This is difficult, as human interactions are harder to manage than numbers and financial statements.

First, managers are often fearful of having to own the consequences of decisions made by front-line employees, especially since employee performance is an important determinant of managerial reward. There is a distinction between what Glover (1993: 57) refers to as managers who develop effective quality teams and take

> the time and effort to build the trust and support necessary for their employees to be able to function in this non-traditional organisational process [and those who] define the limits of employees' power to respond to consumer complaints.

Also, managers are concerned that distributed decision-making might pre-empt a re-definition of their roles and responsibilities and hence are cautious about the realities of taking an active line on involvement. This is an important issue, particularly when it is considered that initiatives concerned with widening employee responsibilities are often preceded by rationalisation programmes aimed at reducing employee numbers for associated cost advantages.

This serves to complicate the effective operation of involvement programmes for two reasons. First, employees can confuse a sense of greater involvement in decision-making with an overall company concern for cost-cutting and rationalisation. Second, the accompanying benefits, such as increased involvement in decision-making, can often be resisted by middle management who view involvement as a means of reducing their managerial authority and discretion at the unit level. Such resistance on the part of middle managers may result in low priority being given to the implementation of strategic activities and actions being taken to obstruct deliberately the operation of strategic decisions.

Moreover, changing "hearts and minds" is extremely problematic in current conditions of uncertainty. The American Society for Training and Development claims that the management of change has become more difficult because managers themselves have lost credibility: employees are scared and organisational trust has hit rock bottom. They suggest that the real reason trust has disappeared is that managers have handled workplace changes poorly. This point has relevance for management and employees within the hospitality industry where employees are often treated inconsistently. In the haze of mixed messages, as the report suggests, employees don't know what to believe, so they have stopped believing — or trusting — anything. What can be done? Again we draw from the American research.

First, it should be understood that developing trusting relationships should be the responsibility of everyone in an organisation. It should involve listening to employees to understand their feelings about management actions. What are employees telling each other? What would they say to management if they could? Why have they become so sceptical? When this information has been gathered and management agree that there is a trust problem, the problem can then begin to be addressed.

Second, communication must be made with employees to restore trust, because in an age of uncertainty, nothing is more important to staff than honesty. Open, honest communication is what fosters employee confidence.

One organisation that understands the importance of having a culture based on trust and fairness is Swissotel. The company has overcome many of the reported problems associated with evolving a quality culture and now actively engages its staff on decisions relating to quality improvement on a regular basis.

Exhibit 6.6: Quality Culture as an All-embracing Code of Practice

Swissotel, through a programme called "Quality Wins", have set themselves the ambitious target of trying to distil the spirit that makes customer service work and to inject it into their corporate culture. Though the vision of total quality service in everything done by everybody is hugely ambitious, implementation is actually by way of quite modest, and achievable, steps. What they do is to produce visible results within a short period of time; and they involve everyone — the metaphorical head cook as much as the equally metaphorical bottle washer. In the case of "Quality Wins", these small steps are described as "standards".

Take the way the telephones are answered. Many a service organisation falls down right there at the first point of contact with the customer. The standard for Swissotel's telephone operators is to answer within three rings and to get back to the caller if the person they asked for has not replied within thirty seconds. Obvious, perhaps — and a lot of the standards sound like enshrining commonsense, but commonsense is not as common as it's cracked up to be and the obvious gets overlooked with the passage of time. In Switzerland, the need to have things like this set down is not simply a watchmaker-ish desire for orderly systems. Instead it reflects a genuine concern for the quality of service provided to customers.

The programme is not confined to the upper levels, either. When Swiss Trainers, a subsidiary of Swissair itself, introduced the programme they made the point that quality knows neither boundaries nor hierarchies. The key is to make people aware that they are part of a chain of internal customers, each dependent on the other.

> The management team believe that the market will ensure that custom will not stale "Quality Wins". Customers are getting more sophisticated and demanding — like those in other fields. This, as Hans Peter Durr, General Manager, comments, is what keeps the programme on track: "If we find we are repeating a lot of our standards, we ought to be wondering if we're being innovative enough".

Source: Golzen, G. (1994), "Star Qualities", *Human Resources*, Winter, pp. 41–44.

However, in many situations the actions reported in Exhibit 6.6 tend to be the exception rather than the rule. Often hospitality organisations — although acknowledging the requirement to embrace notions of "involvement" and "empowerment" through the application of approaches such as "Investors In People" — appear loathe to distribute the necessary authority and responsibility for decision-making to lower levels in the organisation. Others have also alluded to this problem. In fact, one of the most frequently mentioned sources of quality failure involves senior management's failure to back up their quality talk through daily personal actions. Such actions might include: rewarding quality over production; maintaining a physical presence in quality training programmes; personally conducting quality systems reviews; getting involved in customer and employee quality efforts; and empowering their own subordinates (middle managers) in the same way they exhort these middle managers to empower first-level employees (Olian and Rynes, 1991). Thus, although the language of involvement and employee discretion over decision-making is finding its way into the hospitality industry, its effective application is constrained by the traditional "command-and-control" type structure through which it is operated. The practical challenges required to apply the "consensus-based" approach show how difficult it is to achieve a closer integration between top and bottom. While companies within the hospitality industry acknowledge the business and competitive significance of evolving a quality culture they are not fully committed to its practical application. In addition, the tourism and hospitality industry has to cope with the added problem of seasonal employment. With staff changing every four to six months and staff turnover, by definition, high, encouraging a loyal, quick-thinking, empowered workforce is a difficult task. Middle managers may find such staff easier to direct, rather than to encourage and extol the virtues of quality.

Customer Orientation

The quality culture alluded to above is centred around a concern for effectively managing relationships with customers. The change and uncertainty witnessed in recent years has intensified the difficulties inherent in managing customer expectations. Across all industries, customers have become more knowledgeable, and increasingly they are shifting their loyalties between firms. These problems have been even more acute within service industries — such as the hospitality industry — where the specific characteristics of services make customer orientation a challenging task. The common approach that has been applied within the industry has been to offer a form of industrialised service via the development of specific product brands. The brand format allows one to pre-select the type of customer one intends to serve and thereby reduce the chances of a customer making a request that the organisation cannot meet (Lockwood and Ghillyer, 1996).

We would add to the problems identified by these contributors and argue that two key issues in particular complicate the management of customer expectations. First, customers don't know what they want. Hence, the challenge for hospitality managers is to find new, engaging ways to find out. There is a requirement not just to respond to existing needs but also to lead and create those still emerging and those imagined. Second, it should be noted that customers are also undergoing major change. As they adapt to the conditions of uncertainty in the marketplace, customers will be looking for a redefinition of the role of the companies with whom they deal, one which will make better, simpler and more productive their personal and professional lives as they grow and develop. In this sense, we need to address both the substance of what needs changing and the process by which we intend to change it (Vandermerwe, 1996).

Exhibit 6.7 reinforces the above points and shows that customer care needs to be ingrained within the firm's culture and needs to influence and shape training and development activities. It also emphasises the importance of steering customer care initiatives from the top and linking them closely to the organisation's quality policy.

Exhibit 6.7: Training for Customer Care

Customer service is not just about selling. Getting orders is relatively easy: after-sales service and winning repeat orders is the tough part. The skills needed to provide consistently good customer service are not hard to develop. They involve listening to customers to understand their needs, communicating lucidly, delivering what was promised, and managing one's time and resources efficiently.

However, to develop these skills alone is not enough. The real training need is to stimulate a change in attitudes in which the whole business activity becomes focused on the customer. Customer service depends not only on the individual dealing with the external customer, but also on the people behind that individual. To have everyone, at all levels, thinking of their job in terms of satisfying the needs of their personal customers, both internal and external, imposes a valuable discipline.

Customer care is not a matter of logic alone. It is no good arguing that customers are irrational or unreasonable and that their expectations are governed by emotional feelings rather than logic. How a customer "feels" is a business fact with which we have to work. If training courses in customer service are to be worthwhile, and not just lip service to the idea, there are two prerequisites. Firstly, the corporate culture must be clearly oriented to the customer. Secondly, overall training and development policies and practices must be focused on the needs of customers — both internal and external.

> Customer service must come from the top. It is inextricably linked to the pursuit of total quality throughout the organisation. As a recent advertisement pointed out: "If your failure rate is one in a million, what do you tell that one customer?"

Source: Schofield, P., "Missing You Already", *Human Resources*, Winter 1993/1994.

Evidence suggests that managers within the hospitality industry are concerned about the competitive requirement to develop quality policy around the "language of the customer". The requirement to organise and deliver on market demands is gaining ground within the industry. However, although studies suggest that executives within the industry are aware and knowledgeable of the substance of some of the changes needed to nurture a customer orientation, they are less able to deal with the process issues. In quality management initiatives, managers are going to be evaluated by their process and political skills in bringing about and sustaining change.

This issue is especially relevant for European operators, as evidence suggests that, relative to the US, the uptake of interest in quality initiatives in European hospitality firms and their subsequent success with implementation is low. For example, the American Hotel and Motel Association has had a quality-assurance committee for a number of years. In the early 1980s, it commissioned a report into quality, out of which emerged a quality programme. A widely known adopter of this programme in the 1980s was the Boca Raton Hotel and Club. Other hotel chains have followed suit, most notably Sheraton in the 1980s, and have adopted quality strategies.

Additionally, data concerning customers and markets is widely available in the US from a number of sources, which include market researchers, consultants, industry associations and academics. Such detailed information is available at national, regional and city levels. Recent studies suggest that analyses are regularly conducted, ranging from simple purchase behaviour

research and demographics to psychographic and lifestyle pro-
filing (JHIC, 1998). Industry associations also contribute with the
dissemination of information and regularly supply members with
a wide range of data. For example, the National Restaurant Association Monthly (*Restaurants USA*) places particular emphasis on
market intelligence and provides regular updates on consumer
trends covering a wide range of issues (JHIC, 1998).

In contrast, it would appear that European operators are more
concerned with the rhetoric of quality management than the reality. In many European hospitality firms, the strong emphasis on
meeting customer expectations is often not seen to parallel
equally strong concern for providing employees with the necessary support to manage the customer interface effectively. As
Willmott (1995: 460) cautions in a review of developments in organisation theory:

> . . . elements . . . such as the much-vaunted idea of employee
> empowerment rarely arise from any value-commitment by
> employees to extend their autonomy and responsibility.
> Rather, it is usually bestowed, or imposed, by managers in the
> hope or calculation that some competitive advantage (e.g. in
> relation to quality, customer responsiveness, wage cost) can
> be secured.

Although it has been suggested that new work arrangements,
with their inherent focus on the customer, are more facilitating
towards employee involvement and participation, there is evidence to suggest that these arrangements merely represent new
forms of employee control. In the case of the hospitality industry,
with significant employee/customer interaction, customers are
made to function in the role of management. These forms of employee control are oppressive in new ways:

> . . . by stipulating behavioural standards, installing new tech-
> nologies of surveillance (such as consumer reports, "profes-
> sional" customers and random staff visits) associated with

attempts to define and structure employees' subjective meanings and identities (Du Gay and Salaman, 1992: 621).

It is fair to say that these have been features of many of the quality programmes introduced in Europe in recent years. Most of the programmes such as the quality awards and Investors in People (UK) have been paid lip service by operators within the tourism and hospitality sector. The increasing sophistication of tourism products requires operator knowledge and appreciation of general management techniques and specific skills such as human resource management, disciplines commonly used in other sectors. However, from our experiences, these have not been incorporated as significant considerations in European hospitality firms. In fact, in a wider sense, few examples of successful programmes have been reported, and of the small number of "success stories", many still encounter problems. This is an issue to which we will return in our discussion of quality implementation in Chapter 7.

Do quality objectives therefore preclude an emphasis on providing benefits to employees and instead focus primarily on the requirements of the market? If so, what are the consequences? Consider the following statement from Wilkinson and Willmott (1995: 3) who argue that:

> For quality management gurus, "quality" does not necessarily mean the attainment of exceptionally high standards with regard to employees' terms and conditions of work. Instead, it means the development of "uniform and dependable" work practices that are congruent with delivering products or services at low cost with a quality suited to the market.

Others have also attempted to distinguish between the concepts of quality management and customer care and employee involvement. In particular, attempts have been made to examine the compatibility of these two concepts and to question whether employee involvement supports quality management or whether quality management practices are best used to promote the notion of employee involvement. Although these approaches represent substantial departures from the traditional bureaucratic approach to managing organisations, they are not necessarily interchangeable or even compatible. Although they share common themes and place emphasis on giving employees more responsibility, power, information and knowledge, they are different in that they recommend different approaches to rewards, leadership, work structure and organisation structure (Lawler, 1993: 74).

Again, we draw from the US experience. In the US, an extensive study of quality management and employee involvement practices (Lawler et al., 1992) showed that the concepts of quality management and employee involvement can be compatible with each other. However, the organisations that demonstrated such compatibility were the ones who had closely integrated the concepts of quality management and employee involvement and had applied techniques that were appropriate to the context within which the organisation operated (Lawler et al., 1992). These studies demonstrate the importance of achieving compatibility and integration between standards with regard to employee terms and conditions of employment and standards with regard to the effective provision of quality service for the customer alluded to earlier. Only when compatibility is achieved between these can an organisation hope to deliver on customer expectations.

Employee Resourcefulness

The effective delivery of service quality also rests on the degree to which employees manage the interface with customers. This also is an important part of the infrastructure for quality management. Giving employees more authority and decision-making flexibility encourages greater responsiveness and provides customers with more efficient service and quicker solutions to difficult situations. Employee competencies and skills in effecting quality delivery are strongly related to both the quality and degree of training offered by the organisation, and also to the extent to which management distributes power and authority within the company.

The case for involving employees in the implementation of quality initiatives has been made previously. Quality is inextricably linked to human resource considerations because of the importance of a committed workforce to the achievement of quality goals; because the effectiveness of the quality initiative is highly dependent on management's treatment of the workforce; and, as outlined in the previous section, because quality, with its emphasis on commitment and involvement, implies a high-trust organisation (Guest, 1992).

Employees with the necessary training and education, and responsibilities to effect quality service for the customer, need to be "resourced". There are a number of issues of importance here. Firstly, "training" refers to the skills and knowledge base required to deal with a specific task, project or current job. Secondly, "education" is the development of people regardless of the job(s) they are doing. It is futuristic and based on the belief that well-educated people can contribute more effectively because their creative potential has been raised. In addition, better-educated people are more flexible and more adaptable to change (Zairi, 1994: 2).

Also of significance in this respect are the procedures in place to evaluate, and if appropriate reward, individual performance. Equally important are the "responsibilities" conferred on employees by those in senior positions within the firm. In particular, the level and extent of distributed decision-making that exists throughout the organisation is under examination here.

Exhibit 6.8 suggests that, although the notion of giving power to employees is a challenging exercise, it is nevertheless here to stay. As the business environment has become more competitive and uncertain, managers are looking to their employees to create advantages in the marketplace.

Exhibit 6.8: Empowerment: Trendy Slogan or Effective Management Tool?

"Empowerment" — in its current usage — is supposed to herald a departure from the traditional methods of control and command which characterise hierarchical organisations, and moves towards making things happen through coaching and facilitation. So, by removing layers of supervision from the organisation, the role of manager can be changed from one of command and control to one of support, coach, provider of direction and resources.

While some organisations would claim to have made this transition very successfully, the reality for others is somewhat different. Some organisations that consider themselves to be "empowering", still have many managers who talk in the sort of terms that imply an inherent power differential between themselves and staff. Empower-ment is, instead, used to describe what the manager will empower the employee to do.

But if the employee is to feel properly empowered, then it is necessary for that employee to feel totally trusted, requiring significant commitment from the senior management team. Empowerment is not delegation. It is about making the most of people's potential, an understanding that people have the ability to do more things than they have been asked to do in the past.

There is no doubt that, for some organisations, empowerment works. But is important to manage the managers who are often the ones who have most to lose from empowerment and are well placed to launch counter-offensives or delaying tactics. Although change can be a very satisfying experience, thinking about it beforehand can be very frightening — as anyone who has been involved in the upheaval of an organisation can testify. But even those who believe empowerment is just another way of getting more for less, must acknowledge that it is a technique that is here to stay.

As the Industrial Survey concludes from its survey: "Empowerment presents a fundamental change to the way people are managed [and] the benefits make the journey worthwhile."

Source: "Power to the People", *The Guardian*, Saturday, 11 May 1996.

Such are the requirements of a modern competitive marketplace which places a high premium on the knowledge and capabilities of organisational employees:

> . . . the perspective of employees may be difficult to ignore
> when it comes to the practicalities of quality implementation
> in many organisations (Snape et al., 1995: 49).

We therefore reinforce the need for managers to involve employees in decisions regarding the application of quality procedures if they are to bridge the gap between outlined policy and implemented procedures. As identified earlier, top-down procedures for implementing service quality are not sufficient if operationalised without the consideration of, and input from, key front-line employees.

This is an area of particular significance for operators in Ireland and Britain who lag behind their counterparts in continental Europe and the US in supporting initiatives designed to broaden the range of skills that individual employees possess. There is an urgent requirement that management approaches be updated in this regard to reflect international best practices. This is important, as the input of front-line employees will increasingly underpin the provision of quality services in international markets. Recent initiatives in these countries have, however, been encouraging. In Great Britain, the development of the national vocational qualification (NVQ) system, which develops and accredits work-based learning, has proved an important initiative in this area. In Ireland, CERT, the state tourism training agency, has played a proactive role in promoting training and education, focusing on "training the trainers" and other initiatives to promote the concept of systematic training in industry.

Exhibit 6.9 emphasises the importance of engaging employees in decisions relating to quality improvement. It suggests that, although there are risks associated with empowering people to take more control of their jobs, the additional risk is more than compensated for by the increased loyalty which employees attach to their roles.

Exhibit 6.9: Employee Resourcefulness — Risk and Reward?

At the level of the grand design, cost-cutting as a strategy doesn't work. Research in the US shows that companies which choose this route as their main focus are still cost-cutting years later. Low morale is not a good platform for high productivity. At the level of daily management, the attempt by human resources departments to rationalise the developments of the 1980s as "employability" has also had mixed results.

Years ago, Abraham Maslow in his hierarchy of needs posited that not until requirements for food, shelter and basic security were satisfied would people motivate themselves with loftier ambitions. As most current change hits squarely at security, it is not surprising that so much of the employment superstructure is wobbly. To stop people wasting energy on the things they can no longer control (the job, company) and focus them on the one thing that they can (themselves) the most important (and cheapest) ingredient is information.

Where people understand the reasons for change, they view it much less negatively than if they believe it is just cost-cutting — even when their own jobs are at risk. Better still, get them to plan the changes themselves. Trials involving teams in the restructuring process often have proved the positive effect on business results of improved staff morale. This has been achieved by helping the teams to make all the key decisions about how the new structure should be organised.

As one manager commented: "The only way to keep them is to risk losing them. You have to give them room to develop, which at the same time makes them marketable. But ironically that's how you create loyalty. True, it's a gamble. But there isn't much choice. It's a game with high stakes, and the enforcers are at the door."

Source: Caulkin, S., "The New Avengers", *Management Today*, November 1995, pp. 49–53.

However, we also need to address some wider issues relating to employee resourcefulness. Often, managers work on the assumption that employees, like themselves, are desirous of increased involvement in decision-making and its accompanying rewards. Frequently, however, employees express dissatisfaction with the notion of having increased responsibility within the company.

This arises both from a fear of being burdened with the consequences of a poor decision, and from a fear of having to take a more active line on managerial matters.

The notion of employee involvement may also raise concerns in relation to the way in which employees are appraised and rewarded for outstanding performance. Employee involvement operates most effectively when it evolves into an overall organisational effort to improve service quality for the customer. However, employee involvement can have a reductionist focus. By placing emphasis on individual performance as the basis for overall system effectiveness, employees direct their efforts towards improving their own individual performances at the expense of the external customer. In fact, frequently, it is beneficial for the overall system if employees make individual sacrifices from time to time.

Consider what "Dilbert's Management Handbook" has to say about employee recognition programmes (Exhibit 6.10). Is this the attitude that prevails in organisations within the hospitality industry or is there reason to believe that things are changing?

Exhibit 6.10: Employee Recognition Programmes

Employees like to feel that their contributions are being valued. That's why managers try to avoid that sort of thing. With value comes self-esteem, and with self-esteem come unreasonable requests for money. There are many ways to tell employees that their work is not valued. Here are some of the crueller methods, which incidentally work the best:

- Leaf through a magazine while the employee voices an opinion. Ask for information "urgently", and then let it sit on your desk untouched for weeks. Have your secretary return calls for you.

- Then there are recognition programmes. These send an important message to all the employees in the group, not just the "winners". Specifically, the message is this: "Here is another person who won't be downsized until after we nail you."

I once won a recognition award and as I approached the front of the room to accept my award, it became apparent that the executive running the programme didn't know what I did for a living. Thinking quickly, he invented an entirely fictitious project for the benefit of the audience and thanked me for my valuable contribution to its success.

I felt "happier" after that, but my self-esteem didn't increase enough for me to think it was a good time to ask for a raise. Morale-wise, this was a home run for the company. I was so motivated that I gave serious thought to working right through my siesta that afternoon.

Source: S. Adams (1996), *Dilbert's Management Handbook*, New York: Harper Collins.

Notwithstanding these issues, however, there is a need to align human resource considerations closely with overall strategic concerns in the achievement of quality objectives.

Evidence suggests that human resource policies emphasising employee involvement and commitment can be made to work by increasing employee mobility, skills and responsibilities within the organisation. For instance, Marriott Corporation has succeeded in applying the above concepts to its method of organising work. Specifically, the company provides employees with the opportunity to participate in the design of their own 90-day training programme to allow movement into higher paid, more responsible positions within the company. Similarly, teamwork and lateral service were two of the key dimensions that helped Ritz-Carlton achieve its quality focus. Ritz-Carlton completely integrates human resources and operations, so that an outside observer might be hard pressed to figure out who were the human resources people and who were the operations people (Partlow, 1993: 22). Exhibit 6.11 shows how human resource considerations are increasing in significance in organisations across the globe. At the same time, however, the example shows that there are challenges associated with "being nice to people".

Exhibit 6.11: Making Quality Work for Staff?

There is nothing particularly new about being nice to workers. The idea is now much in vogue, however. *Fortune,* a business magazine, estimates that half of America's large companies are experimenting with self-managing teams. Teams eliminate waste by reducing the number of managers. They also institutionalise innovation by involving the whole workforce in upgrading products and processes, and reduce errors by keeping people interested in their work.

There are also other benefits associated with adopting worker-friendly practices. For example, high wages attract and retain good workers. Job security can persuade workers to try harder for their bosses. Performance-related pay encourages and rewards effort. And critically, training reduces staff turnover and raises productivity.

However, being nice to people is harder than it sounds. Flexibility is extremely hard to manage and worryingly easy to subvert, because it depends on everybody pulling their weight and using their initiative. Another problem is that many people have a vested interest in resisting change. Middle managers, who risk losing their power and status, not to mention their jobs, are good at sabotaging teamwork. And many workers do not want an increase in responsibility.

It is tempting to be starry-eyed about the new corporate paternalism. However, generous employment policies cannot make up for poor strategies. Even the most altruistic firms have to make a choice between stability and flexibility, between keeping old retainers and generating other profits for employees. To be responsive, they need to be as flexible in their approach to their workforce as to everything else; to introduce changes, they need to be much choosier about whom they employ. Organisations have spent much of the last decade cutting their workforces to the bone. It may be time for bosses to be nice to those workers who are lucky enough to have kept their jobs.

Source: *The Economist,* "Nicely Does It", 19 March 1994, p. 94.

The issues raised in Exhibit 6.11 reinforce our own concerns regarding notions of "involvement", "niceness" and "participation". Often we argue that, instead of being used positively as part of the organisation's quality policy, employee involvement/

participation is perceived negatively at middle levels within an organisation and, as a consequence, is used in a limited manner within the hospitality industry. There appears to be confusion about the nature and role of employee involvement in quality management. Should involvement allow greater opportunities for participation in power and decision-making or does it merely represent a subtle means through which greater control can be exercised over employees' work? (Rees, 1995; Ashness and Lashley, 1995).

Strategies concerned with the development of a quality orientation are frequently abstracted from the thrust of overall corporate strategy. Although managers appear committed to the development of quality, this commitment does not translate into positive action in the form of reducing employee turnover or instilling a sense of pride into those who show a willingness to take responsibility for managing the service encounter. A consequence of increased competitiveness should be a closer integration between quality objectives and the overall strategy of the organisation.

However, from our own work in the area, we feel that there is a lack of consistency between espoused quality objectives and actual implemented policies. Often managers appear more at ease listing the strategic benefits and advantages of subscribing to a quality orientation than outlining the initiatives enacted to effect implementation.

This situation will need to change if tourism operators are to achieve differentiation through the provision of high-quality service. Quality initiatives have lacked a strategic dimension in tourism operations precisely because training and management development have not been regarded as key considerations within the industry. First it has proved difficult to recruit sufficient, suitably qualified staff into the industry; and secondly, if recruited, such staff are difficult to retain. In the US, programmes have been initiated, such as those at the Disney Institute in Florida and others delivered by Cornell Hotel School, which have been successful in attracting and retaining staff. However, the experience has not been the same in Europe. A recent report by JHIC (1998) reinforces the above points. It suggests that active commitment to education and training in the US has been achieved through a number of means:

- Internationally acclaimed educational programmes under the auspices of the major industry associations, the National Restaurant Association (NRA) and the American Hotel and Motel Association (AHMA);

- Local support for educational providers through sponsorship and an active role in curriculum guidance and development;

- Active interchange of faculty and industry professionals on a short-term and career progression basis;

- Active profile of academic consulting on behalf of the industry; and

- Active sponsorship and support for education at all levels — for example, industry partners provide support in excess of $250,000 per annum for CHRIE, the professional association for hospitality educators.

Such initiatives greatly assist the process of recruiting quality graduates and also the professional development of existing personnel.

In Great Britain, the Hotel and Catering International Management Association (HCIMA) has been attempting to promote continuing training and development programmes to businesses in recent years but has been disappointed with the level of interest shown.

Because it is primarily concerned with the management of human interaction either at the customer or employee interface, quality implementation is a complex exercise. There are no step-

by-step procedures to guarantee success. However, the development of an infrastructure promoting, amongst other things, continuing training and development activities should be an important part of any quality development exercise. So too should be a
thorough examination of the evidence to evaluate how different
organisations world-wide approach the task of implementing
quality initiatives. By doing so, we can illustrate the challenges
and associated difficulties involved and help hospitality organisations to plan effectively for quality management programmes.
A consideration of such issues will form the basis of the next
chapter.

Summary

In this chapter, we considered the necessary infrastructure for
quality management. Too often, quality implementation is presented as a series of actions which, if applied accordingly, will
guarantee success. However, the management of quality does not
proceed in a step-by-step fashion; nor is it without challenges or
obstacles. Achieving continuous improvement, customer satisfaction and long-term profitable growth requires an infrastructure to
be in place to manage the delivery of high standards of service to
customers. Increasingly, organisations are looking to their employees to help them provide quality for the customer. However,
companies have been less concerned about how they should
achieve this objective. We argue that hospitality organisations
must place greater emphasis on the strategic significance of their
staff and examine ways in which they can encourage and nurture
their commitment to quality improvement.

The management of such initiatives requires a quality infrastructure that promotes awareness and encourages involvement
in matters relating to quality management. A number of issues
are of importance here.

First, there must be an understanding that quality cannot be managed effectively without the commitment and support of senior executives. This gives impetus and strategic significance to quality improvement.

Second, efforts must be made to integrate "top" and "bottom" parts of the organisation in quality initiatives. Configurations emphasising openness, involvement and participation must be encouraged.

Third, these issues need to be reflected within the organisation's culture. Again, if given the necessary support, a quality culture concerned with improving both customer and employee "terms and conditions" will evolve. Otherwise, a form of "manufactured" quality will prevail and only a "plastic, themed" service will be offered to customers, and greater control exerted on staff.

Fourth, in all instances staff and management need to be reminded of where the customer fits into this. Orienting systems and procedures towards customers for the sake it will not work. Instead, dedication to customer satisfaction needs to be reflected honestly within the employment practices and culture of the organisation.

Finally, it should be noted that these initiatives are predicated on the willingness and abilities of staff to commit to the quality process. In this case, the "why" is as important as the "how". There is more to quality management than mere compliance; staff need to feel part of the process and engage and commit to it if it is to work effectively. The implementation of such initiatives is proving difficult for many organisations engaged in quality management efforts partly because of negative attitudes towards continuing training and development activities.

In the next chapter, we consider evidence and evaluations of quality implementation in practice: How is quality management working? What are the challenges and difficulties associated with implementation?

Review Questions

1. Evaluate the strategic significance of human resource management within the hospitality sector? Consider human resource practices in a hospitality organisation of your choice. How would you rate these practices? How do they compare with employment practices in other industry sectors?

2. You have been appointed "Head of Human Resources" at a large hotel group. You have been asked to develop a strategic approach to human resource management. What actions would you take and what changes would you wish to institutionalise?

3. What is the significance of a quality management infrastructure? What are the components of such an infrastructure and how might they relate to each other in a practical context?

4. Elaborate, with examples, on the challenges involved in developing a quality infrastructure at an organisation of your choice. What are the key considerations involved?

5. In your opinion, how successful have hospitality organisations been in developing an infrastructure for quality management? Do you consider the notion of an infrastructure valuable or would you advise a different approach to managing quality? Illustrate your answers with examples.

Chapter 7

Evaluating Quality Management

Introduction

The development of a quality infrastructure, with its emphasis on giving employees better training and more opportunities to participate in decision-making, has proven a difficult challenge for hospitality and other organisations. The problem with TQM is that it has increased in importance at precisely the time when organisations have been forced to de-layer and restructure their activities. Hence, the question presents itself for workers: is quality management a process through which employees are forced to work harder for the same rewards, unwilling to resist through fear of being made redundant, or is TQM a way of providing workers with more responsibility and more interesting work? These questions have not been adequately addressed and in this chapter we seek to evaluate the quality management phenomenon.

In particular, we evaluate the prevalence and effectiveness of quality management practices within hospitality organisations. Specifically, the intention is to investigate the challenges and difficulties apparent in the implementation of service quality initiatives within the sector. However, to be of value, we will need to draw on experiences and evidence from other industry sectors; hence the material addressed is wide-ranging.

Unlike other contributors, therefore, we acknowledge the challenges and associated difficulties involved in applying a quality ethos. In doing so, we are widening the debate on quality management and are alerting managers to some of the obstacles inherent in its application.

Quality to Date

From an analysis of published studies and from our own experiences in the area, it is fair to say that quality management works. The quality movement has assumed importance because it has been viewed as an effective way in which to improve work practices. It provides individuals with a model, social support, a powerful language and the motivation to carry through progressive changes in organisational contexts. The movement has done more than almost anything else to stimulate serious efforts at workplace change in ways consistent with achieving competitive advantage through human resources development (Pfeffer, 1996). The evidence to suggest that TQM can, on its own, successfully improve the bottom line in the short term is, however, sketchy.

The quality philosophy works when it is carefully applied as a means of achieving customer satisfaction and long-term growth. It has found successful application across countries and cultures and across different industry sectors. Exhibit 7.1 provides support for this view and shows the strong level of interest in quality management amongst US organisations. However, the example also shows the difficulties involved in applying the concept, especially in current conditions of uncertainty, and suggests that the real challenge is in sustaining momentum for quality management initiatives.

Exhibit 7.1: More Quality than You Think

It makes a quality guru sad to think that common wisdom may be right: only five per cent of US businesses actually use high-performance work practices like TQM. But that common wisdom may be wrong. Professor Paul Osterman of MIT's Sloan School of Management found that, in 1992, 35 per cent of US organisations had at least some quality or productivity initiatives in place.

> Of his survey of 875 establishments, he found that cutting edge workplaces had common traits, among them concern for their employees and extensive worker training. Independent of the productivity gains to be had, establishments that believed they were responsible for employee welfare were more likely to adopt innovative work practices.
>
> Mastering these practices requires a spirit of co-operation, but he found that relentless downsizing is taking its toll on morale: "It's very hard to empower the labour force while laying so many people off," he notes. Thus the real question about quality initiatives is, will they stick?

Source: *Fortune*, 18 April 1996, pp. 27–29.

What this and other examples also show is that there are no short cuts to achieving a quality culture. Customers may be satisfied with the standard and quality of service initially but after a suitable period of time they come to expect and demand a consistently high level of service. Thus, satisfying a customer at this level is a treadmill that organisations cannot get off easily, because quality of service is something which customers demand.

Organisations offer high standards of service because greater customer satisfaction leads to long-term profitable growth. In this sense, it is customers who set the agenda for the management of quality in hospitality organisations. Those organisations that anticipate and recognise this achieve significant improvements in performance. Those that fail to deliver services around customer requirements are the ones that report problems with implementation and subsequently abandon quality programmes because of their poor short-term effects on the bottom line. One company that has built its reputation around the provision of consistently high standards of customer service is the Ritz-Carlton hotel group. After successfully winning the Malcolm Baldrige National Quality Award in 1993, Ritz-Carlton is now aiming for zero defects in its encounters with customers. Exhibit 7.2 sets out the principles which guide its approach to anticipating and managing customer expectations.

Exhibit 7.2: Getting Down to the Basics of Quality Management

Ritz-Carlton became the first hospitality organisation to win the coveted Malcolm Baldrige National Quality Award in 1993. Most small hotel operators would be content with winning such an award. Some would be happy with a 30 per cent turnover rate in an industry in which the average is close to 100 per cent. Some would be happy with a customer satisfaction rate of 97 per cent and with being rated the best hotel chain by travel agents and meeting planners. Some would be delighted that out of every one million transactions with customers, fewer than 60,000 could be counted as defects. Not so Ritz-Carlton. Now the company is aiming for zero defects: employees will aim to decrease defects in 18 key processes involving customers to just four defects for every million encounters. The following is an extract from the company's "20 Basics of Customer Service", a central component of its overall quality implementation strategy:

- All employees will successfully complete training certification to ensure that they understand how to perform to the Ritz-Carlton standards in their positions.

- Each employee will continuously identify defects throughout the hotel.

- Any employee who receives a customer complaint "owns" the complaint.

- Instant guest pacification will be ensured by all employees. React quickly to correct the problem immediately. Follow up with a telephone call within 20 minutes to verify that the problem has been resolved to the customer's satisfaction. Do everything you possibly can to never lose a guest.

- Be an ambassador of your hotel, in and outside of the workplace. Always talk positively — no negative comments.

- Escort guests rather than pointing out directions to another area of the hotel.

- Be knowledgeable of hotel information so that you can answer guest queries.

- Use proper telephone etiquette. Answer within three rings and with a "smile". Do not screen calls. Eliminate call transfers when possible.

- Uniforms are to be immaculate; wear proper and safe footwear and a name tag.

- Ensure that all employees know their roles during emergency situations.

Source: Galagan, P.A. (1993) "Putting on the Ritz", *Cornell Restaurant and Administration Quarterly*, December, pp. 41–47.

Achieving such high quality levels holds out important challenges for hospitality operators in Europe. For example, it has been shown that many British hotel companies are reporting problems with quality management, mainly because of their failure to understand customers. Using a comparison study of 23 British hotels and 11 US hotels, it was shown that insufficient feedback and poor market research have led to problems with quality service. It was also suggested that the problem is compounded by the reluctance of British consumers to complain and a tendency for staff to ignore customers. It recommended that a more open-minded approach is needed to maximise worker potential. Such an approach should incorporate ways of making employees' jobs more interesting, adopting teamworking practices and offering additional responsibilities to workers (Teare, 1997).

Strategic Quality: The Question of Implementation

In the late 1990s, quality management is at a crossroads. Undoubtedly, there have been success stories, but recently managers have been reporting problems with the application of TQM principles within their organisations. They have also grown critical of the purported benefits of subscribing to the quality philosophy, arguing that quality implementation has not led to any great improvements in overall business performance. Thus, there has been a tendency to attach the label "quality management" to any improvement programme undertaken in organisations and to report

problems when such initiatives fail to achieve their desired outcomes. Exhibit 7.3 shows that, although there has been an uptake
of interest in quality management within the business community, there have been difficulties with the application of the concept. These are challenges that have often been overlooked by the
"quality evangelists".

Exhibit 7.3: Applying the Quality Philosophy

Today, only Neanderthals deny the importance of strong and sustained corporate purpose, or the evidence that quality has changed
the name of management's game. The front-end ethos has shifted
decisively to training and retraining, constructive leadership instead
of order-giving, elimination of fear as a means of control, removal of
barriers between functions and substitution of improved systems for
slogans, exhortations, targets and quotas.

With these steps taken, as world-wide experience shows, pride of
workmanship can rise again. The whole process hinges on two further, familiar developments: the extension of training and retraining
throughout, including top management, and working in teams. The
latter is rapidly becoming the dominant organisational mode: teams,
as Deming insisted, are more likely than not to cross functional and
departmental borders.

Practice, however, lags far behind preaching. The difficulty is
familiar in management. You don't need great intelligence to see the
disadvantages of departmental barriers. You do need great determi-
nation to break down their supports — custom, conservatism, pride,
obstinacy and inertia. Consequently, managers dodge the confron-
tation. Turf wars, conflicting goals and uncoordinated actions therefore continue to waste time and money and blunt competitive prow-
ess. Shortly before his death in 1993, Deming proclaimed: "I'm
desperate. There's not enough time left." For companies that haven't
fully adopted the ideas and practices that Deming, as much as any
man, made universal, those last five words will be their epitaph, not his.

Source: Heller, R. (1994), "Fourteen Points that the West Ignores at its Peril",
Management Today, March, pp. 17–19.

In consequence, questions have been posed about quality management implementation. The interest in implementation has

risen because of the difficulties which organisations are experiencing in introducing quality management initiatives. Studies have found that the lack of results has led to the demise of as many as two-thirds of quality programmes that are less than two years old (Day, 1994: 46). Also, attention has been given to implementation because there has been a tendency to focus on issues that allow firms to compete effectively and on the context within which strategies are chosen, as opposed to considering how strategies are implemented effectively. As Hardy (1995: 224) remarks:

> . . . business success depends not only on finding the right strategy, but also ensuring it actually materialises in the form of a pattern of strategic actions. This is the part of the strategy-making process that we know relatively little about.

Indeed, much of the published material on strategic management has emphasised the importance of planning and its proposed benefits for business performance at the expense of implementation issues. Managers are frequently not trained or prepared for the execution of plans, being generally "strategy sophisticated" and "implementation bound" (Cespedes and Piercy, 1996: 137). In many instances, the process of selecting a strategic blueprint for the future is considered a more fundamental task than that of developing an approach to implementing a chosen strategic direction.

If organisations concerned with quality issues are to gain market advantage, they need to address the implementation variable effectively: the process matters as much as the product. It matters so much that implementation becomes a source of strategic advantage. Quality-obsessed companies have learnt this well. However, while the process of, and indeed the difficulties involved in, managing the strategy formulation process are fully specified, there are obvious difficulties with the treatment of implementation practices (Caulkin, 1995: 15). Most of the time, the difficulties lie in the ways in which managers view the process of imple-

mentation. They see it as a bureaucratic process ridden with obstacles and barriers of an administrative nature. Exhibit 7.4 shows
that such views are misleading. Quality management by its nature is anti-bureaucracy and is concerned to find ways in which
the management of customer expectations can be made easier.
Above all, it is common sense.

Exhibit 7.4: Driving the Quality Message

Quality is a culture, a system, and an experience. Quality is not a bureaucracy, but rather a way to manage the reduction and elimination
of bureaucracy. And, most important, quality is a way to increase
sales and profits by strengthening customer relationships.

Quality, in its raw form, is nothing more than the common sense
of seeing things as they are and then doing things as they ought to
be done. One company defines insanity as "doing the same things
over and expecting different results". We all need to be smart
enough to stand back and know something isn't working, then take
some new and daring action that will make things the way they
should be.

Where applied properly, it's a simple approach that will bring success. And there is no aspect of life where quality cannot be applied.

Source: Dannemiler, C. (1994), "Getting Leaders to Lead", *Industry Week*, 18
April, pp. 27–29.

In fact, within the hospitality industry, there are sound theoretical, and indeed practical, reasons for examining quality implementation issues. Today, firms are searching for ways to respond
effectively to the market requirements of change and quality.
Properly resourced and suitably implemented, service quality has
the potential to generate substantial improvements in responsiveness and competitiveness. Excellent service distinguishes otherwise similar competitors in a way that is important to customers. Moreover, after an era during which technology was promoted as a universal panacea for the problems inherent in the
service sector, organisations are keen once again to build business

around the provision of quality and value for the customer. Hence the increased interest in quality implementation.

Most importantly, it has been found, for example, that large numbers of companies have introduced quality initiatives "on the cheap" in the search for a "quick fix", and have, as a result, got it wrong. An examination of the ways in which companies might successfully implement quality initiatives so that continuous improvement is established as a natural organisational concern is long overdue. Indeed, the organisational and competitive costs to the firm of ignoring the implementation issue can be substantial. These include possible failure to achieve sought-after market advantage over rivals and the consequent implications for competitive position; the financial costs of failed plans; and negative impacts of the above for the organisation (Piercy, 1994).

There are also problems with quality initiatives sponsored by the public sector, such as "Investors in People" in Great Britain, which seeks to ensure that certified companies meet various criteria of good practice. The public bodies, often training and enterprise councils (TECs) obviously do not implement the initiative, but set down the criteria for success. In seeking to achieve this success, a prescriptive approach is used whereby companies must follow a set pattern of administration and monitoring. These are often time-consuming to pursue, and lack any obvious merit to managers who are concerned with the day-to-day management of the business operation. Inspections are reasonably frequent and companies can plan for these visits, making last minute adjustments and improvements to their administration. The validity of such a prescriptive approach to quality issues, especially where the programme developer does not implement it, must be questioned.

What Has Gone Wrong with Quality Implementation?

Yet given the importance of implementing quality management across a number of sectors, implementation initiatives have not proven successful. First, as outlined earlier, there has been a tendency to focus attention on the failure of quality programmes to deliver sought-after tangible benefits (for instance, Eskildson, 1995). However, we argue that commentators have not been concerned to examine whether these failures could be avoided by a closer examination of implementation issues in the first place: failure in quality implementation is referred to very often without trying to understand the reasons. It is often thought that quality implementation fails to deliver benefits that impact directly on the bottom line. It is never asked if the failure of quality to deliver is perhaps due to "failure in its implementation in the first place" (Zairi, 1994: 149).

Thus, although others have encouraged the debate for a greater understanding of quality's strategic significance, there has been a reluctance to address the practical issues which may limit the successful development of a quality culture. In many instances, management have not made the effort to prepare themselves fully for the complexities involved in the successful implementation of quality (O'Neill et al., 1994: 37). Despite the upsurge of interest in quality, there has been very little discussion of the problems that managers experience in applying the techniques associated with the quality philosophy. In their comprehensive study of quality initiatives in Irish service organisations, Monks et al. (1996) found that organisations are failing to consider fully the wider implications of the introduction of quality initiatives. They showed that while changes in human resource practices had accompanied quality implementation, these were limited in nature. There was an increased emphasis on reporting systems with the potential to monitor and control employee contributions and there was little evidence that companies were restructuring their reward systems to effect implementation of quality initiatives.

There also has been a tendency to associate service quality programmes with other marketing mechanisms, and managers have adopted them in association with wider organisational initiatives such as customer care programmes. Even within the hospitality industry, some managers have reported that their organisations have combined a variety of approaches to achieve greater response, and hence quality for the customer. Managers have been reluctant to rely on service quality programmes alone in providing excellent service for guests. Instead, service quality objectives are addressed alongside other approaches such as customer care and ISO 9000. This is in part a product of the changing attitudes towards the management of quality in hospitality organisations. Attitudes towards quality have changed considerably in recent times. Total Quality Management has only recently received increased attention within the hospitality industry. Factors such as the intensification of competition and the proliferating demands of customers have meant that an increased significance has been attached to quality within the industry.

On the whole, these "mixed" approaches have evolved out of recessionary conditions where, in many hospitality organisations, care for the customer has necessarily coincided with drives to cut costs and reduce expenditure on business development. The fact that hotel organisations have adopted "mixed" approaches to quality carries implications for the effectiveness with which service quality practices are applied in hotel settings.

There is a danger that departments, or even individuals, will interpret the organisational quality programme differently. By adopting a number of procedures to effect quality objectives, there is an inherent danger that departments, or even individuals, might attend to different aspects of the quality process. Some individuals might interpret quality to mean providing exceptional service for the customer, while others might view it from an internal perspective as a means of reducing organisational expenditures. Lentell and Morris (1995) also report the operation of a variety of approaches to service quality management in their work within the sport and recreation sector. They distinguish between "minimalists" who have not developed any service quality management arrangements or satisfaction monitoring procedures, and "maximalists" who use a variety of techniques including IIP, quality assurance and TQM. The clear danger, as these writers correctly point out, is that in operating a "maximalist" approach, companies run the risk of losing focus by facilitating too many quality programmes and satisfaction monitoring exercises.

Such varied interpretations of the organisation's quality agenda may contribute to a dilution in emphasis on specified quality goals, and accentuate the problems associated with providing clear information to employees on proposed quality initiatives. As Krishnan et al. (1993: 10) make clear:

> Effective quality management requires both differentiation and integration. Even if a shared vision is initially attained, there is still the danger that by pursuing multiple quality initiatives, the original company-wide conception is lost.

These are important issues from a practical perspective. Consider the following account of service quality told by a customer in a recent British publication.

Exhibit 7.5: Quality Street

The receptionist completed two longish telephone calls about her plans for the evening before noticing that I was at the desk, and then expressed what could only be called astonishment at the news that I'd actually reserved a room for an extended period of "two nights".

Once in my room, I sat and waited for an expected telephone call. After half-an-hour of silence, I rang the receptionist and asked if she'd check my phone. Still no sound. I rang her back. "I did ring you," she said. "But there was no one in your room."

> "But I am here in my room now. Standing by the bed. Next to the wardrobe. And the phone never rang."
>
> "Well, we definitely rang 126 and there was no answer."
>
> "But my telephone number isn't 126. That is my room number. The number clearly printed on my telephone is 145."
>
> "Ah," she said reassuringly, "then it is not your mistake, sir. It's just that the wrong telephone's got into your room."
>
> Later in the week, on enquiring about telephone calls received the receptionist replied that "it was a good job that we got the telephone sorted out or you'd have got all the wrong calls". To which I replied that "I might have had a wife I didn't have ringing up to see if I was behaving myself!"

Source: New Statesman and Society, 22 October 1993, p. 25.

In this case, something extremely imprecise had inserted itself into what, in an ideal TQM world, would be the neat symmetrical links of the quality chain — a running joke. Clearly, decentralised decision-making has resulted in a greater concentration of power in employee circles. But it must be understood that with greater power comes greater responsibility and a need to provide customers with satisfying experiences. The above extract emphasises this point and shows that customers are as interested in establishing a sense of common interest and purpose as they are in receiving perfect service from automations. Hence, from a service quality perspective, it is of critical importance that well-defined mechanisms exist for the clear communication of service quality goals.

Problems have also been highlighted with quality implementation in the financial services sector. Particularly, research on the British financial services industry also has found that there are inconsistencies between the notions of employee commitment and empowerment and the ongoing emphasis on rationalisation and job loss. The introduction of quality initiatives within the financial services sector has had no necessary connection with human resource management, suggesting inconsistency on the part of senior management. In this sense, the introduction of quality initiatives is constrained by tensions of a social and organisational nature, which are heightened by the rigid mode through which quality is implemented in organisations.

> . . . it is our view that quality management may promise more than it can deliver. While these tensions derive largely from a limited conception of social and organisational relations that is evident in the designs of those who advocate quality management, they are exacerbated by the managerialist mode through which quality is implemented in organisations (Kerfoot and Knights, 1995: 235).

Consider some of the problems with quality management set out in Exhibit 7.6 by Tom Peters, a leading US management consultant. Are these problems with which you might identify, or is Peters over-critical in his assessment?

Exhibit 7.6: Problems with Quality Management

According to Tom Peters, President of the Tom Peters Group, TQM has failed for three reasons. First, TQM done right is a way of life, not a programme. It becomes the religion, organising logic and culture of the firm. Second, as Dr Deming has said, and most have ignored, the essence is a belief in the capability of the front-line employees. For instance, any employee at the Ritz-Carlton Hotels, even a bellhop, can spend up to $2,000 without approval to fix a customer problem. Third, many quality programmes are not customer-focused. They are internal programmes run by technocrats.

People got the Deming technique but they didn't get the Deming philosophy. Deming said most of the problems are with managers, but managers are not going to voluntarily reject hierarchical steps of the past. The nation, overall, is more concerned with quality than it was in the 1970s, and giant companies will fall by the wayside if they don't get with the programme in as revolutionary and as progressive a way as they need.

Source: Romano, C. (1994), "Report Card on TQM", *Management Review*, January, pp. 22–26.

In the US, it has been shown that the majority of problems arising at the quality implementation stage stem from inadequacies in the design of quality programmes. In general, it is suggested that implementation initiatives fail because of a lack of clarity over the role of quality programmes, particularly in terms of the incompatibility between quality management and corporate restructuring. Also, difficulties arise in relation to the support available from top managers for the implementation of quality programmes (Krishnan et al., 1993). Other US studies have found that diverse beliefs about what the organisation stands for can complicate the implementation process. In particular, it has been shown that:

> . . . a construct that is acceptable to members in one part or level of the organisation might be incomprehensible or opposed by other members. On the other hand, a diversity of organisational identity beliefs may create leverage or entry points into the organisation where TQM may be implemented with relative ease (Reger et al., 1994: 579).

In a comprehensive study of quality practices in British business organisations, it was shown that only eight per cent of companies were "very successful" in implementing quality management programmes. In an international survey of computer, auto, health care and banking industries, it was shown how quality goals are more likely to be achieved if adopted as part of a "team-based human resource system" supporting greater involvement and commitment of organisational stakeholders in quality development (Kochan et al., 1995). Table 7.1 provides a summary of the studies that have examined quality implementation issues.

Table 7.1: Studies of Quality Implementation

Authors	Context	Key Findings
Krishnan et al., 1993 (US)	In-depth analysis of quality implementation	Quality implementation failed due to: confusion over role of quality; different programmes operating simultaneously; lack of support from top management.
Reger et al., 1994 (US)	Conceptual analysis	Posits that inconsistencies between content of quality initiatives and core company values can make implementation difficult.
Witt and Muhlemann, 1994 (Britain)	Conceptual analysis	Emphasised importance of three key issues in implementation of service quality: service package, human aspects and measurement issues.
Kerfoot and Knights, 1995 (Britain)	Conceptual analysis	Highlighted contradictions in the operation of quality practices.
Redman et al., 1995a (Britain)	Survey	Fewer than half reported improvements from introducing quality initiatives; implementation is not a problem-free process.
Kochan et al., 1995 (US, Canada, Germany and Japan)	International survey	Found support for introducing quality as part of a larger transformation of the organisation of work. Emphasised importance of gaining commitment of organisational shareholders.
Monks et al., 1996 (Ireland)	Survey	Top-down approach to quality implementation. Lack of attention given to human resource issues during implementation.

Challenges for Senior *and* Middle Management

Interest is thus beginning to develop in the quality implementation area. Reynolds and Ingold (1994: 2) draw attention to the inadequate treatment of quality implementation when they suggest that, although the successful adoption of quality within the manufacturing industry has been extensively documented in many journals and texts, "documented cases of successful adoption of quality within the British hospitality industry are few and far between".

Increased competition and customer sophistication has led to a greater emphasis being placed on quality within the hospitality industry. However, there are a number of difficulties with the quality concept which represent challenges for those charged with managing the implementation process. Firstly, there is the question as to whether the notion of employee involvement is merely a subtle form of managerial control: although the greater involvement of employees has generally been welcomed by managers, some managers feel threatened by the empowerment of those in junior positions. Secondly, since implementation is occurring simultaneously to "delayering", there are concerns about the motivation of employees, especially as companies are operating under tight financial considerations. Rees (1995: 107) summarises these points as follows:

> All of this raises the question of how real flexibility and empowerment are under QM programmes, and of whether such terms are not merely a rhetorical smokescreen for the assertion of more traditional forms of control.

Exhibit 7.7 illustrates the difficulties of making quality management work in practice. The example reinforces the subtle way in which many organisations practice what they preach.

Exhibit 7.7: Teamwork in Practice!

Here is further evidence of the cynical way in which most organisations practise teamwork. One well-known organisation used to run a
course called "Getting the most out of junior staff". One of the jun-
iors objected to the title, and now the course has been renamed
"Succeeding with teams". The content, needless to say, is identical.
But no one is complaining any more, and, hey presto! The department can now claim to have teams.

Source: Adapted from L. Kellaway (1997), *Financial Times*, 17 July.

Concern has also been expressed about the nature and extent of
senior and middle managerial commitment to the quality process,
particularly that part of the process concerned with implementation. Although it is well established that quality programmes can
only be introduced with a level of senior management commitment, the nature and extent of such commitment has not been examined in any great detail.

Senior managers also have particularly important roles to play
in providing necessary resource support to employees operating
at the encounter with customers. They need to identify implementation issues to which employees are unreceptive, or unwilling to co-operate, and establish the reasons underlying their resistance. Also, there is a requirement for senior management to
market implementation initiatives positively by taking an active
part in understanding organisational response to planned
changes. As Cole (1993a) points out:

> . . . in most cases it is management, and only management,
> which can initiate such activities and command resources to
> consistently support them. . . . it is managers who are in a po-
> sition to provide the resources that can secure worker com-
> mitment . . . (p. 69).

Middle-level management also influence the quality implementation process in important ways. Middle managers' perceptions of

legitimacy and the degree of motivation they give to their participation in quality are likely to depend most upon their own work setting and the particular organisational and market context they are concerned with. Some forms of organisation and markets are likely to be better suited to quality than others (Witcher, 1993: 242).

However, the middle managerial role in facilitating the articulation of a quality ethos is fundamentally undervalued and misunderstood in a great many organisational settings. We argue that the middle management function considerably influences the extent to which organisations are successful in effecting a chosen strategic direction. Often, failure associated with TQM implementation is not really the failure of TQM to deliver results but rather the failure of managers to introduce it effectively (Zairi, 1994: 1). As Ishikawa (1985: 130-5) points out:

> . . . within the management group, middle managers have a distinct place in improvement: they stand at the crossroads of the vertical and horizontal planes, and they are also responsible for the activities that take place between rank and file employees.

Hence, if such strategic actions encompass a quality dimension, it is reasonable to argue that the middle layer of management contributes greatly to the success or otherwise of such initiatives: since an individual hotel is itself a profit centre, its middle manager can be thought of as its CEO. Individual managers of most medium-sized and larger hotels have ample opportunity to engage in a variety of strategic decisions affecting the profitability of their hotels (Nebel and Schaffer, 1992: 235).

A lack of commitment from middle managers may not only result in "passive compliance" but in significant "upward intervention" by middle managers either during the strategy formulation process or during the implementation of the strategy. Such middle managerial actions may be the "hidden reasons" for implementation problems which are apparently explained by other more rational or legitimate reasons. It is important, therefore, not to deny such behaviour because it is perceived to be irrational. Rather, such behaviour "places major constraints on what management can, in fact, decide and implement" (Cespedes and Piercy, 1996: 142).

These issues are not lost on companies with strong reputations for service quality. The masters of customer service haven't achieved their status by accident. They make real efforts to hire the right kind of people and develop them into professional, high quality managers. They also invest earlier and more heavily in training and constantly canvass customers' opinions on service levels achieved. At Marriott and other companies known for good service, the managers that render it are called associates rather than customer service managers. They are free to call on every part of the company in helping customers and earn good bonuses for outstanding work. Similarly, American Express thrives on heroic stories of how its customer service managers rescue customers from civil war and natural disasters, even when that means spending a lot of money (*Fortune*, "Companies That Serve You Best", 7 December 1987).

Another, more everyday, issue with regard to implementation is that quality initiatives are only as strong as their weakest link, and only as successful as perceived by those on the front line who have to implement it. It only takes one error of judgement or an element of poor people-management by senior or middle management for those on the front-line to question the quality philosophy. One poor decision, one questioned judgement and staff will ask, "How was that for a piece of quality management?" The whole process can be undermined, at least for a while. It is important, therefore, that TQM is not seen as "zero tolerance" but as an ongoing management style that will come across management glitches, but should always be heading in the right direction.

Quality Implementation — Some Practical Issues

The question presents itself: for managers, what are the practical difficulties associated with quality implementation? Let's reiterate some of these before discussing the tensions involved in implementation exercises. Firstly, there are difficulties with the notion of involving employees in decisions regarding quality policy. Although employee involvement is central to the quality implementation process, the reality of involving staff is far from straightforward. Most managers would be concerned about distributing decisions with employees, mainly because employee performance is an important determinant of managerial reward. Since they carry responsibilities for the consequences of the decisions made by front-line workers, they are cautious in their attitudes towards employee involvement initiatives.

Secondly, the reluctance of middle managers to support systems based on greater involvement and empowerment may be seen to be reflective of the wider organisational changes affecting their work responsibilities. As competition has intensified in recent years within the hospitality industry, organisations have been concerned to increase front-line employee responsibilities and decision-making authorities. In some instances, this has been seen as a way to weaken resistance to proposed change initiatives; however, in other cases it has been seen to have threatening implications for middle-managerial responsibilities. Consequently, we argue that middle-managerial reluctance to move towards more empowered forms of organisation may be interpreted as a means through which they can protect their positions of authority within the company.

Finally, difficulties are apparent in the ways in which senior managers approach the implementation process. Although senior executives seek to appeal to middle-level management and employees by invoking the use of terms such as "empowerment", "multiskilling" and "investors in people", they often appear unwilling to dilute control from the top to achieve such objectives.

There seems to be a consensus that the accomplishment of tasks within the hospitality industry is still being realised through a "command-and-control" type of structural arrangement. In general, therefore, the rhetoric of weakening hierarchical control to achieve quality objectives has not been matched by practical application. The problem is aptly summarised in Exhibit 7.8 below. The contributor correctly distinguishes between "TQM" and "tqm": while "TQM" is attractive in that managers clearly understand what they are getting for their investment, the latter is nothing more than common sense. However, sometimes even "common sense" can be difficult to nurture and apply!

Exhibit 7.8: When tqm becomes TQM

I don't know when it happened, but somewhere, somehow, total quality management (tqm) became Total Quality Management (TQM). The former — think about the three words individually — pertains to what I consider just plain effective management: creatively, eclectically, courageously doing whatever is necessary and using many tools and methodologies to create a quality organisation, a quality product, a quality culture and quality people — all for the purpose of attaining organisational success.

The latter — TQM — is a product in and of itself. . . . there are nearly a thousand versions of this on the marketplace — each sold, made, delivered, studied, and defended by different professionals. Small wonder then that TQM has become an entire industry, nearly a billion dollar one at that. Lets face it: TQM is big business, and people wrap their careers and identities around it.

Many managers are attracted to TQM, not tqm, and hence make ready customers for an appealing product. TQM is clear and tangible: you know exactly what you are buying and for how much. In contrast, tqm is simply sound management, which is anything but tangible, finite or straightforward. TQM offers the promise of a standard formula, a "one size fits all" solution; tqm offers nothing of the kind. Since so many managers are looking for the magic bullet for quality, it is not surprising that TQM is seductive, and a lot of consultants have capitalised on that market need. That's business.

Source: Harari, O. (1993), "The Eleventh Reason Why TQM Doesn't Work", *Management Review*, May, pp. 31–35.

A further implementation issue concerns whether or not staff wish to be empowered. Tourism and hospitality have, for years, been seen as "candy-floss industries" that employed people on low wages, with unsocial hours, little security and few benefits. This is still, unfortunately, often the case, especially in seasonal jobs in small establishments. Why then should an employee wish to be "empowered"? These poor conditions make the employee merely "go through the motions" to earn their money. If the company is not loyal to them, does not treat them in a quality way, why should the reverse be true? TQM has to work within the whole business environment, not just within the arena of human resource development or front-line service.

It would also appear that, within the hospitality industry, the emphasis on quality evaluation has resulted in a form of results evaluation. Systems such as quality audits and the evaluation of employee service performances have merely supplanted traditional hierarchical systems and represent a subtle form of managerial control. Indeed, such results-oriented systems have made it easier for managers to exert control, operating as they often do under the guise of involving employees. Further, the systems have been legitimised by their emphasis on the notion of "two-way" evaluation, where employees are also given the opportunity to evaluate their peers. However, it is unlikely that employees would resort to such channels to evaluate their managers critically, especially given the current global economic climate where employees are under increasing pressure to conform to organisational requirements of them.

These findings are a cause for concern, since it is well known that customers tend to recall bad experiences more vividly than good ones. Several studies show that customers will tell only a handful of friends about the great service they have received but will tell as many as 20 people about poor service experiences. It is no wonder that Jan Carlzon, during his years at Scandinavian Airline Systems (SAS), stated that every year his employees' contacts with customers create "50 million 'moments of truth'". Far from costing money, therefore, good service and recovery procedures boost overall business performance. As competition intensifies and as quality differences between companies' offerings become less pronounced, effective procedures for monitoring customer satisfaction will be key in the race for competitive advantage.

Tensions in Quality Implementation

Although receptive to organisational change concerned with quality improvement, managers of hospitality operations tend to be less sympathetic towards the procedures that facilitate such change. There tends to be general scepticism towards practices designed to facilitate service quality implementation. Although managers are often accepting of the notion of sharing responsibility for implementation issues, they appear reluctant to involve employees in the decision-making process. As Glover (1993: 57) remarks:

> When quality is introduced as a new way of doing things, it is often difficult for traditional managers to give up this perceived power. They fear that employees will create anarchy, they will lose some of the management privileges which they have accumulated, or they may even lose their jobs if employees begin to do things like make decisions.

Similarly, managers tend to be equally cautious in their views about distributing additional powers to employees, arguing that the trustful support of employees on which empowerment is based is difficult to create. This problem arises because of the "anti-expert" nature of quality management. The philosophy necessarily implies a sharing of expertise and associated power for the accomplishment of quality objectives: it is anti-expert because it emphasises that all employees can, and should, contribute to quality. It does this by its emphasis on teamwork and cross-functional working (Wilkinson and Witcher, 1993: 54). In many hospitality organisations, employee involvement is thus practised in a limited fashion and the reality of involvement is some way short of its literal meaning:

> In reality, the term is typically much more dilute, likely to refer to the opportunity for employees to make suggestions for change or have responsibility for decision making in severely constrained boundaries (Marchington, 1995: 56).

Indeed, other studies have reached similar conclusions. In their work within the hospitality industry, Ashness and Lashley (1995: 31) showed that although hospitality organisations appear to be:

> . . . moving from a control to a more trust-orientated culture, . . . trust is exercised within the boundaries of control set by management. Although there appears to be a greater emphasis on involvement this tends to be within a managerial defined agenda.

Indeed, in this light, we perceive quality measurement techniques as serving twin purposes: in addition to the effective monitoring of customers that quality measurement procedures provide, the use of elaborate and sophisticated customer feedback data may also be perceived as a

> . . . method for measuring, monitoring and ultimately managing service employees . . . thereby achieving sufficient control without destroying the very behaviour that is required (Du Gay and Salaman, 1992: 622).

What this and the example below demonstrate are the challenges implicit in applying quality management and other participative techniques effectively. There must be a sense of purpose about quality management initiatives if they are to work in practice.

Exhibit 7.9: Solutions for Maintaining Top Performance?

> Even the soundest of notions is subject to ridicule as it matures in the marketplace of ideas. Such is now the case with TQM. TQM's abundant merits will enable it to endure the slings and arrows of outrageous contrarians and cynics. Still, the grousing is useful: it exposes our lingering and troublesome penchant for quick, "magic bullet" cures. More important, it sheds light on a shortcoming that hampers not only TQM but also other participative-management and quality-of-worklife strategies. In adopting them, their champions tend to assume that all employees will embrace these strategies with gusto, and have the skills, desires, and self-discipline required to make them work.
>
> The trouble is, not all employees do. As long as work exists, there will be those who shoot themselves in the foot with antics and attitudes that boggle the mind and betray the very organisations and individuals striving to give them more satisfying and rewarding jobs. Some of these inane deeds are deliberate. Others aren't. But not even TQM can eliminate them all. So even though a kick in the pants is not currently in vogue as a primary management tool, we'd better not eliminate it either.

Source: Day, C. (1993), "What About Blob?", *Industry Week*, 18 January, pp. 7–9.

In our experience, tensions are also evident in the attitudes of employees and middle-level managers towards senior management. From our work in the area, we feel that, although managers are keen to emphasise the key contribution which senior executives bring to the implementation process, they appear critical of the short-term nature of such contributions. Front-level employees are also often less-than-positive in their remarks concerning the ways in which senior executives approach the management of quality implementation, criticising in particular their reluctance to share information with subordinates. Morris and Pitt (1994: 68), in their study of marketing implementation practices, found a similar reluctance on the part of CEOs to share the "real strategy" with middle managers and employees:

> ... very often the real strategy is in the chief executive's head. The strategy is implicit, rather than explicit; the chief executive assumes that everyone understands it, while often they do not (p. 68).

Equally, however, while proposing that senior executives identify with resistance to organisational quality policy, middle managers can also be reluctant to rely on employees to effect decisions regarding quality procedures. Indeed, we extend the above point and argue that often middle-level managers share responsibility for the persistence of the "command-and-control" type of structures of which they are critical. Notwithstanding instances where senior managers preserve control at the top, the middle-level managers can often obstruct the transformation to more empowered forms of organisation by their reluctance to support decentralised decision-making arrangements.

Further, managers within the hospitality industry are cautious about relying overly on employees to effect decisions on quality-related issues. Case studies within the hospitality and banking industries found that, while managers were concerned to show how quality management had allowed employees to express their opinions openly and take responsibility for their work, at the same time it acknowledged clear trends towards the closer monitoring and tighter control of that work (Rees, 1995: 108). Also, within the hotel sector, it has been shown that generally:

> ... there was no widespread attempt to empower hotel employees to take responsibility for service quality . . . a strong marketing orientation was not matched by internal marketing activity (Hales and Mecrate-Butcher, 1994: 324).

This also supports the view that middle managers share responsibility for the persistence of the hierarchical systems of which they are critical.

Tensions associated with the introduction of quality initiatives in the tourism organisations include:

- Limited involvement

- Diluted commitment

- Results orientation

- Controlled participation

- Quantitative-based evaluation techniques.

These tensions show up the difficulties involved in applying quality principles in practice. They reveal how quality implementation cannot be achieved by adherence to a strict set of standards or prescriptive guidelines. Standards-based measuring systems place emphasis on job control and standardisation and do not encourage flexibility or loosely coupled work arrangements. Thus, it is essential that tensions between measurement and control on the one hand, and flexibility and autonomy on the other, be alleviated if the organisation is to achieve its quality implementation objectives.

Building flexibility into workforce arrangements will become increasingly important in the future. Customers will demand flexibility in their dealings with tourism organisations and expect high standards from staff. They are quite willing to say what kind of service they want and to rate the service they are getting. In this respect, employees need to be flexible and to listen carefully to customer complaints. Too often, companies rely on toll-free telephone lines and comment cards to evaluate quality. The best companies, however, use these to supplement their well-trained, empowered staff who are well equipped to handle customer queries. This need not be a major problem for companies; instead, with the talented management of people and intense commitment, service should be consistently delivered to a high standard.

Exhibit 7.10 emphasises the importance of promoting and encouraging flexibility in the workplace. It suggests that quality management should be concerned with open communication and a sense of shared responsibility for decision-making. Above all, the exhibit highlights the importance of using mistakes as learning opportunities for growth and development.

Exhibit 7.10: Is Total Quality Fading as a Strategy?

Albert Einstein once said: "You cannot solve a problem with the thinking on the level that created it." That maxim applies to the relative lack of success with quality efforts. If you keep doing things the way you have always done them, you will keep getting the same results. If those results are unsatisfactory, then you must find a new way to approach the problem. Executives in a number of companies report that employee morale seems to have dropped rather than risen since they have implemented TQM. Tension between management and employees seems to have intensified. Meanwhile the strategic plans in these companies called for empowered people to make decisions that affect them and their jobs. The training was designed to provide employees with needed skills. The company's leaders embraced the creation of a total quality, high-involvement environment. The problem is, nothing in these companies changed but the words. The rewards stayed the same, employees still feared making mistakes, managers were not trained to become coaches, obstacle removers, resource providers and communicators, true power was not transferred to employees.

Companies must show managers how change can enrich their jobs and how new responsibilities will truly allow them to contribute to success. They must promote open communication, provide employees with decision-making information and drive fear from the workplace by using mistakes as learning opportunities. And finally, top managers must demonstrate by their behaviours that they support a life of continuous improvement.

Source: Ryan, J. (1995), *HR Focus*, October, pp. 14–16.

These contradictions show how difficult it is to apply quality principles in practice. As outlined earlier, the practical application of service quality procedures has not been sufficiently addressed by commentators. The academic, and even the practitioner, accounts which have dealt with implementation issues have largely

been prescriptive studies which use anecdotal evidence to support their recommendations. These prescriptive studies operate
under the assumption that organisational variables such as culture, service quality, strategy, structure, etc., can be manipulated
to effect business objectives, and improve performance. Here we
argue that organisations are more complex than that, and the task
of implementing quality cannot be accomplished by following a
set of prescriptive guidelines. If quality implementation were that
straightforward, then the business press would not be reporting
difficulties with quality implementation.

The tensions reported above have been caused largely by a
lack of integration between the organisation's quality philosophy
and overall business strategy. It would appear that the recent
strategic attention given to service quality has been pre-empted
by other strategic concerns, such as the need for improved responsiveness and performance. Hence, service quality does not
necessarily carry strategic weight, in the sense that it is a planned
and co-ordinated activity, in hospitality organisations. Instead, it
would appear that its strategic significance has evolved from a
wider organisational concern for improving business results and
performance. Decisions about quality policy are often margi-
nalised from those concerned with the organisation's overall
strategy, suggesting a lack of integration between overall strategy
and quality management strategy.

An analysis of 150 organisational quality programmes similarly found that quality improvement's role was considerably less
than quality gurus would suggest: cost reductions, not quality
improvement, predominated (Eskildson, 1995). The prevalence of
staff reductions reported in the companies examined suggests a
much different and more limited role for employee involvement
and empowerment (p. 32). The primary problems with quality
appear to be the implementation methods typically employed
within quality programmes. It seems that some quality programmes have been introduced as "a result of external pressure

rather than as a positive and proactive step" (Redman et al., 1995b: 30).

Indeed, achieving a closer integration between quality and the organisation's business-level strategy is an important concern:

> If HRM were more closely integrated with senior executive decision-making, perhaps the tension of seeking greater employee trust and commitment while, at the same time, handing out redundancy notices, would not be so blatant. It might also facilitate a greater integration of HRM and quality management practices whereby accountability, empowerment and the development of a workforce aware of, and committed to, achieving the strategic goals of the organisation could be more readily achieved (Kerfoot and Knights, 1995: 233).

There is also evidence to suggest "partial" operation of quality management practices such as employee involvement. Middle managers within the industry generally regard the development of quality policy as a managerial prerogative and, as stated above, view systems of involvement with scepticism. Hence, it appears that a limited degree of attention is accorded to issues such as involving employees in decision-making about quality; such issues are not attached the strategic significance which one might have expected.

Further, in extending the above point, it would appear that participative approaches such as empowerment and involvement have been popularised in hospitality organisations to weaken resistance to proposed changes rather than to facilitate the employee input in quality implementation exercises. It was noted earlier that employee participation is often treated with caution, fearing such participation might involve a dilution of managerial authority. While managers are keen to show an awareness of the importance of involving management, staff and guests in the development of quality policy, such actions might be interpreted as a mechanism to support hierarchical decision-making by giving employees the impression that they are contributors to quality policy making. This again lends credibility to the view that a lack of integration between organisational strategy and quality philosophy is serving to obstruct the effective implementation of service quality initiatives within the hospitality industry.

Summary

Despite the general upsurge of interest in quality management and the strategic significance attached to quality programmes, this enthusiasm has been limited somewhat by the lack of support for the practical application of quality procedures. Generally, the strong desire to project awareness of, and enthusiasm towards, the quality philosophy has not been matched by a simultaneous consideration of the practical concerns involved in transforming awareness into policies for improvement.

In this chapter we attempted to evaluate the quality management philosophy. In particular, we sought to highlight the challenges involved in applying quality programmes and examined the experiences of those charged with managing implementation initiatives. In summary, we reinforce a number of important issues that emerge from our discussion and elaborate the tensions which complicate the quality implementation process. We question the general managerial reluctance to share information and decision-making responsibilities with subordinates and warn of the dangers of applying coercion to enforce quality procedures. We are also concerned by the evidence suggesting that the introduction of quality management is often pre-empted by other strategic issues such as organisational concern for improving business performance and/or reducing costs. This approach leads to interpretation problems and may dilute the quality message and culture. Significantly, however, we suggest that middle managers are in part responsible for some of the practical difficulties associated with implementing quality initiatives. From our own work in the area, there appears to be a reluctance on the part of middle managers to distribute decision-making responsibilities to employees, fearing the performance consequences of such actions.

There are also structural issues within the hospitality industry that militate against quality implementation. Terms and conditions of employment, the seasonal nature of jobs and the departmentalised, often very hierarchical structures of hotels and attractions makes empowerment difficult to sell to both front-line staff and middle management.

We suggest that, in view of the tensions highlighted and discussed within the chapter, there exists a requirement to challenge and rethink our attitudes and approach to managing quality in hospitality operations. We need to consider new directions in applying quality concepts. In particular, the following questions need to be posed:

- How does quality management sit alongside the poor pay and conditions of employment within the hospitality sector?

- Will current trends towards reengineering and de-layering replace the general interest in quality management?

These and other issues will be examined in Chapter 8.

Review Questions

1. Does quality management work in practice? What are the challenges to effective quality implementation?

2. As a practising manager, how would you sustain momentum for continuous improvement? Set out the approach you would take.

3. Employee involvement can often be seen by managers as a way of exerting increased control over subordinates. What is your view on participative management approaches such as employee involvement? Using an organisation of your choice,

elaborate on how employee involvement might be made to work effectively.

4. Are there tensions in quality implementation? Illustrate in detail key discussion points, using practical examples to support your analysis.

5. How would you evaluate quality management? Discuss how you would evaluate quality management initiatives in an organisation of your choice.

6. Why should front-line employees in the hospitality sector sign up to the TQM philosophy?

Chapter 8

Future Challenges
for Quality Management

Introduction

Within this text, we have tried to give a fresh perspective on quality management and have sought to bring critical account to bear on an important management philosophy. We have also focused attention on an industry that is too often neglected within the business area: the tourism and hospitality sector. Studies on quality management within this sector are still in their infancy and it is hoped that this contribution will add in an important way to the material. In this sense, we are positioning our contribution amongst a growing number of writers who are considering the broad implications of quality management initiatives in a variety of industry sectors.

This concluding chapter attempts to draw together the key issues reported in the previous chapters to reflect on the implications for the tourism and hospitality industries of applying quality initiatives. Particularly, we consider the main themes that have emerged from our study and experiences within the quality domain. The ideas presented within the chapter, it is hoped, will help alert managers and researchers to the challenges and complexities involved in implementing quality management programmes. Also, we would hope that our concluding comments will help stimulate further work in the area, especially within the tourism sector where, increasingly, quality service will be used as a key differentiating factor.

Growing Importance of the Tourism Industry

An important theme that emerges in this book is that of the global nature of the tourism industry. As a result of globalisation and competitive pressures, the tourism industry will become increasingly important to national economies. This trend is likely to continue, as companies need to become "global" in order to seize opportunities. The following statistics place the argument in context. Services, within which tourism occupies an important position, are now a critical element of a developed market infrastructure and comprise an ever-larger share of international trade, investment and employment. In 1997, trade in services amounted to over £1 trillion. In the EU, over 46 per cent of the workforce is employed in commercial services and services account for over 52 per cent of GDP. An estimated 60 per cent of foreign direct investment flows are directed towards services. Tourism as a service industry is now estimated to be employing 10 per cent of the world's workforce. By 2006, it is predicted that the number of jobs in travel and tourism world-wide will have increased to 365 million. In the European Union, tourism generates 19 million jobs and employs 13 per cent of the workforce. Along with telecommunications and information technology, tourism will be one of the three "superservices" that will drive economic growth in the twenty-first century.

Notwithstanding the growth prospects for tourism, markets are facing unprecedented change because of changing lifestyles and rapidly evolving technologies. As discussed in earlier chapters, the widening range of choice, within and between sectors, combined with growing access to information, will facilitate the opportunity for consumers to exchange one supplier for another. With consumers shifting loyalties between firms, "relationships" will be difficult to develop and nurture. This changing profile of customers makes it difficult to determine future tastes and preferences and the complexity of the market has made the concept of the "average traveller" redundant. This changing consumer profile will encourage a blurring between the categories within the sector with facilities encompassing a wider range of hospitality/ leisure/retail offerings. Consumers will require immediate service and products and services will increasingly be sold on the basis of a company's ability to respond to their customers' needs for flexibility. This is a strategy which has informed the approaches used by the Dusit Thani group in Thailand. The management team has attempted to develop a unique character for each of the hotels within the group. Fashion shows, art contests and fitness events are all part of the "activity marketing" mix that has helped raise the profile of Dusit hotels. The group has attempted to combine retailing and hotel concepts in an effort to boost profitability.

In addition, developments in technology have increased consumers' knowledge of and accessibility to a wider range of suppliers. By 2006, 50 per cent of households will own a PC and a large majority of these will have access to the Internet. The associated changes in distribution technology will require a review of supplier pricing strategies. Within international tourism markets, market access commitments need to be expanded and standards and procedures for ensuring professional competence and performance of service providers will need to be more transparent. As competition intensifies, inconsistency in expected service delivery will have to be replaced by "better practices" throughout. Ireland is an excellent example of a country that has kept abreast of the wider changes occurring in international tourism markets and has successfully transformed itself into a modern, innovative and economically aggressive nation. Exhibit 8.1 details the approaches adopted by the Irish tourism industry and charts the changes underway within the sector.

Exhibit 8.1: Managing Change within the Irish Tourism Industry

The Irish tourism industry has achieved record-breaking levels of success over the last number of years. In 1993, about 91,000 people were fully employed in tourism and related sectors, an increase of 24,000 since 1988. Overseas visitors in 1997 totalled 4.7 million, with a value to the economy of £1.5 billion. Tourism is also a powerful instrument of regional balance, tourism revenue being widely spread throughout the country. All available statistics point to the fact that tourism will be the biggest industry by 2000.

The function of developing a comprehensive approach to the education and training of personnel within the tourism industry in Ireland is delegated to an executive agency, CERT. In helping to achieve change within the industry, the agency provides the following important services: identification of manpower and training needs; development of national training structures and programmes; industry-based training for tourism managers and workers; recruitment and training of school-leavers through college-based training courses; provision of business development and advisory services to the industry; and basic skills training for the unemployed.

Bord Fáilte, the Irish Tourism Board, assists in the development and promotion of Ireland as a tourism destination in international markets. The board was completely restructured in 1995 to create a newly focused and more dynamic organisation to market Irish tourism world-wide aggressively and professionally in close partnership with the industry. The restructuring has involved outsourcing the inspection of tourism accommodation, although Bord Fáilte will continue to set high standards.

A new Tourism Council, representative of the industry and chaired by the Minister for Tourism, Recreation and Sport, has been appointed to operate for a two-year term and a total of £1 million has been allocated for a new home holiday initiative, with industry co-financing to encourage greater marketing of home holidays, particularly in the off-peak season. A key factor in Ireland's success has been the improved competitiveness of all aspects of the visitor's experience — access transport, accommodation, and other facilities and services. Even more significantly, there has been increased competition on access routes, resulting in a real-term decrease in all promotional fares. Further, Ireland is increasingly being viewed as a "trendy" location and as a place to visit in terms of culture, and the positive international attention given to this niche destination.

Source: "Operational Programme for Tourism, 1995–1999", Department for Tourism, Recreation and Sport, 1994.

The issues raised above, highlighting change and competition, mean that the tourism industry will continue to go through a process of continuous restructuring and updating of its services to meet changing customer requirements and compete effectively in a global marketplace. As we argued in our earlier chapters on strategy and international competition, the quality of the offering will be critical as it attempts to meet increasingly fragmented consumer needs. Attention to quality will not merely centre around improvements in standards of service to customers; it will also symbolise a new business strategy and method of management. It is to this theme that we now turn our attention.

Quality: a New Method of Management

Throughout this book, we have attempted to examine quality issues in a comprehensive way and address studies, published data, research and practical examples from a wide number of sources. Too often, accounts of quality management are presented without supporting data or without knowledge of relevant research studies. We have sought to present and report upon these contributions and in so doing develop our own views on the quality philosophy.

Throughout, we have sought to locate quality in a strategic context characterised by rationalisation and job cuts, insecurities, cost reduction, new technologies and the search for customers through service quality. In adopting this view, we wish to take account of the "context" as well as the "content" of quality initiatives. Although the 1990s have been described as the "decade of quality", it is important to be clear about both the challenges as well as the purported benefits of subscribing to the philosophy.

One of the attractions of "quality" and "quality systems" is that nobody is against it and everybody wants it. Yet quality and quality systems can be misleading. However, companies are going to have to become more aware of quality issues and managers

will play an important role, particularly middle-level management executives. In the late 1980s, accreditation of quality systems
to ISO norms was an important issue for businesses. Certification
came to be seen as a necessary condition for marketing products
and services effectively. Introducing quality systems and having
them accredited was also supposed to boost companies' competitiveness. However, as discussed in earlier chapters, many individuals involved in the implementation of quality systems found
the benefits to be intangible and internal. There was also a perception that quality systems had only limited impact on business
competitiveness and in most companies they were introduced for
entirely the wrong reasons. Indeed, some commentators suggested that quality systems were monopolised by a small group of
experts who focused their efforts on assessing quality standards
and neglecting the ultimate objective of improving quality to increase customer satisfaction. On the other hand, those companies
that viewed the quality system, not as an end in itself, but as part
of a wider process, performed more effectively.

Thus, while the competitive benefits of adopting quality systems are acknowledged (in many situations, having an accredited
quality system in place is a condition for doing business), it needs
to be complemented by an effective business strategy and appropriate method of management. A second theme emerging from
this text suggests that for quality management to be effective it
needs to be viewed from a wider context. Industry should be encouraged to move beyond the scope of ISO 9000 and introduce
full quality management programmes, where customer and staff
satisfaction, results and impact on society are integral. Responsibility should be regularly and boldly emphasised. Often, the development of quality policies is theoretical and internal. The
alignment of customer specifications with design, process and delivery should be given more prominence. Thus, for organisations
to satisfy their customers, they need to be able to detect the implied as well as the obvious requirements of a potential consumer.

The American approach is illustrative in this regard. US companies are hugely sophisticated in the ways in which they track customer satisfaction and manage the complaint process. In the US, consumers are very willing to complain when things go wrong. A recent *Wall Street Journal* article showed that consumers scored hotels at 71 out of 100 points in the most recent nationwide customer satisfaction survey, a drop from 75 points in 1994 when hotel companies were struggling to pull themselves out of recession. The score was the lowest since Andersen began its US customer satisfaction index five years ago (*Wall Street Journal*, 13 August 1998).

In consequence, US firms are proactive in their approach to designing "service recovery" systems into their complaint handling procedures. These include such systems as policies on corrective action and front-line employee empowerment to take action if things should go wrong. Organisations must therefore strive for more proactive, credible and transparent quality management approaches if they are to remain competitive under present conditions of uncertainty.

In the US and elsewhere, customers are becoming increasingly discerning and there is a real need for initiatives that help employees to engage more actively with customers. This is an important consideration, especially when viewed within the context of changes outlined in Exhibit 8.2. It is becoming extremely difficult to anticipate customer expectations effectively; hence, the growing realisation in many organisations of the need to distribute decision-making responsibilities to front-line employees.

Exhibit 8.2: Tracking Customers' Expectations of Quality Initiatives

A growing number of small, chic hotels are finding that hostility sometimes sells better than hospitality. Places like New York's Royalton, Miami's Delano hotel and San Franciso's Diva Hotel charge $200 to $400 per night and tend to offer small rooms, weird furniture, little conference space and the aloof service of an exclusive restaurant.

> But they also have something else: 90 per cent occupancy rates, even at prices that can run 20 per cent higher than competitors. Most of these hotels' decidedly unglamorous occupants say they just cannot resist the glitter. The managers of such hotels say they don't promote disdainful behaviour, but they try to be more casual and edgy than traditional luxury hotels. Some liken running a hotel to a stage production, where sets and appearances are crucial and where "casting calls" are often used as part of the recruitment procedure.
>
> At the Mondrian hotel, the bellmen wear cream coloured *faux* Armani suits, and the lobby resembles a museum of contemporary furniture. The company has even gone so far as to hire talent agents, who contact modelling and acting agents to find desirable workers. Some customers do complain that the interior decor isn't always functional; however, for all their complaining, guests keep coming back for more. It is all part of the process of anticipating and responding to customers' expectations.

Source: Wall Street Journal, "Hotels Find Hostility Sells Better than Hospitality", 8 November 1997, p. 12.

Training for Quality

A consistent theme in this text is the importance of employee training in the achievement of product and service quality. In earlier chapters, we noted that employers are increasingly dependent on the skills of all their employees for improvements in efficiency, quality and customer service. Quality products and services depend on a quality workforce. This idea is not new. It was an issue raised by Deming in the formulation of his 14 maxims to aid in the reduction of variation. Deming's argument was that if workers were inadequately trained, they would each carry out the same task in a different way, increasing variation. In this sense, training for quality means thinking about what is being done, why it is being done and what the associated outcomes are.

However, while acknowledging the early work on quality management, we argue in this text that the tourism industry has a different need for training. After all, quality customer service is not often achieved by homogeneity — by treating all customers the same. Instead, training forms a vital part of the cure, particularly training which allows staff to empathise with customers, or to use company systems more effectively. With the pace of change quickening and competition intensifying, obsolescence of employee skills and abilities is emerging as a critical issue in many companies. To address this problem, companies must foster a learning-oriented culture where the emphasis should be placed on lifelong learning for everyone. We also argue that such initiatives should focus not only on the "hard" system components but also on the "softer" process skills associated with managing change, innovation and learning. These issues should not be discarded as overworked buzzwords; instead, they should be incorporated as important components of the training intervention. Such convergence of employee and employer interests to pursue learning and employee development will culminate in a workforce that possesses the knowledge and skills required in the future.

Exhibit 8.3 shows how McDonald's have applied this philosophy to the organisation of work. Across the globe the company has applied very high standards to the recruiting and training of staff. This has served to enhance their market profile and has helped the company achieve a strong market position worldwide.

Exhibit 8.3: Can't get this Big without HR Deluxe

Every three to four hours, a new McDonald's opens its doors. More than 20,000 Golden Arches shine from Singapore to the Netherlands to Russia, with an additional 2,000 to 3,000 new stores planned a year. What does it mean to be this big, this ubiquitous, this well known? It means you would better have some fairly amazing people — and fairly amazing HR policies to support those people. McDonald's does. From recruiting to training, from expanding world-wide to leveraging diversity, McDonald's has a people plan in place. Its on-the-ball HR agenda earned the company a "Personnel Journal General Excellence Optimas Award", which means that the company excels in six of the ten Optimas categories. These six are:

- Competitive Advantage

- Quality of Life

- Partnership

- Financial Impact

- Innovation

- Global Outlook

It doesn't stop here. To sustain its success with human resource management, the company has initiated a "HR Regeneration" programme consisting of three parts. First, a "solution centre" will take over HR transactions. But this solution centre will also include a consultative piece. When management people have questions about a particular HR venue, they can access the Internet and Lotus Notes for just-in-time information and training. If this doesn't solve the issue, management then can go straight to the company's HR experts. If it's a staffing issue, they can access the top staffing people. They will deal directly with the best of the best in all the HR areas: compensation and benefits operations, staffing, etc. The second area is creating "business partners". These people will work with management, taking all business strategies and interpreting the implications from a HR perspective. Thirdly, they work with people in the "design centre", ensuring the HR's new systems and processes are addressing the business's needs.

As Stan Stein, senior VP, HR and Labour Relations, points out: "If we are going to stay ahead of the game, we have got to be looking forward in this way. That way we can manage 40,000 or 50,000 stores as well as we can manage 20,000". With McDonald's serving up this kind of HR excellence, that goal seems quite achievable.

Source: *Personnel Journal*, Vol. 75, No. 12, December 1996, pp. 1–9.

This point is also beginning to emerge as a serious consideration within the tourism industry. In a labour-intensive industry such as tourism, the effective management of human resources can provide a competitive advantage. Organisations must develop human resource practices that will enable them to recruit, select and retain competent employees who can contribute to the achievement of their objectives. Otherwise they will not be able to compete effectively in the new global tourism and hospitality environment.

Evidence that this position has been gaining considerable acceptance is clear and has been outlined consistently throughout this text. However, there is a great deal of resistance and apathy to it as well. Often, the strong emphasis on meeting customers' expectations is often not seen to parallel equally strong concern for providing employees with the necessary support to manage the customer interface effectively.

Equally, it is arguable that the support which employers apparently commit to the training and development of their employees can be questioned, given the high levels of turnover reported within the tourism industry. Continuous high levels of staff turnover and major skills shortages are areas meriting serious consideration. They highlight the requirement for improvements in the image and status of the industry and the need for additional investment in education, training and lifetime learning.

Exhibit 8.4 below illustrates the benefits of training in supporting the company's quality effort. It is an approach propounded by Michael Governey at the Conrad Hotel, Dublin. An emphasis on quality supported by large investments in training permeates the company's operations. From decisions on strategy through marketing planning to positioning, the Conrad has adopted a quality focus which has helped it achieve enormous growth in the buoyant marketplace.

Exhibit 8.4: Quality Focus Keeps Hands-on Host 100 Per Cent Occupied

> Michael Governey has brought Dublin's Conrad Hotel through difficult times to a position where it can afford to focus on corporate clients. The 200-bedroom hotel is aimed at the corporate market, which currently accounts for up to 70 per cent of its sales. It aims for and is currently achieving 80 per cent occupancy.

In line with other tourism businesses, the Conrad came under enormous pressure in the early 1990s, with sales figures plunging and competitors engaging in aggressive price-cutting. However, while rivals cut prices and compromised on standards, Governey made it clear that he was not prepared to sacrifice high quality standards in the short term. This stance, he believes, has helped the hotel to capitalise on the huge growth in corporate and leisure business from 1994 onwards.

Governey's philosophy places strong emphasis on quality in all aspects of the business. He maintains that while people will select a hotel based on the brochure and facilities available, it is the staff that make a difference. Specifically, he states: "My philosophy on staff is that their attitude is the most important thing. You can teach skills but you cannot teach attitude. When I came here in 1990, I explained to our personnel manager what I would be looking for and I have to say that, of all of the hotels I have managed, I have the greatest pride in the staff here".

Also, he stresses the importance of positioning your offering at the right end of the market. He argues that five-star operations cannot afford to mix their business: "You cannot mix top corporate clients with a different level of business, by taking a chance on a cheap tour, for instance. People will notice a change in standards." Clearly his approach is paying off with the Conrad well positioned to take advantage of changing demand patterns within the industry.

Source: *Irish Times*, "The Director's Chair", 31 October 1997, p. 24.

Governey's approach shows the important role which senior managers have to play in providing necessary resource support and training to employees operating at the front-end with customers. It is not enough that management simply throws money at quality; it also needs to ensure that the *"processes"* of quality are working in an everyday sense and at the sharp end of the business where customers are affected. In most cases, it is management, and only management, that can initiate such activities and command resources to support service encounters consistently. It is managers who are in a position to provide the resources that can secure worker commitment.

Implementing the Quality Initiative

The challenges associated with quality implementation are also emerging as an important theme. We argue the requirement to examine quality implementation from two different, but related, perspectives. On the one hand, it is pointed out that, for quality to be implemented, it needs to be managed from the top. This point has been alluded to earlier, particularly in the case of quality issues at the Conrad (see Exhibit 8.4). Attention needs to be directed to the requirement to secure support and commitment from senior management when implementing service quality initiatives.

There is also a need for bottom-up involvement from employees to ensure that commitment is translated into actionable policy at the front-end with customers. The implementation process needs to be informed by those who operate closest to the customer, so that the approach adopted by the organisation can be assessed on a continual basis. Our arguments, emphasising the requirement for quality implementation to take account of both "top" and "bottom" organisational interests, challenge the "top-downist" emphasis in much of the material on quality management. In particular, there is need for a greater consideration of a consensual approach to implementation initiatives.

Although accepting of the important contribution that senior executives bring to the implementation of quality initiatives, we also caution against an exclusive emphasis on the concerns of top managers. Current trends emphasise the need to facilitate the views of managers and employees at various levels within the organisation. Effective implementation can only be achieved if understanding and commitment is shared between members at all levels within the organisation. In complex or changing environments, individuals rarely appreciate all the intricacies of the situation, and organisations benefit from the variety of viewpoints represented by middle and operating managers.

It is suggested that, in pursuing service quality initiatives, senior executives within the organisation need to be supportive of a participative style of managing where they openly engage with employees to identify any obstacles which might obstruct the implementation process. Consider the following information given to prospective employees at Sabena airlines. The Exhibit shows the increasing importance attached to service quality in the competitive airline business and highlights the significance of distributing responsibility to where it matters most: the front line.

Exhibit 8.5: New Wave Management Techniques at Sabena

We have all heard the saying, "All airlines are the same". To a degree, they are. Indeed, most aircraft are alike: seats are similar and the same limitations are shared by airlines when it comes to serving food and drink abroad. The big difference is in the attitudes of the people employed. There is a popular book whose subtitle is "Attitude is a little thing that makes a difference". Who could be more receptive to such an idea than an international airline?

Management at Sabena believe that employees can succeed only if they are given the freedom to take decisions at the front-line and if they can be flexible and adaptable in carrying out work tasks. To sustain competitiveness, the airline is focusing its attention on passenger satisfaction. In this regard, the company is providing permanent training for experienced cabin crew so that every single member of the 1,400-strong Sabena corps is equipped to respond to evolving passenger expectations. Also, since September 1997, the organisation conducts training sessions at the Belgian Aviation School for its employees. They master behavioural theory and develop an awareness of cultural diversity. They perfect flight preparation and service skills, practice safety and security drills and learn other specialised airline procedures. This approach, according to Paul Reutlinger, President and CEO, lies at the heart of Sabena's success in the international airline business and serves to help the company differentiate itself from other operators in the marketplace.

Source: Company documentation (1997).

However, we see difficulties with commitment to quality at a number of different levels. Firstly, from our experience there appears to be a lack of strong senior managerial commitment to quality implementation. Despite the emphasis that middle managers often place on this dimension, evidence suggests difficulties with senior managerial commitment in practice, particularly in relation to the extent to which senior managers are willing to communicate and involve themselves with middle level executives. Some managers have become fixated on the word "quality" and have lost sight of the word "management". Ironically, the result is that key quality management precepts are being ignored; customers' responses are being taken for granted instead of continuously monitored and evaluated; selected processes are not improved upon, and their effect on other equally important processes are not being considered; changes are not tested on a small scale first before being implemented corporate-wide; and there is little attempt made to measure costs and benefits along the way.

There are also structural issues affecting the implementation of quality initiatives in many hospitality and tourism companies and organisations, namely seasonality. Many of the accounts given in published work have focused on hotels with high annual occupancy rates, and often those aiming at the corporate market. However, the vast majority of smaller and resort hotels, attractions and resort support services show distinct seasonality both in terms of turnover and in staff numbers. How can an inclusive HRM style, which requires the building of trust between managerial levels and operative staff, be developed when this relationship may only last for the three or four months of the season? Further, the tourism sector in general has been broadly criticised for lacking a structural career path.

This debate on the viability of quality initiatives has not quelled enthusiasm for it; rather, it has given a healthy dose of realism to those companies that embraced it as a simple-minded ethos to cure all their ills. It may even open the way for more cynically minded managers who have so far been put off quality management by the almost evangelical hype that has accompanied it. Nevertheless, as outlined in earlier chapters, despite the current revisionist push, quality management is still seen as the most viable source of effective corporate change.

Integration with Strategy

Equally significant is the requirement that quality be incorporated as a key strategic consideration within the organisation. It is suggested that a general increase in quality initiatives has the beneficial effect of including more people in discussions of strategy-related issues. The upsurge of interest in quality management should therefore serve to improve management–employee relations and improve communications at lower levels in the organisation. This concurs strongly with contemporary views of strategy. In recent years, emphasis on the customer and the requirement to provide high quality service have been incorporated as key strategic concerns for the organisation. As we discussed earlier in the text, hotels and other tourism-related organisations have thus encouraged their staff to think of departments as "internal customers" in order to increase overall standards of service. These will continue to be important concerns in the future.

We will probably find that our travel and tourism industries will be forced up-market. There will be rising pressure to give value for money. Of course, that pressure always exists in every business; the point is that it will intensify. If companies do not respond by improving the quality of output, they will find that they are losing customers and ultimately market share.

What does going "up-market" mean in practice? It is easy to understand the process in a manufactured product. It is harder to see in a service industry. For example, in the airline business, there has been a revolution in productivity over the last decade; the planes are the same, but in general the service is better and in real terms the fares are lower. In hotels, the Scandinavian model has been accustomed to using labour much more frugally than has been common in Britain and the US. Hotels in these countries have invested to create luxury environments that need relatively little labour to keep clean, while staff are trained to meet guests' needs in the most efficient ways possible (*The Independent*, 18 September 1997). Clearly, there is a role for the government in all this. It needs to invest in travel infrastructure and tax sensibly. But in the end, it is critical that tourism businesses appreciate the pace and rate of the changes affecting their industry and that quality and productivity issues assume greater importance in their strategic management activities.

Indeed, despite the general perception that quality has assumed increased strategic importance within the tourism industry, we suggest that quality management is not a planned and co-ordinated initiative. Instead, the emphasis on quality has arisen possibly as a consequence of an overall concern for improving organisational performance. Initiatives such as employee involvement and participation are operated so as to weaken resistance to hierarchical authority and decision-making, as opposed to being viewed as positive and proactive steps in the development of effective internal systems for quality provision. Over the last decade, organisational downsizing has put many experienced managers, particularly those in middle management positions, out of work. This has introduced acute shortages in many organisations' human resource base. While there appears to be a general consensus that downsizing and restructuring are necessary to maintain profitability and reduce overheads, others argue that such initiatives bring many negative long-term effects.

Exhibit 8.6: Reengineering Initiatives in the Tourism Sector

During the past decade, it has been reported that US companies have eliminated 4.7 million jobs, or approximately one-quarter of their workforce. Now, both people and businesses are feeling the hangover from headier times. As businesses downsize, many workers are worrying less about accumulating goods and more about hanging on to their jobs. And they are often scrambling to keep their heads above water.

This is a growing trend within the tourism industry. According to a recent survey of the top 200 restaurant chains in the US, nearly two-thirds of respondents have undertaken some level of reengineering effort in the past three or four years. While reengineering has taken place at all levels of the industry, it is most noticeable in the reduction of staff at corporate headquarters. Reengineering, with its extensive process analysis and regrouping of companies' corporate staffs, has resulted in a sharp rise in optimism among top executives about company performance, if not productivity.

However, it is difficult to be clear about the implications of reengineering projects. The impact of downsizing cannot always be determined, because there is rarely a clear measurement of the level or impact of individual burnout. Part of the reason is that corporate staff members and other middle managers are adept at masking job dissatisfaction and the strains of working with too few personnel. Hidden costs to productivity and quality of performance are incalculable but real nonetheless. The loss of individual capital due to workload stress could well negate the supposed productivity gains of recent years. When the losses reach noticeable proportions and demand costly attention, we may find that the next wave of management buzzwords will proclaim human reinvestment.

Source: D.J. Lombardi and T. Miner (1995), *Cornell Hotel and Restaurant Administration Quarterly*, December 1995, pp. 43–7.

The hospitality industry has in recent years been very "fluid" in terms of ownership. Major changes have taken place, the largest being the takeover of Forte by Granada. Such "fluidity" is itself unsettling. Newspaper reports of the new companies' strategies being to increase rack rates, reduce management levels, sell off non-core-brand hotels and change fundamental principles, such as nationwide pricing of roadside lodges, do not give good and encouraging signals to the staff, at any level, who must try to maintain enthusiasm through such change. Driving through the necessary changes to implement quality initiatives works best in an environment where all sides, including customers, can trust and understand each other. They also operate effectively when managers share a commitment to continued learning and development and possess the necessary competences to integrate management and employee development into the competitive strategy formulation process.

To this end, more attention needs to be given to management development in tourism organisations. In general, little is known of the role of management in creating effective organisations in the hospitality industry and the research to date has been unable to isolate the competences used by effective senior managers. Exhibit 8.7 reports some of the findings of a doctoral study of management competences within the Irish tourism sector, which was carried out in an attempt to address some of these deficiencies.

Exhibit 8.7: Management Competences in the Irish Tourism Industry

It is well established that the hospitality industry is important to national economies, yet little is known about the characteristics of its senior managers and the ways in which they influence organisational performance. Managers ensure that business opportunities are identified and that the industry's reputation for friendliness and quality service is maintained. A comprehensive study of Irish tourism organisations was thus undertaken to establish the nature of management practices and the competences used by general managers in Irish tourist companies.

Specifically, the study allowed for the development and application of a framework of performance indicators for use in the Irish tourism and hospitality sector. The research also provided for the formulation of a competence profile of general managers, including a comprehensive assessment of the skills, abilities, knowledge and personal strengths required for the effective execution of critical tasks and activities.

The methodology employed the critical incident technique, an administered survey and semi-structured interviews to examine management competences. The research showed that general managers in effective hotels identified 144 critical incidents and in managing these incidents they used 67 dominant competences. The study also allowed for the development of an "Integrated Model of Management Practices, Competences and Organisational Effectiveness" illustrating linkages between organisational performance, management practices and management competences.

> In general, however, the findings revealed a diversity of management activities and practices in the organisations studied and showed that management is dominated by operational activities and issues. As the industry continues to evolve and develop, organisations must not only have experienced managers who can recognise and adapt to changing market conditions, but also depend on those individuals to mobilise internal resources to capitalise on potential new market opportunities. The findings from this study contribute in important ways to the achievement of such objectives.

Source: T. Lenehan (1996), "A Study of Management Practices and Competences within Effective Organisations in Tourism", Proceedings, British Academy of Management Conference, Sheffield University, September.

Competence development and management will assume a more significant degree of importance within the tourism sector in future as organisations compete to secure and retain talented, competent, experienced and adaptable managers. With the exception of a small number of major international companies, programmes for the continuing professional development of managers appear to be relatively underdeveloped within the tourism and hospitality sector. If management within the tourism sector is truly to be regarded as a profession, managers must recognise that it is essential to update their skills on a continual basis. We suggest greater consideration of the nature and role of management competences in tourism and in particular the possible links that may exist between underlying competences and quality performance. This is an emerging area of interest and one that warrants increased attention from commentators in the area. Hitherto, participation by managers in management development programmes offered by management institutes and training organisations has tended to be low. In the future, professional development programmes will provide the catalyst for the anticipation of change and the effective allocation of organisational resources.

Tensions, Complexities and Future Challenges for the Tourism Sector

A final theme to emerge in our assessment of quality management practices is that of the challenges and complexities inherent in achieving quality objectives. By this we mean the insufficient attention given to understanding how quality measures can be implemented under conditions of uncertainty. This issue has been raised a number of times within the text because we feel it is often side-stepped or ignored in the material on quality. There appears to be an overabundance of material outlining the benefits of adhering to quality principles, and indeed a plethora of reports suggesting prescriptive approaches to achieving a quality focus. However, these have failed to address the wider implications of adopting quality initiatives. In line with a growing number of authors, we are suggesting that future work will need to address tensions in the application of quality initiatives. This is important from a theoretical and practical perspective. In particular, we need to understand how the "softer" side of quality management can be illuminated and how it can be "worked" more effectively within tourism organisations. We also need to address the difficulties of introducing greater involvement and empowerment under conditions of rationalisation and job cuts.

Long-term neglect of human resources is undermining the competitiveness of many organisations. For example, many US firms within the tourism sector have invested billions of dollars in capital equipment, only to learn later that there was a shortage of skilled labour to operate the equipment. This situation will change in the decade ahead as increased levels of competition, a more sophisticated customer base and the international presence of high quality tourism organisations operating through franchising, agreements, joint ventures and mergers, will force changes to current attitudes towards training.

Greater attention will also need to be given to organisational political issues when examining quality management initiatives.

Achieving quality objectives has more to do with "social and political" considerations than with technical issues. Individuals compete for power and influence within organisations; therefore we need to take political account of quality issues. Quality needs to recognise the political reality of organisational life: this does not mean that quality cannot get off the ground, but merely that an awareness of this is likely to lead to a clearer picture of the obstacles to implementation.

The successful implementation of quality goals will therefore be dependent upon fundamental changes in organisational processes and strategies which will drive and reinforce changes in the behaviour of key stakeholders. A particular issue to address in the tourism sector is the inter-organisational problem. Tourists go on holiday first to a destination, then to an accommodation unit, be this a camp site or a hotel. The quality philosophy must be seen to be active throughout the destination; no company or organisation can act alone in a resort or city. Whilst commentators have, as reported, considered intra-organisational quality issues, the time is ripe for inter-organisational, destination-wide issues to be addressed. This is a particular issue in the tourism sector. When buying manufactured goods, quality issues are easily assessed for the customer through, say, reliability studies. In tourism, this may not be the case.

In the future, customers will increasingly look for innovation in destinations and activities and will seek fulfilling experiences. They will have more transparent price structures, especially with the introduction of EMU and, as users of the Internet, will seek immediate information and interactive reservations facilities (see, for instance, Lenehan, 1998). Never has it been so important, therefore, for tourism organisations to have effective quality strategies in place to meet changing customer expectations. Such initiatives, if they are to be successful, will need to be framed with the above considerations in mind. Many companies have in recent years undergone a quiet revolution in their thinking and approaches to managing quality. However, there is still much to be accomplished. With the globalisation of service expectations, quality will emerge as a key differentiating factor in competitive markets. Either companies accept this reality or they face being forced out of the market by their more sophisticated, quality-driven rivals. Hopefully, this text will point interested companies in the right direction.

Summary

In line with other service industries, competition within the tourism industry has intensified in recent years with the growing sophistication of customer demand and the pressures for technological advancement and globalisation. In this climate, service quality has become an important issue for many tourism organisations. The adoption of quality management techniques is generally regarded as having positive implications for business performance and viewed as an effective means by which an organisation can achieve competitive advantage through differentiation. However, with some notable exceptions, the published work to date has not included comprehensive analyses of quality management practices in tourism businesses. Compared to other service industry sectors, the tourism industry has received less attention from management writers and researchers.

Also noticeably absent from the published material on quality management are accounts incorporating a critical dimension. A review of available material suggests that there are clear deficiencies in the treatment and attention given to critical studies of the quality concept.

Our contribution has sought to address such shortcomings and has argued for greater emphasis to be placed on an examination of service quality practices within the tourism industry. As outlined earlier, the economic realities of change and increased competitiveness have encouraged tourism companies to embrace quality as a medium through which they can appeal to a discerning public. Moreover, research carried out within the industry has tended to be insular in nature and could usefully be informed by wider theoretical and empirical investigations. In consequence, we have aimed to broaden the current research perspective and consider tourism quality issues from a wider strategic perspective. Admittedly, such a goal is necessarily ambitious; however, we feel that we have given comprehensive coverage of the available material on quality management and have sought to include both underlying theory and practical exhibits to support the arguments presented.

Overall, we feel that while the service quality philosophy has gained in importance within service industries and in the tourism sector in particular, there are deficiencies in the treatment of the implementation variable. A clear distinction is perceived to exist between managerial awareness of quality procedures and their actual implementation at the organisational level. We also feel that a perception exists at middle managerial level in many tourism organisations that quality implementation is best approached by applying a consensual, involvement-based strategy for achieving quality objectives. However, there are internal barriers that obstruct such an implementation process. Specifically, the barriers relate to internal organisational tensions, which limit the successful application of quality initiatives and serve to illustrate the complicated nature of the implementation process. Account must be taken of both these issues — the practice of consensual-based implementation strategies and associated tensions in the application of such approaches — in quality implementation exercises, as strategic benefits will increasingly be accorded to those organisations that can successfully translate the quality rhetoric into implemented practice. To quote Zairi (1994: 2), a leading contemporary thinker in the area:

The challenge for all of us is perhaps to make TQM work effectively in any sector, to ensure that organisations optimise its benefits, to develop it as a philosophy of modern management so that it can address future challenges, to disseminate widely ideas, definitions, examples of TQM and its workings and to integrate it in our education systems.

Review Questions

1. How effective are quality programmes? Comment on effectiveness using an organisation to illustrate your answer.

2. As a practising manager, how would you ensure that quality initiatives are translated into actionable policies for improvement?

3. What changes will affect tourism operations in the decade ahead? How might a manager implement quality policies so as to anticipate such changes?

4. After reading the textbook, what advice would you have for tourism organisations wishing to undertake a quality management programme?

Bibliography

Adams, S. (1996), *Dilbert's Management Handbook*, New York: Harper Collins.

Aguilo, E. (1996), "Research into Policies on Tourism", *The Tourist Review*, Vol. 1, pp. 12–17.

Akehurst, G. (1985), Editorial, *Service Industries Journal*, Vol. 5.

Andrews, K. (1980), *The Concept of Corporate Strategy*, Homewood, IL: Irwin.

Andrews, K.R. (1991), "The Concept of Corporate Strategy", in H. Mintzberg and J.B. Quinn (eds.), *The Strategy Process*, London: Prentice Hall, pp. 47–55.

Ansoff, I. (1994), "Comment on Henry Mintzberg's Rethinking Strategic Planning", *Long Range Planning*, Vol. 27, No. 3, pp. 12–21.

Armistead, C.G. and G.R. Clark (1992), *Customer Service and Support: Implementing Effective Strategies*, London: Financial Times/Pitman.

Arrebola, J.L.S. (1995), "Spanish Tourist Resorts: New Initiatives", *The Tourist Review*, No. 3, pp. 40-3.

Ashness, D. and C. Lashley (1995), "Empowering Service Workers at Harvester Restaurants", *Personnel Review*, Vol. 24, No. 8, pp. 17–32.

Athiyaman, A. and R.W. Robertson (1995), "Strategic Planning in Large Tourism Firms: an Empirical Analysis", *Tourism Management*, Vol. 16, No. 3, pp. 199–205.

Babakus, E. and G.W. Boller (1992), "An Empirical Assessment of the SERVQUAL Scale", *Journal of Business Research*, Vol. 24, pp. 253–68.

Babakus, E. and W.G. Mangold (1992), "Adapting the SERVQUAL Scale to Hospital Services: an Empirical Investigation", *Health Service Research*, Vol. 26, No. 6, pp. 768–786.

Baker, M. and P. Cave (1995), "The Cardiff Copthorne: Squeezing the most from Quality Registration" in A. Lockwood, M. Baker and A. Ghillyer, *Quality Management in Hospitality: Best Practice in Action*, London: Cassell.

Ballantyne, D., M. Christopher and A. Payne (1995), "Improving the Quality of Services Marketing: Service (Re)design is the Critical Link", *Journal of Marketing Management*, Vol. 11, pp. 7–24.

Band, W.A. (1992), "Listening to the Customer", *Sales and Marketing Management*, October, pp. 15–16, 36.

Barke, M. and J. Towner (1996), "Urban Tourism in Spain", in M. Barke, J. Towner and M.T. Newton (eds.), *Tourism in Spain: Critical Issues*, Wallingford: CAB International.

Barnes, J.G. and W.J. Glynn (1993), "The Customer Wants Service: Why Technology is No Longer Enough", *Journal of Marketing Management*, Vol. 9, pp. 43–53.

Barsky, J.D. (1992), "Customer Satisfaction in the Hotel Industry: Meaning and Measurement", *Hospitality Research Journal*, Vol. 16, No. 1, pp. 51–73.

Barsky, J.D. (1996), "Building a Program for World-Class Service", *Cornell Hotel and Restaurant and Administration Quarterly*, February, pp. 17–27.

Bateson, J.G. (1977), "Do We Need Service Marketing?" in *Marketing Consumer Services: New Insights*, Marketing Science Institute, Report No. 77–115, December.

BDO Hospitality Consulting (1994), *UK Hotel Industry*, London: BDO Hospitality Consulting, p. 6.

Becker, C. and M.D. Olsen (1995), "Exploring the Relationship between Heterogeneity and Generic Management Trends in Hospitality Organisations", *International Journal of Hospitality Management*, Vol. 14, No. 1, p. 39.

Beer, M. and B. Spector (1985), "Corporate-wide Transformations in Human Resource Management" in Walton, R.E. and P.R. Lawrence (eds.), *Human Resource Management: Trends and Challenges*, Boston, MA: Harvard Business School Press.

Belohlav, J.A. (1993), "Quality, Strategy and Competitiveness", *California Management Review*, Vol. 35, No. 3, pp. 55–67.

Bendell, A. (1992), *The Quality Gurus*, London: DTI.

Benjamin, R.I., J.F. Rockart, M.S. Scott-Morton and J. Wyman (1984), "Information Technology: a Strategic Opportunity", *Sloan Management Review*, Spring, pp. 3–10.

Berry, L.L. (1980), "Services Marketing is Different", *Business*, May/June, pp. 24–9.

Berry, Leonard L. (1983), "Relationship Marketing" in Leonard L. Berry, G. Lynn Shostack and Gregory D. Upah (eds.), *Emerging Perspectives on Services Marketing*, Chicago, IL: American Marketing Association, pp. 25–8.

Berry, Leonard L., D.R. Bennett and C.W. Brown (1989), *Service Quality: A Profit Strategy for Financial Institutions*, Homewood, IL: Dow-Jones/Irwin.

Berry, L.L. and A. Parasuraman (1992), "Prescriptions for a Service Quality Revolution in America", *Organisational Dynamics*, Vol. 20, Spring, pp. 29–41.

Berry, L.L., A. Parasuraman and V.A. Zeithaml (1994), "Improving Service Quality in America: Lessons Learned", *Academy of Management Executives*, Vol. 8, No. 2, pp. 32–52.

Blanchard, R.F. and R.L. Galloway (1994), "Quality in Retailing Banking", *International Journal of Service Industry Management*, Vol. 5, No. 4, pp. 5–23.

Bonoma, T.V. (1985), *The Marketing Edge: Making Strategies Work*, New York: Free Press.

Bord Fáilte (1998), "Consumer Journeys", Dublin: Bord Fáilte.

Bowen, D.E. and E.E. Lawler (1992), "The Empowerment of Service Workers: What, Why, How and When", *Sloan Management Review*, Spring, pp. 31–9.

Brogowicz, A.A., L.M. Delene and D.M. Lyth (1990), "A Synthesised Service Quality Model with Managerial Implications", *International Journal of Service Industry Management*, Vol. 1, No. 1, pp. 27–45.

Brown, S.W. and T.A. Swartz (1989), "A Gap Analysis of Professional Service Quality", *Journal of Marketing*, Vol. 53, pp. 92–8.

Burns, P. and A. Holden (1995), *Tourism: A New Perspective*, London: Prentice Hall.

Callan, R.J. (1989), "Small Country Hotels and Hotel Award Schemes as a Measurement of Service Quality", *Service Industries Journal*, Vol. 9, No. 2, pp. 223–246.

Callan, R.J. (1992), "Quality Control at Avant Hotels: the Debut of BS 5750", *Service Industries Journal*, Vol. 12, No. 1, pp. 17–33.

Callan, R.J. (1993), "An Appraisal of UK Quality Grading Schemes", *International Journal of Contemporary Hospitality Management*, Vol. 5, No. 5, pp. 10–18.

Callan, R.J. (1994), "Quality Assurance Certification for Hospitality Marketing, Sales and Customer Services", *Service Industries Journal*, Vol. 14, No. 4, pp. 482–98.

Callan, R. (1996), "Attributional Analysis of Customers' Hotel Selection Criteria by Grading Scheme Categories", Proceedings, *Fifth Annual Hospitality Research Conference*, Nottingham, Trent University, April 10–11, pp. 116–43.

Carmen, J.M. (1990), "Consumer Perceptions of Service Quality: an Assessment of the SERVQUAL Dimensions", *Journal of Retailing*, Vol. 66, No. 1, pp. 33–56.

Caruna, A., L. Pitt and M. Morris (1995), "Are there Excellent Service Firms and do They Perform Well?" *The Service Industries Journal*, Vol. 15, No. 3, pp. 243–56.

Caulkin, S. (1995), "Just Get Me to the Market on Time", Management Section, *The Observer*, 1 October, p. 15.

Caulkin, S. (1995), "The New Avengers", *Management Today*, November.

CERT (1997), "Annual Report", Dublin: CERT Publications.

Cespedes, F.V. and N. Piercy (1996), "Implementing Marketing Strategy", *Journal of Marketing Management*, Vol. 12, pp. 135–60.

Chandler, A. (1962), *Strategy and Structure*, Cambridge, MA: MIT Press.

Christopher, M., A. Payne and D. Ballantyne (1993), *Relationship Marketing*, London: Butterworth-Heinemann.

Clark, F., C. Tynan and A. Money (1994), "Senior Managers' Views on Quality: a Strategic Perspective", *Journal of Strategic Marketing*, Vol. 2, pp. 61–84.

Cole, R.E. (1993a), "Introduction" to Special Issue on Quality Management, *California Management Review*, Spring, pp. 7–11.

Cole, R.E. (1993b), "Quality, Participation and Competitiveness", *California Management Review*, Spring, pp. 68–81.

Collins, B. and A. Payne (1991), "Internal Marketing: a New Perspective for HRM", *European Journal of Marketing*, Vol. 9, No. 3, pp. 261–70.

Confederation of British Industry (1994), *A Wealth of Attractions: a New Agenda to Boost Britain's Tourism Potential*, London: CBI.

Confederation of British Industry (undated, circa 1996a), *World Hosts: International Benchmarking in the Hospitality Industry*, London: CBI.

Confederation of British Industry (1996b), *Visitors Welcome: Tourism in the Third Millennium*, London: CBI.

Counsel, S. (1991), "Fifty-seven-fifty and All That", *International Journal of Contemporary Hospitality Management*, Vol. 3, No. 3, pp. iii–iv.

Cravens, D.W. (1997), *Strategic Marketing*, Homewood, IL: Irwin.

Crosby, P. (1979), *Quality is Free*, New York: McGraw-Hill.

Cruise O'Brien, R. and C.A. Voss (1992), "In Search of Quality", Working paper 92/02, London Business School.

Cruise O'Brien, R. (1995), "Employee Involvement in Performance Improvement", *Employee Relations*, Vol. 17, No. 3, pp. 110–20.

Daneshkhu, S. (1995a), "Drive to Lift Hotel Standards", *Financial Times*, 4 May, p. 10.

Daneshkhu, S. (1995b), "Accommodating the Views of Guests", *Financial Times*, 16 October, p. 9.

Daneshkhu, S. (1996), "Ownership Loses its Appeal", *Financial Times*, 11 April, p. 3.

Dannemiler, C. (1994), "Getting Leaders to Lead", *Industry Week*, 18 April.

Davenport, T.H. (1993), "Process Innovation: Reengineering Work through Information Technology", *Harvard Business School Press*, Boston.

Dawson, P. (1994), *Total Quality Management*, Oxford: Oxford University Press.

Day, A. and J. Peters (1994), "Rediscovering Standards: Static and Dynamic Quality", *International Journal of Contemporary Hospitality Management*, Vol. 6, No. 1/2, pp. 81–4.

Day, C. (1993), "What About Blob?", *Industry Week*, 18 January.

Day, G.S. (1994), "The Capabilities of Market-Driven Organisations", *Journal of Marketing*, Vol. 58, October, pp. 37–52.

De Keyser, R. and N. Vanhove (1997), "Tourism Quality Plan: an Effective Tourism Policy Tool", *The Tourist Review*, No. 3/1997, pp. 32–7.

Dean, J.W. and D.E. Bowen (1994), "Management Theory and Total Quality: Improving Research and Practice through Theory Development", *Academy of Management Review*, Vol. 19, No. 3, pp. 392–418.

Demetriadi, J. (1995), "Academic Research in Hospitality and Tourism: a WHAT-CD User's View", *International Journal of Contemporary Hospitality Management*, Vol. 7, No. 7, pp. 20–7.

Deming, W.E. (1986), *Out of the Crisis: Quality, Productivity and Competitive Position*, Cambridge: Cambridge University Press.

Department of National Heritage (1995a), *Tourism: Competing with the Best*, London: DNH.

Department of National Heritage (1995b), *Tourism: Competing with the Best – Hotels: The Consumer View*, London: DNH.

Department of National Heritage (1996a), *DNH Guidance to Successor Authorities on Tourism*, London: DNH.

Department of National Heritage (1996b), *Tourism: Competing with the Best – Benchmarking for Smaller Hotels*, London: DNH.

Department of National Heritage (1996c), *Tourism: Competing with the Best – People Working in Tourism and Hospitality*, London: DNH.

Department of National Heritage (1997), *Success through Partnership: a Strategy for Tourism – Competing with the Best*, London: DNH.

Department of Tourism, Sport and Recreation (1994), *Operational Programme for Tourism, 1994–1999*, Dublin: Department of Tourism, Sport and Recreation.

Dodwell, S. and P. Simmons (1994), "Trials and Tribulations in the Pursuit of Quality Improvement", *International Journal of Contemporary Hospitality Management*, Vol. 6, No. 1/2, pp. 14–18.

Doyle, P. (1995), "Marketing in the New Millennium", *European Journal of Marketing*, Vol. 29, No. 13, pp. 23–41.

Du Gay, P. and G. Salaman (1992), "The Cult[ure] of the Customer", *Journal of Management Studies*, Vol. 29, No. 5, September, pp. 615–33.

Economist Intelligence Unit (1996), *The International Hotel Industry*, London: EIU.

Economist (1992), "The Cracks in Quality", 18 April.

Edgar, D. and S. Taylor (1996), "Strategic Management Research in Hospitality: from Slipstream to Mainstream", *Proceedings of the Fifth Annual Hospitality Research Conference*, Nottingham Trent University, April 10–11, pp. 264–78.

Edgett, S. and S. Parkinson (1993), "Marketing for Marketing Industries — a Review", *The Services Industries Journal*, Vol. 13, No. 3, pp. 17–35.

English Tourist Board (1997), *Agenda 2000: Shaping the Future of English Tourism*, London: ETB.

English Tourist Board (1998), *Action 2000: Brief*, London: ETB.

Eskildson, L. (1995), "TQM's Role in Corporate Success: Analysing the Evidence", *National Productivity Review*, Autumn, pp. 25–38.

European Commission (1996), *Tourism and the European Union: a Practical Guide*, Brussels: European Commission DGXXIII.

Fahy, J. (1992), "How Service Firms can Attain a Sustainable Competitive Advantage", *Irish Marketing Review*, pp. 29–37.

Fayos-Sola, E. (1996), "Tourism Policy: a Midsummer Night's Dream?" *Tourism Management*, Vol. 17, No. 6, pp. 405–12.

Fick, G.R. and J.R.B. Ritchie (1991), "Measuring Service Quality in the Travel and Tourism Industry", *Journal of Travel Research*, Fall, pp. 2–9.

Figueiredo, K., J. Rivera Latas and D. Gomes (1995), "A Strategic Service Vision in the Hotel Industry: Some Conclusions from Case Studies", in R. Teare, and C. Armistead (eds.), *Services Management: New Directions, New Perspectives*, London: Cassells.

Filipo, J.P. (1986), "Service Firms: Interdependence of External and Internal Marketing Strategies", *European Journal of Marketing*, Vol. 20, No. 8, pp. 5–14.

Financial Times (1995), *Survey of International Conferences and Exhibitions*, 22 February, Part II.

Financial Times (1996), *International Hotels Survey*, April, pp. I–IV.

Fisk, R.P., S.W. Brown and M.J. Bitner, (1993), "Tracking the Evolution of the Services Marketing Literature", *Journal of Retailing*, Vol. 69, No. 1, pp. 61–103.

Fitzgerald, L., R. Johnston, S. Brignall, R. Silvestro and C. Voss (1993), *Performance Measurement in Service Businesses*, London: Black Bear Press.

Flood, R. (1995), *Beyond TQM*, New York: Wiley.

Floyd, S.W. and S. Wooldridge (1992), "Managing Strategic Consensus: the Foundation for Effective Implementation", *Academy of Management Executive*, Vol. 6, No. 4, pp. 27–39.

Foreman, S., and A. Money (1995), "Internal Marketing: Concepts, Measurement and Application", *Journal of Marketing Management*, Vol. 11, pp. 755–68.

Fortune (1995), "More Quality Than You Think", 18 April, p. 28.

Fortune (1995), "Winning Ideas in Management", 15 May.

Fox, A. (1974), *Man Mismanagement*, London: Hutchinson.

Freeman, K.D. and J. Dart (1992), "Measuring the Perceived Quality of Professional Business Services", *Journal of Professional Services Marketing*, Vol. 9, No. 1, pp. 27–47.

Frohman, M. (1994), "Remything Management: the New Myths are Just as Counterproductive as the Old Ones", *Industry Week*, 21 March.

Galagan, P.A. (1993), "Putting on the Ritz", *Cornell Hotel and Restaurant and Administration Quarterly*, December.

Galloway, L. (1995), "Towards an Operations Centred Definition of Service Quality" in R. Teare and C. Armistead (eds.), *Services Management: New Directions, New Perspectives*, London: Cassells.

Gamble, P. and P. Jones (1991), "Quality as a Strategic Issue" in R. Teare and A. Boer (eds.), *Strategic Hospitality Management*, London: Cassells, pp. 73–82.

Garavan, T.N. (1991), "Strategic Human Resource Development: Characteristics, Conditions and Benefits", *Journal of European Industrial Training*, Vol. 15, No. 1, pp. 3–19.

Garvin, D.A. (1987), "Competing on the Eight Dimensions of Quality", *Harvard Business Review*, Vol. 65, November/December, pp. 101-9.

Garvin, D.A. (1988), *Managing Quality: The Strategic and Competitive Edge*, New York: Free Press.

Gilbert, D. and I. Joshi (1992), "Quality Management and the Tourism and Hospitality Industry" in C. Cooper and A. Lockwood (eds.), *Progress in Tourism and Hospitality Management*, Vol. 4, pp. 149-68.

Gilbert, D. and R. Kapur (1990), "Strategic Marketing Planning and the Hotel Industry", *International Journal of Hospitality Management*, Vol. 9, No. 1, pp. 47-52.

Giles, E. and K. Starkey (1988), *The Japanisation of Xerox, New Technology, Work and Employment*, Vol. 3, No. 2, pp. 125-33.

Gilmore, A. and D. Carson (1995), "Managing and Marketing to Internal Customers" in W.J. Glynn and J.G. Barnes (eds.), *Understanding Services Management*, Dublin: Oak Tree Press, pp. 295-321.

Gilpen, S. (1996), "Hospitality", in F. Buttle (ed.), *Relationship Marketing*, London: Paul Chapman, pp. 145-59.

Glover, J. (1993), "Achieving the Organisational Change Necessary for Successful TQM", *International Journal of Quality and Reliability Management*, Vol. 10, No. 6, pp. 47-64.

Go, F. and R. Pine (1995), *Globalisation Strategy in the Hotel Industry*, London: Routledge.

Goffee, R. and R. Scase (1995), *Corporate Realities*, London: Routledge.

Gomez, V.B. (1996), "Research in Spain on Tourism and Economic Development", *The Tourist Review*, No. 1/1996, pp. 5-11.

Gremler, D.D., M.J. Bitner and K.R. Evans (1993), "The Internal Service Encounter", *International Journal of Service Industry Management*, Vol. 5, No. 2, pp. 34-56.

Grindley, K. (1991), *Managing IT at Board Level*, London: Pitman.

Gronroos, C. (1983), *Strategic Management and Marketing in the Service Sector*, London: Chartwell Brat.

Gronroos, C. (1984), "A Service Quality Model and its Marketing Implications", *European Journal of Marketing*, Vol. 18, pp. 36-44.

Gronroos, C. (1988), "Service Quality: the Six Criteria of Good Perceived Service Quality", *Review of Business*, Vol. 9, pp. 10-13.

Gronroos, C. (1990), *Service Management and Marketing: Managing the Moments of Truth in Service Competition*, Lexington, MA: Lexington Books.

Gronroos, C. (1990), "Relationship Approach to Marketing in Service Contexts: the Marketing and Organisational Behaviour Interface", *Journal of Business Research*, Vol. 20, pp. 3–11.

Gronroos, C. (1994), "From Scientific Management to Service Management: a Management Perspective for the Age of Service Competition", *International Journal of Service Industry Management*, Vol. 5, No. 1, pp. 5–20.

Guerrier, Y. and A. Lockwood (1989a), "Core and Peripheral Employees in Hotel Operations", *Personnel Review*, Vol. 18, No. 1, pp. 9–15.

Guerrier, Y and A. Lockwood (1989b), "Managers in Hospitality: a Review of Current Research" in C. Cooper (ed.), *Progress in Tourism, Recreation and Hospitality Management*, Vol. 2, pp. 151–67, London: Belhaven.

Guerrier, Y. (1996a), "Managers and Management in the UK Hotel Industry", *Service Industries Journal*, (forthcoming).

Guerrier, Y. (1996b), "Hospitality Human Resource Management", *Internet Conference*, May, MCB Press.

Guerrier, Y. (1996c), Book Review, *Management Learning*, (in press).

Guest, D. (1987), "Human Resource Management and Industrial Relations", *Journal of Management Studies*, Vol. 24, No. 5.

Guest, D. (1992), "Human Resource Management in the UK", in B. Towers (ed.), *A Handbook of Human Resource Management*, Oxford: Blackwell.

Gummesson, E. (1993), "Service Management : an Evaluation and the Future", *International Journal of Service Industry Management*, Vol. 5, No. 1, pp. 77–96.

Gummesson, E. (1991), "Marketing Orientation Revisited: the Crucial Role of the Part-time Marketer", *European Journal of Marketing*, Vol. 5, No. 2, pp. 60–75.

Gummesson, E. (1992), "Quality Dimensions: What to Measure in Service Organisations", *Advances in Services Marketing and Management*, Vol. 1, pp. 177–205.

Guth, W.D. and C. MacMillan (1986), "Strategy Implementation versus Middle Management Self-interest", *Strategic Management Journal*, Vol. 7, pp. 313–27.

Hackman R.J. and G. Oldman (1980), *Work Design*, Reading, MA: Addison-Wesley.

Hackman, J.R. and R. Wageman (1995), "Total Quality Management: Empirical Conceptual and Practical Issues", *Administrative Science Quarterly*, Vol. 40, pp. 309–42.

Hales, C. (1995), "Internal Marketing as an Approach to Human Resource Management: a New Perspective or a Metaphor Too Far?" *Human Resource Management Journal*, Vol. 5, No. 1, pp. 50–71.

Hales, C. and J. Mecrate-Butcher (1994), "Internal Marketing and Human Resource Management in Hotel Consortia", *International Journal of Hospitality Management*, Vol. 13, No. 4, pp. 313–26.

Hampden-Turner, C. (1990), "Henry Mintzberg: a Profile", *Business Strategy Review*, Vol. 1, No. 1, pp. 57–70.

Harari, O. (1993a), "Ten Reasons Why TQM Doesn't Work", *Management Review*, January, pp. 33–8.

Harari, O. (1993b), "The Eleventh Reason Why TQM Doesn't Work", *Management Review*, May.

Hardy, C. (1995), How Understanding Power can Help Bring about Strategic Change", Proceedings, *British Academy of Management Annual Conference*, pp. 222–32.

Harrington, D. (1997), "Empirical Analysis of Quality Implementation Practices within the UK Hotel Industry", unpublished PhD Thesis, South Bank University, London.

Harrington, D. and G. Akehurst (1996a), "An Exploratory Study Of Quality Practices in Selected UK Hotels", *Progress in Tourism and Hospitality Management*, Vol. 1, No. 3.

Harrington, D. and G. Akehurst (1996b), "An Exploratory Analysis of Quality and Performance in the UK Hotel Industry", *International Journal of Hospitality Management*, Vol. 16, No. 3.

Harrington, D. and G. Akehurst (1996c), "Managerial Perceptions of Service Quality in the UK Hotel Industry", *Proceedings of the Learning Edge Conference of the European Foundation for Quality Management*, Paris, 24–26 April, pp. 483–94.

Harrington, D. and R. Stearn (1996), "Service Delivery: Some Practical Issues", Working Paper, Centre for International Business, South Bank University, London.

Harrison, A. (1996), "Small Business and Distribution as a Value System", Proceedings, *Fifth Annual Hospitality Research Conference, Nottingham Trent University*, 10–11 April, pp. 279–300.

Hart, C. and L. Schlesinger (1991), "Total Quality Management and the Human Resource Professional: Applying the Baldrige Framework to Human Resources", *Human Resource Management*, Vol. 30, No. 4, pp. 433–54.

Hart, C.W.L., J.L. Heskitt and W.L. Sasser Jr. (1990), "The Profitable Art of Service Recovery", *Harvard Business Review*, July/August, pp. 148–56.

Hendry, C. (1995), *Strategy through People*, London: Routledge.

Heskitt, J.L. (1986), *Managing in the Service Economy*, Boston, MA: Harvard Business School Press.

Heskitt, J.L. (1987), "Lessons in the Service Sector", *Harvard Business Review*, Vol. 65, March–April, pp. 118–26.

Hill, S. and A. Wilkinson (1995), "In Search of TQM", *Employee Relations*, Vol. 17, No. 3, pp. 8–25.

Hill, S. (1991), "Why Quality Circles Failed but Total Quality Management might Succeed", *British Journal of Industrial Relations*, Vol. 29, No. 4, December, pp. 541–68.

Hine, K. (1995), "American Affairs", *Hotel Management International*, London: Cornhill Publications.

Hodgetts, G. (1996), "Implementing TQM in Small and Medium Sized Organisations", *Industry Week*, 1 June, p. 12.

Hooley, G.J. (1993), "Market-led Quality Management", *Journal of Marketing Management*, Vol. 9, pp. 315–35.

Hope, V. and J. Hendry (1995), "Corporate Cultural Change: Is it Relevant for the Organisations of the 1990s?", *Human Resource Management*, Vol. 5, No. 4, pp. 61–73.

Hopper, A. (1995), *Institutional Investment in the UK Hotel Industry*, London: Pannell Kerr Forster.

Horwath and Horwath (1988), *Hotels of the Future*, London: Horwath and Horwath.

Horwath and Horwath (1991), *UK Hotel Industry*, London: Horwath Consulting.

Horwath and Horwath (1993), *UK Hotel Industry*, London: Horwath Consulting.

Horwath and Horwath (1995), *Worldwide Hotel Study*, London: Horwath and Horwath.

Hotel and Catering Training Company (HCTC) (1994), *Catering and Hospitality Industry – Key Facts and Figures*, London: HCTC.

Hotel Data (1994), *UK Hotel Industry*, London: Molton Street.

Hubrecht, J. and R. Teare (1993), "A Strategy for Partnership in Total Quality Service", *International Journal of Contemporary Hospitality Management*, Vol. 5, No. 3, pp. i–v.

Industrial Relations Services (1994), "Investors in People: an IRS Survey of Employers' Experiences", *Employee Development Bulletin*, 52, *Industrial Relations Review and Report 558*, April.

Irish Tourist Industry Confederation (ITIC) (1998), *Strategy for Growth Beyond 2000: Strategic Framework for Irish Tourism*, Dublin: Tourism and Leisure Partners.

Ishikawa, K. (1985), *What is Total Quality Control? The Japanese Way*, Englewood Cliffs, NJ: Prentice Hall.

Jackson, Barbara (1985), "Build Customer Relationships that Last", *Harvard Business Review*, November/December, pp. 120–128.

Jarpennaa, S.L. and B. Ives (1993), "Organising for Global Competition: the Fit of Information Technology", *Decision Sciences*, Vol. 24, No. 3, pp. 547–79.

Johns, N. (1992), Quality Management in the Hospitality Industry: Definition and Specification, *International Journal of Contemporary Hospitality Management*, Vol. 4, No. 3, pp. 14–20.

Johns, N. (1995), "The Developing Role of Quality in the Hospitality Industry" in M.D. Olsen, R. Teare and E. Gummesson (eds.), *Service Quality in Hospitality Organisations*, London: Cassells, pp. 9–27.

Johnston, R. and B. Morris (1985), "Monitoring Control in Service Operations", *International Journal of Operations and Production Management*, Vol. 5, pp. 32–8.

Johnston, R., R. Silvestro, L. Fitzgerald and C. Voss (1990), "Developing the Determinants of Service Quality" in E. Langeard and P. Eiglier (eds.), *Marketing, Operations and Human Resource Insights into Services: First International Research Seminar on Services Management*, IAE, Aix-en-Provence, 375; 393.

Joint Hospitality Industry Congress (JHIC) Report (1998), *Anything They Can Do We Can Do Better*, London: JHIC.

Jones, P. and A. Ioannou (1993), "Measuring Guest Satisfaction in UK-based International Hotel Chains: Principles and Practice", *International Journal of Contemporary Hospitality Management*, Vol. 5, No. 5, pp. 27–31.

Jones, P. (1989), *Management in Service Industries*, London: Pitman.

Jones, P. (1996), "Hospitality Research — Where Have We Got To?", *International Journal of Hospitality Management*, Vol. 15, No. 1, pp. 5–10.

Jordans Report (1991), *The British Hotel Industry*, Bristol: Jordan & Sons Ltd.

Juran, J. (1986), "The Quality Trilogy", *Quality Progress*, Vol. 19, No. 8, pp. 19–24.

Kano, N. (1994), "A Perspective on Quality Activities in American Firms", *California Management Review*, Spring, pp. 12–31.

Kaplan, R. (1991), "Why Empowerment Often Fails", *Executive Excellence*, December, p. 9.

Karger, J. and R.A. Blumenthal (1994), "Successful Implementation of Strategic Decisions in Small Community Banks", *Journal of Small Business Management*, Vol. 32, April, pp. 10–22.

Kay, E. (1974), *The Crisis in Middle Management*, New York: American Management Association.

KBS (1994), *Kleinwort Benson Securities*, London: KBS.

Kearney, A.T. in association with *TQM Magazine* (1992), *Total Quality: Time to Take off the Rose Tinted Spectacles*, Kempston: IFS Publications.

Keller, P. (1997), "A Review of the 47th AIEST Congress: Quality and Quality Management in Tourism — Towards a Synthesis", *The Tourist Review*, No. 4/1997, pp. 2–6.

Kerfoot, D. and D. Knights (1995), "Empowering the Quality Worker," in A. Wilkinson and H. Willmott (eds.), *Making Quality Critical*, London: Routledge.

Keynote Report (1994), *UK Hotel Industry*, London: Keynote Publications.

Kochan, T., R. Grant and R. Shani (1995), "TQM's Challenge to Management Theory and Practice", *Sloan Management Review*, Vol. 36, Winter, pp. 25–35.

KPMG (1995), *UK Hotel Trends*, December, London: KPMG.

Krishnan, A.B., R. Shani, R.M. Grant and R. Baer (1993), "In Search of Quality Improvement: Problems of Design and Implementation", *Academy of Management Executive*, Vol. 7, No. 4, pp. 7–20.

Lapierre, J. and P. Filiatrault (1996), "The Foundation of Research on the Quality of Professional Services to Organisations" in P. Kunst and J. Lemmink (eds.), *Managing Service Quality*, Volume II, London: Paul Chapman, pp. 97–105.

Larkin, T.J. and S. Larkin (1996), "Reaching and Changing Frontline Employees", *Harvard Business Review*, May–June, pp. 95–104.

Lawler, E.E. (1992), *The Ultimate Advantage: Creating the High Involvement Organisation*, New York: Maxwell Macmillan.

Lawler, E.E. (1993), "Debate", *Harvard Business Review*, May–June, p. 34.

Lawler, E.E., S.A. Mohrman and G.E. Ledford (1992), "Employment Involvement and Total Quality Management: Practices and Results in Fortune 1000 Companies", San Francisco, CA: Jossey Bass.

Laws, E. (1991), *Tourism Marketing: Service and Quality Management Perspectives*, Cheltenham: Stanley Thornes.

Leblanc, G. and N. Nguyen (1988), "Customer Perceptions of Service Quality in Financial Institutions", *International Journal of Bank Marketing*, Vol. 6, pp. 7–18.

Lee-Mortimer, A. (1991), "The Customer is King", *Total Quality Management*, Vol. 3, p. 26.

Legge, K. (1995), *Human Resource Management: Rhetorics and Realities*, London: Macmillan.

Lehtinen, U. and J.R. Lehtinen (1982), "Service Quality: a Study of Quality Dimensions", Unpublished working paper, Helsinki: Service Management Institute.

Lehtinen, U. and J.R. Lehtinen (1991), "Two Approaches to Service Quality Dimensions", *The Service Industries Journal*, Vol. 3, pp. 289–303.

Lehtinen, U., J. Ojasola and K. Ojasola (1995), "On Service Quality Models, Service Quality Dimensions and Customers' Perceptions" in P. Kunst and J. Lemmink (eds.), *Managing Service Quality*, Volume II, London: Paul Chapman, pp. 109–15.

Lenehan, T. and I. Filby (1995), "A Study of Management Practices and Competences within Effective Organisations in Tourism", Proceedings, British Academy of Management Conference, September, Sheffield University, UK.

Lenehan, T. (1996), "A Study of Management Practices and Competences within Effective Organisations in Tourism", unpublished PhD thesis, University of Surrey.

Lenehan, T. (1998), "Important Role for Tourism in EMU Transition", *Irish Times*, 18 May.

Lentell, B. and B. Morris (1995), "Service Quality Management in Sport and Recreation Services" in R. Teare and C. Armistead (eds.), *Services Management: New Directions, New Perspectives*, London: Cassells.

Leonard, F.S. and W.E. Sasser (1982), "The Incline of Quality", *Harvard Business Review*, November–December, pp. 163–71.

Levin, I.M. and J.Z. Gottlieb (1993), "Quality Management: Practice Risks and Value-added Roles for Organisation Development Practitioners", *The Journal of Applied Behavioural Science*, Vol. 29, No. 3, pp. 296–310.

Levitt, T., (1972), "Production-line Approaches to Services", *Harvard Business Review*, May/June, pp. 168–78.

Levitt, T, (1976) "The Industrialisation of Service", *Harvard Business Review*, September/October, pp. 63–74.

Levitt, T. (1981), "Marketing Intangible Products and Product Intangibles", *Harvard Business Review*, May–June, pp. 94–102.

Lewis, B. (1989), "Quality in the Service Sector: a Review", *International Journal of Bank Marketing*, Vol. 7, No. 5.

Lewis, B.R. (1991), "Service Quality: an International Comparison of Bank Customers' Expectations and Perceptions", *Journal of Marketing Management*, Vol. 7, pp. 47–62.

Lewis, B.R. (1993), "Service Quality: Recent Developments in Financial Services", *International Journal of Bank Marketing*, Vol. 11, pp. 19–25.

Lewis, R.C. (1987), "The Measurement of Gaps in the Quality of Hotel Services", *International Journal of Hospitality Management*, Vol. 6, No. 2, pp. 83–8.

Lewis, R.C. and B.H. Booms (1983), "The Marketing Aspects of Service Quality" in L. Berry, G. Shostack and G. Upah (eds.), *Emerging Perspectives on Services Marketing*, Chicago: American Marketing Association.

Linney, C.J. and R. Teare (1991), "Addressing the Human Resource Challenges of the 1990s", *International Journal of Contemporary Hospitality Management*, Vol. 3, No. 2, pp. iii–iv.

Littler, D. and D. Wilson (eds.) (1995), *Marketing Strategy*, London: Butterworth-Heinemann.

Lockwood, A. and A. Ghillyer (1996), "Empowerment: the Key to Service Quality — an Operations Perspective", *Proceedings of the Fifth Annual Hospitality Research Conference*, Nottingham Trent University, pp. 208–24.

Lockwood, A., E. Gummesson, J. Hubrechtand and M. Senior (1992), "Developing and Maintaining a Strategy for Service Quality" in R. Teare and M. Olsen (eds.), *International Hospitality Management Corporate Strategy in Practice*, New York: John Wiley and Sons.

Lovelock, C. (1981), "Why Marketing Management Needs to be Different for Services" in J. Donnelly and W. George (eds.), *Marketing of Services*, Chicago: American Marketing Association.

Marchington, M. (1995), "Fairy Tales and Magic Wands: New Employment Practices in Perspective", *Employee Relations*, Vol. 17, No. 1, pp. 51–66.

Martin, P. (1996), "The Death of Geography", *Financial Times*, 22 February, p. 20.

Maxon, J. (1991), "Total Quality Management", in *International Manufacturing Strategy Resource Book*, Zurich: Strategic Direction Publishers, pp. 189–202.

McRae, H. (1995), *The World in 2020 — Power, Culture and Prosperity: a Vision of the Future*, London: Harper Collins.

Medlik, S. (1989), *The Business of Hotels*, London: Heinemann.

Mintzberg, H. (1979), "An Emerging Strategy of 'Direct' Research", *Administrative Science Quarterly*, Vol. 24, No. 4, pp. 582-9.

Mintzberg, H. (1992), "Five Ps for Strategy" in H. Mintzberg and J.B. Quinn (eds.), *The Strategy Process: Concepts and Contexts*, London: Prentice Hall, pp. 12-19.

Mintzberg, H. (1994), "Rethinking Strategic Planning — Part I: Pitfalls and Fallacies", *Long Range Planning*, Vol. 27, No. 3, pp. 12-21.

Monfort Mir, V.M. (1996), "Spanish Research on Quality Tourism: the State of the Art", *The Tourist Review*, No. 1/1996, pp. 41-5.

Monks, K., A. Sinnott and F. Buckley (1996), "Implementing Quality Initiatives in Ireland: the Practice in Service Organisations", *QUIS Annual Conference*, Madrid, April.

Moore, J.I. (1992), *Writers on Strategy and Strategic Management*, London: Penguin.

Moore, S. (1995), "Making Sense of Strategic Management", *Management Decision*, Vol. 33, No. 1, pp. 19-23.

Morgan, N.A. and Piercy, N. (1992), "Market-led Quality", *Industrial Marketing Management*, Vol. 21, pp. 111-18.

Morris, M. and L. Pitt (1994), "Implementing Marketing Strategies in the US and South Africa", *Long Range Planning*, Vol. 27, No. 1, pp. 56-71.

Mullins, L.J. (1993), "The Hotel and the Open Systems Model of Organisational Analysis", *Service Industries Journal*, Vol. 13, No. 1, January, pp. 1-16.

Nadler, L. and G.D. Wigge (1986), "Managing Human Resource Development — a Practical Guide", San Francisco, CA: Jossey Bass.

Nailon, P. (1982), "Theory in Hospitality Management", *International Journal of Hospitality Management*, Vol. 1, No. 3.

Nankervis, A.R. and Y. Debrah (1995), "Human Resource Management in Hotels: a Comparative Study", *Tourism Management*, Vol. 16, No. 7, pp. 507-13.

Narver, J.C. and S.F. Slater (1990), "The Effect of a Marketing Orientation on Business Profitability", *Journal of Marketing*, Vol. 54, No. 4, pp. 28–53.

National Economic Development Office (NEDO) (1992), *UK Tourism: Competing for Growth*, London: NEDO.

Nebel, E.C. and J.D. Schaffer (1992), "Hotel Strategic Planning at the Business and Unit Level in the USA" in R. Teare and M. Olsen (eds.), *International Hospitality Management Corporate Strategy in Practice*, New York: John Wiley & Sons, pp. 228–54.

Newton, M.T. (1996), "Tourism and Public Administration in Spain" in M. Barke, J. Towner and M.T. Newton (eds.), *Tourism in Spain: Critical Issues*, Wallingford: CAB International.

Nightingale, M. (1986), "The Hospitality Industry: Defining Quality for a Quality Assurance Programme", *Service Industries Journal*, Vol. 5, pp. 9–22.

Oakland, J.S. (1993), *Total Quality Management: The Route To Improving Performance*, London: Butterworth-Heinemann.

Oberoi, U. and C. Hales (1990), "Assessing the Quality of the Conference Hotel Product: towards an Empirically Based Model", *Service Industries Journal*, Vol. 10, No. 4, pp. 700–21.

O'Farrell, P.W., D.M. Hitchens and L.A.R. Moffat (1993), "The Competitive Advantage of Business Service Firms: a Matched Pairs Analysis of the Relationship Between Generic Strategy and Performance", *The Service Industries Journal*, Vol. 13, p. 54.

Olian, J.D. and S.L. Rynes (1991), "Making Total Quality Work: Aligning Organisational Processes, Performance Measures and Stakeholders", *Human Resource Management*, Vol. 30, No. 3, pp. 303–33.

Oliver, N. (1990), "Employee Commitment and Total Quality Control", *International Journal of Quality and Reliability Management*, Vol. 7, No. 1, pp. 21–9.

Olsen, M.D. (1992), "Strategic Management in the Hospitality Industry: a Literature Review" in C. Cooper (ed.), *Progress in Tourism, Recreation and Hospitality Management*, London: John Wiley & Sons, pp. 215–31.

Olsen, M.D. (1992), "Expectations of the Future Given Events of the Past" in R. Teare and M.D. Olsen (eds.), *International Hospitality Management: Corporate Strategy in Practice*, London: Pitman, pp. 346–51.

Olsen, M.D. (1993), "International Growth Strategies of Major US Hotel Companies", *EIU Travel & Tourism Analyst*, No. 3, pp. 51–64.

Olsen, M.D., R. Teare and E. Gummesson (1995), "Exploring the Service Quality Paradigm: an Overview" in M.D. Olsen, R. Teare and E. Gummesson (eds.), *Service Quality in Hospitality Organisations*, London: Cassell, pp. 9–27.

O'Neill, M. and M. Black (1994), "Current Quality Issues in the Northern Ireland Tourism Sector", *The TQM Magazine*, Vol. 8, No. 1, pp. 15–19.

O'Neill, M., H. Watson and M. McKenna (1994), "Service Quality in the Northern Ireland Hospitality Industry", *Managing Service Quality*, Vol. 4, No. 3, pp. 36–40.

Oster, S. (1994), *Strategic Management*, Oxford: Oxford University Press.

Page, C. (1994), "Sutcliffe Catering's Approach to Continuous Improvement", *International Journal of Contemporary Hospitality Management*, Vol. 6, No. 1/2, pp. 19–24.

Pannel Kerr Forster (PKF) (1995), *UK Hotel Industry*, London: PKF.

Parasuraman, A. (1995), "Measuring and Monitoring Service Quality" in W. Glynn and J.G. Barnes (eds.), *Understanding Services Management*, London: Wiley, pp. 143–77.

Parasuraman, A., L.L. Berry and V.A. Zeithaml (1993), "More on Improving Service Quality Measurement", *Journal of Retailing*, Vol. 69, pp. 140–7.

Parasuraman, A., V.A. Zeithaml and L.L. Berry (1985), "A Conceptual Model of Service Quality and its Implications for Future Research", *Journal of Marketing*, Vol. 49, pp. 41–50.

Parasuraman, A., V.A. Zeithaml and L.L. Berry (1988), "SERVQUAL: a Multiple Item for Measuring Consumer Perceptions of Service Quality", *Journal of Retailing*, Vol. 64, pp. 12–40.

Parsons, D. and P. Cave (1991), *Developing Managers for Tourism*, London: NEDO.

Partlow, G. (1993), "How Ritz-Carlton Applies TQM", *Cornell Hotel & Restaurant Quarterly*, Vol. 34, No. 4, pp. 15–23.

Paxson, M.C. (1993), "A Review of the Organisational Commitment Literature as Applied to Hospitality Organisations" in A. Lockwood and C. Cooper (eds.), *Progress in Tourism and Hospitality Management*, Vol. 5, pp. 211–28.

Peppard, Joe (1993), *IT Strategy for Business*, London: Pitman.

Peters T. and R. Waterman (1982), *In Search of Excellence*, New York: Harper-Collins.

Pfeffer, J. (1996), *Competitive Advantage through People*, London: McGraw-Hill.

Piercy, N. and N. Morgan (1991), "Internal Marketing: the Missing Half of the Marketing Programme", *Long Range Planning*, Vol. 24, No. 2, pp. 82–93.

Piercy, N. (1994), "Marketing Implementation and Internal Marketing" in M. Baker (eds.), *The Marketing Book*, pp. 586–606.

Piore, M. and C. Sabel (1984), *The Second Industrial Divide: Possibilities for Prosperity*, New York: Basic Books.

Pitt, L.F., S. Foreman and D. Bromfield (1995), "Organisational Commitment and Service Delivery: Evidence from an Industrial Setting in the UK", *The International Journal of Human Resource Management*, Vol. 6, No. 1, pp. 368–89.

Pizam, A. and T. Knowles (1994), "The European Hotel Industry" in C.P. Cooper and A. Lockwood (eds.), *Progress in Tourism, Recreation and Hospitality Management*, Vol. 6, p. 291.

Porter, M. (1980), *Competitive Strategy: Techniques for Analysing Industries and Competitors*, New York: Free Press.

Porter, M. (1985), *Competitive Advantage: Creating and Sustaining Superior Performance*, New York: Free Press.

Porter, M. and V. Millar (1985), "How Information Gives you a Competitive Advantage", *Harvard Business Review*, July/August, pp. 149–60.

Powell, T.C. (1995), "Total Quality as Competitive Advantage: a Review and Empirical Study", *Strategic Management Journal*, Vol. 16, pp. 15–37.

Prahalad, C.K. and G. Hamel (1990), "The Core Competence of the Corporation", *Harvard Business Review*, May/June, pp. 79–91.

Price, L. (1994), "Poor Personnel Practice in the Hotel and Catering Industry: Does it Matter?", *Human Resource Management Journal*, Vol. 4, No. 4, pp. 44–62.

Pruett, M. and H. Thomas (1996), "Thinking about Quality and its Links with Strategic Management", *European Management Journal*, Vol. 14, No. 1, pp. 37–46.

Purcell, K. (1994), "Equal Opportunities in the Hospitality Industry: Custom and Credentials", *International Journal of Hospitality Management*, Vol. 12, No. 2, pp. 127–40.

Purcell, K. and J. Quinn (1995), "Hospitality Management Education and Career Trajectories", Report, Oxford Brookes University.

Quest, M. (1996), "Year of Excitement as Industry Enters Boom Period", in *Hospitality Yearbook*, London, Vol. 9–15.

Quinn, J.B. (1980), *Strategies for Change: Logical Incrementalism*, Homewood, IL: Irwin.

Quinn, J.B. (1995), *The Strategy Process*, London: Prentice Hall.

Quinn, T. (1992), "ISO 9000 — the Route to Success", Conference Proceedings, *Competitive Advantage through Quality*, Dublin, 29 April.

Rafiq, M. and P.K. Ahmed (1993), "The Scope of Internal Marketing: Defining the Boundary between Marketing and Human Resource Management", *Journal of Marketing Management*, Vol. 9, pp. 219–32.

Rajagopal, S., S. Balan and E.E. Scheuing (1995), "Total Quality Management Strategy: Quick Fix or Sound Sense?", *Total Quality Management*, Vol. 6, No. 4, pp. 335–44.

Randall, L. and M. Senior (1990), "Measuring Quality in Hospitality Services", *International Journal of Contemporary Hospitality Management*, Vol. 4, No. 2, pp. vi–viii.

Redman, T., E. Snape and A. Wilkinson (1995a), "Is Quality Management Working in the UK?", *Journal of General Management*, Vol. 20, No. 3, Spring, pp. 44–59.

Redman, T., B. Mathews, A. Wilkinson and E. Snape (1995b), "Quality Management in Services: is the Public Sector Keeping Pace?", *International Journal of Public Sector Management*, Vol. 8, No. 7, pp. 21–34.

Rees, C. (1995), "Quality Management and HRM in the Service Industry: Some Case Study Evidence", *Employee Relations*, Vol. 17, No. 3, pp. 99–109.

Reeves, C.A. and D.A. Bednar (1994), "Defining Quality: Alternatives and Implications", *Academy of Management Review*, Vol. 19, No. 3, pp. 419–45.

Reger, R., T. Loren, S. Gustafson and J.V. Mullane (1994), "Reframing the Organisation: Why Implementing Total Quality is Easier Said Than Done", *Academy of Management Review*, Vol. 19, pp. 565–84.

Reichheld, F.F. and W.E. Sasser (1990), "Zero Defections: Quality Comes to Services", *Harvard Business Review*, Vol. 68, September/ October, pp. 105–11.

Reynolds, S. and T. Ingold (1994), "An Evaluation of Total Quality Management Tools and Techniques in the UK Hotel Industry", Proceedings, *CHME Annual Hospitality Management Conference*.

Robertson, M. and Y. Guerrier (1998), "Events as Entrepreneurial Displays: Seville, Barcelona and Madrid" in D. Tyler, Y. Guerrier and, R. Robertson, *Managing Tourism in Cities: Policy, Process and Practice*, Chichester: J. Wiley and Sons.

Rocha, G. (1995), "Seeing the Future First", *Hotel Management International*, London: Cornhill Publications, pp. 23–4.

Ross, G.F. (1994), "Service Quality Ideals among Hospitality Industry Employees", *Tourism Management*, Vol. 5, pp. 273–80.

Ross, J.E. and K.Y. Shetty (1985), "Making Quality a Fundamental Part of Strategy", *Long Range Planning*, Vol. 18, pp. 53–8.

Rust, R.T. and R.L. Oliver (eds.) (1994), *Service Quality: New Directions in Theory and Practice*, London: Sage Publications.

Rust, R.T., A.J. Zahorik and T.L. Keiningham (1994), *Return on Quality*, Chicago: Probus.

Rust, R.T., A.J. Zahorik and T.L. Keiningham (1995), "Return on Quality (ROQ): Making Service Quality Financially Accountable", *Journal of Marketing*, Vol. 59, pp. 58–70.

Saleh, F. and C. Ryan (1991), "Analysing Service Quality in the Hospitality Industry Using the SERVQUAL Model", *Service Industries Journal*, Vol. 11, pp. 324–45.

Sangster, A. (1994), "Hotels See Tangible Returns on Investors", *Caterer and Hotelkeeper*, November.

Sasser, W.E. and P.R. Olsen and D.D. Wyckoff (1978), *Management of Service Operations: Text and Cases*, Boston: Allyn and Bacon.

Scarborough, H. and J. Martin Corbett (1992), *Technology and Organisation: Power, Meaning and Design*, London: Routledge, pp. 38-9.

Schneider, B. and D.E. Bowen (1985), "Employee and Customer Perceptions of Service in Banks: Replication and Extension", *Journal of Applied Psychology*, Vol. 70, pp. 423-33.

Schneider, B. (1994), "HRM — a Service Perspective: Towards a Customer Focused HRM", *International Journal of Service Industry Management*, Vol. 5, No. 1, pp. 64-76.

Schuler, R.S. and D.L. Harris (1992), *Managing Quality: The Primer for Middle Managers*, Reading, MA: Addison-Wesley.

Seddon, J. (1997), *In Pursuit of Quality: The Case Against ISO 9000*, Dublin: Oak Tree Press.

Segal-Horn, S. (1994), "Are Service Industries Going Global?" in C. Armistead (eds.), *The Future of Services Management*, London: Pitman, pp. 41-62.

Senior, M. and R. Morphew (1993), "Examining Structure in Decision Making in Hotels", *International Journal of Contemporary Hospitality Management*, Vol. 2, No. 3, pp. 3-9.

Shadur, M.A. (1995), "Total Quality Systems Survive, Cultures Change", *Long Range Planning*, Vol. 28, No. 2, pp. 115-25.

Shostack, G.L. (1977), "Breaking Free from Product Marketing", *Journal of Marketing*, Vol. 41, No. 2, pp. 73-80.

Silvestro, R., R. Johnston, L. Fitzgerald and C. Voss (1991), "Quality Measurement in Service Industries", *International Journal of Service Industry Management*, Vol. 1, No. 2, pp. 54-66.

Simmons, D.E., M.A. Shadur and A.P. Preston (1995), "Integrating TQM and HRM", *Employee Relations*, Vol. 17, No. 3, pp. 75-86.

Slattery, P. (1995), "Quoted Hotel Companies: International Developments", *International Hotel Association*, 33rd Annual Congress, Tel Aviv, November.

Smith, A.M. and B.R. Lewis (1988), "Customer Care in the Service Sector: the Supplier's Perspective", Manchester: Financial Services Research Centre, UMIST.

Smith, A.M. (1995), "Measuring Service Quality: is SERVQUAL now Redundant?", *Journal of Marketing Management*, Vol. 11, pp. 257–76.

Snape, E., A. Wilkinson, M. Marchington and T. Redman (1995), "Managing Human Resources for TQM: Possibilities and Pitfalls", *Employee Relations*, Vol. 17, No. 3, pp. 42–51.

Steininger, D.J. (1994), "Why Quality Initiatives are Failing to Address the Foundation of Human Motivation", *Human Resource Management*, Winter, Vol. 33, No. 4, pp. 601–16.

Sternberg, L.E. (1992), "Empowerment: Trust Vs Control", *Cornell Hotel & Restaurant Quarterly*, Vol. 33, No. 1, pp. 69–72.

Stewart, S. and N. Johns (1996), "Total Quality: an Approach to Managing Productivity in the Hotel Industry", *International Association of Hospitality Management Conference*, Vol. 1, 1–15.

Sunday Business Post (1997), "ISO 9000 can Damage your Company's Position", June.

Tahir, T. (1994), "Total Quality Management" in M. Baker (ed.), *Perspectives on Marketing Management*, Vol. 4, London: Wiley.

Taylor, P. (1992), "Why Customers Must Come First", *Financial Times*, Management Section, 26 October.

Teare, R. (1995), "The International Hospitality Business: a Thematic Perspective", *International Journal of Contemporary Hospitality Management*, Vol. 7, No. 7, pp. 55–73.

Teare, R., (1997), "UK Hotels Trail USA", *Caterer and Hotelkeeper*, 9 October, p. 10.

Thompson, R. (1993), "An Employee's View of Empowerment", *HR Focus*, July.

Tse, E.C. (1995), "Towards a Strategic Total Quality Framework for Hospitality Firms" in M.D. Olsen, R. Teare and E. Gummesson, (eds.), *Service Quality in Hospitality Organisations*, London: Cassell, pp. 299–315.

UK Hotels Group Directory (1992/3), Hotel and Catering Research Centre, University of Huddersfield.

van Biema, M. and B. Greenwald (1997), "Managing Our Way to Higher Service Sector Productivity", *Harvard Business Review*, July/August, pp. 87–95.

Vandamme, R. and J. Leunis (1993), "Development of a Multiple-Item Scale for Measuring Hospital Service Quality", *International Journal of Service Industry Management*, Vol. 4, Vol. 30–49.

Vandermerwe, S. (1996), *The Eleventh Commandment*, London: Wiley.

Vandermerwe, S.A. and C. Lovelock (1994), *Competing Through Services*, Englewood Cliffs, NJ: Prentice Hall.

Vandermerwe, S.A. (1993), "Jumping into the Customer's Activity Cycle: a New Role for Customer Services in the 1990s", *Columbia Journal of World Business*, Vol. XXVIII, pp. 47–65.

Vandermerwe, S.A. (1994), *From Tin Soldiers to Russian Dolls*, London: Butterworth-Heinemann.

Vera, F and R. Rippin (1996), "Decline of a Mediterranean Tourist Area and Restructuring Strategies: the Valencian Region" in K. Priestley, J.A. Edwards and H. Coccosis, *Sustainable Tourism? European Experiences*, Wallingford: CAB International.

Vlitos Rowe, I. (1995), *Impact of Technology on the Travel Industry: Developments and Trends*, London: Financial Times Management Report.

Voss, C.A. and K. Blackmon (1995), "Does Investment in TQM and ISO 9000 Pay Off? Data from Europe", Working Paper, London Business School, November.

Walker, O.C. and R.W. Reukert (1987), "Marketing's Role in the Implementation of Business Strategies: a Critical Review and Conceptual Framework", *Journal of Marketing*, Vol. 51, July, pp. 15–33.

Westley, F.R. (1990), "Middle Managers and Strategy: Micro-dynamics of Inclusion", *Strategic Management Journal*, Vol. 11, pp. 337–51.

Whiteley, R. and D. Hessan (1996), *Customer-Centred Growth*, London: Century Business Press.

Wilkinson, A. and B. Witcher (1993), "Holistic Total Quality Management must Take Account of Political Processes", *Total Quality Management*, Vol. 4, No. 1, pp. 47–56.

Wilkinson, A. (1992), "The Other Side of Quality: 'Soft' Issues and the Human Resource Dimension", *Total Quality Management*, Vol. 3, No. 3, pp. 323–9.

Wilkinson, A. (1994), "Managing Human Resources for Quality" in B. Dale (ed.), *Managing Quality*, Second edition, London: Prentice Hall International, pp. 273–88.

Wilkinson, A. and H. Wilmott (eds.) (1995), *Making Quality Critical*, London: Routledge, pp. 1–32.

Wilkinson, A., M. Marchington, P. Ackers and J. Goodman (1991), "Total Quality Management and Employee Involvement", *Human Resource Management Journal*, Vol. 2, No. 4.

Wilkinson, A., T. Redman and E. Snape (1993), *Quality and the Manager*, London: Institute of Management.

Williams, B. (1998), "Micro-millions Tourism", *The Journal of the Tourism Society*, Vol. 95, p. 14.

Willmott, H. (1995), "What has been Happening in Organisation Theory and Does it Matter?", *Personnel Review*, Vol. 24, No. 8, pp. 33–53.

Witcher, B. (1993), "TQM and the Creation of Market Responsive Organisation" in M. Baker (ed.), *Perspectives in Marketing Management*, Vol. 3, London: Wiley, pp. 169–245.

Witcher, B. (1994), "The adoption of TQM in Scotland", *The TQM Magazine*, Vol. 6, No. 2, pp. 48–53.

Witt, C. and A. Muhlemann (1994), "Service Quality in Airlines", *Tourism Economics*, Vol. 1, No. 1, pp. 33–49.

Wood, R.C. (1983), "Theory, Management and Hospitality: a Response to Philip Nailon", *International Journal of Hospitality Management*, Vol. 2, No. 2, pp. 102–18

Wood, S. and R. Peccei (1995), "Does Quality Management Make a Difference to Employee Attitudes?", *Employee Relations*, Vol. 17, No. 3, pp. 52–62.

Zairi, M. (1996), "TQM: What is Wrong with the Terminology?", *The TQM Magazine*, Vol. 6, No. 4, pp. 1–3.

Zairi, M., S.R. Letza and J.S. Oakland (1994), *TQM: Its Impact on Bottom Line Results*, London: Technical Communications.

Zairi, M. and M.A. Youssef (1995), "Quality Function Deployment", *International Journal of Quality and Reliability Management*, Vol. 12, No. 6, pp. 9–23.

Zeithaml, V., A. Parasuraman and L.L. Berry (1991), *Delivering Quality Service*, New York: Free Press.

Zeithaml, V.A. and M.J. Bitner (1997), *Services Marketing*, London: McGraw-Hill.

Index

acquisitions, *see* hospitality
industry (consolidation)
airlines, 39, 40–1, 45, 49, 53, 153,
231, 256
American Hotel and Motel
Association, 21, 193, 205

benchmarking, 6, 78–9, 81, 84, 85,
111–16, 137
competitiveness stage, 114
effectiveness stage, 113
Bord Fáilte (Irish Tourist Board),
21, 144, 246
brand affiliation, 37–8, 45–6
business travel, 49–50, 153

CERT, 23, 88, 89, 169–70, 246
Choice Hotels, 38, 46, 47
communications, 69, 80, 85, 92,
94, 131, 158–9, 178, 189, 221,
236
competition, 64, 65, 77, 225, 247,
263, 265
intensity, 77–8, 232, 251
internationalisation, 247, 253
see also strategy
competitive advantage, 1, 25, 54,
86, 93–123, 252
quality as, 108–11
competitiveness, 84, 92, 97, 198,
204, 216, 248, 263, 265; *see also*
competitive advantage
complaints, 21, 249
as source of information, 21

computerised reservation
systems, 48–9, 50, 153–4; *see also*
information technology;
technology
Condominiums International, 27
Confederation of British
Industry, 76, 77, 78, 83, 114–15
consolidation *see* hospitality
industry
construction, 80
continuous improvement, 69,
130–5, 217; *see also* total quality
management
Crosby, P., 6
customer
data on, 20–22, 193–4
demands, 6, 9, 10, 11, 78, 236
expectations, 16, 66, 67, 82,
117, 159–60, 191, 194, 216,
236, 249, 253
experiences, 66–7, 74, 79, 80,
112, 231
feedback, 120–21, 236
interface, 180, 184, 194, 196
orientation, 8–9, 66, 75, 165,
184, 191–6
perceptions, 11–12, 20, 66, 67,
118–19, 160
satisfaction, 75, 88–9, 100, 106,
120, 133, 150, 211, 221, 232,
233, 248, 249
sophistication of the, 102, 225,
263, 265

decision-making, 128, 144, 145, 159, 169, 179–80, 181–2, 184, 187, 188, 190, 197, 199, 200, 209, 221, 229, 232, 235, 237, 239, 240, 241, 249

Deming, W. Edwards, 4, 5, 6, 214, 250

destination-level policy, 66–77, 91, 264

differentiation, 101–3, 108, 232

downsizing, 96, 259–60

Doyle Hotel Group, 37

economic
   growth, 4
   recession, 1, 32, 231

employee involvement, *see* staff

empowerment, *see* staff

environment, 70–1, 72, 86

European Union, 4, 16, 38, 64–5, 89, 90, 182, 193, 199, 244, 264

Feigenbaum, Armand, 4

financial services, 221–2

flexibility, 49, 156, 165, 236–7

Forte, 37, 45, 50–1

Four Seasons, 38, 54–5, 109–10

franchising, 38, 45–7, 51, 263

globalisation, 1, 36, 40, 265

government, 71–3, 76–8, 80, 84, 86–7, 91, 106

Great Britain, 18, 25, 31–2, 35, 37, 38, 91, 94, 103, 107, 112, 114–15, 117, 121, 129, 141, 147, 148, 152, 169, 171, 199, 205, 213, 217, 225, 258
   tourism performance, 33–4, 77
   tourism policy, 54, 64, 75–86

Gulf War, 1, 32, 95, 104

Hilton International, 44, 45, 55, 119

holiday companies, 27; *see also* tour operators; travel agencies

Holiday Inn, 45, 47, 51, 59, 97–8

hospitality industry, 31–61, 147, 165, 188, 191, 219, 241, 243
   characteristics of, 34–6
   consolidation, 36–9, 51, 52–3, 263
   fragmentation in, 36, 51, 53, 70, 260
   organisations, 3, 20, 172, 174, 179, 190, 209, 213, 233, 239, 258
   quality in, *see* quality
   strategic alliances, 39, 40–3, 51
   strategic analysis of, 31–61
   see also hotels; tourism

Hotel and Catering International Management Association (HCIMA), 141, 205

hotels, 13, 27, 32, 35, 40, 43–4, 45, 56, 60–1, 81, 94, 140, 179, 245, 249, 258–9
   investment in, 79
   occupancy rates, 34, 52, 103, 253
   see also hospitality industry

human resource development (HRD), 165, 174, 231
   definition, 166–7
   strategic, 167, 173
   and tourism, 168–75

human resource management (HRM), 8, 15, 79, 94–5, 141–2, 165–208, 218, 223, 239, 252, 257, 263; *see also* staff

Hyatt Hotels, 38, 55

implementation, quality, 3, 96, 147–8, 165, 178, 193, 199, 205–6, 213–17, 229–42, 255–8, 260
  challenges, 209, 225–8
  complexity of, 218
  failure of, 218–23, 224
  practical issues, 229–32, 240
  resistance to, 178–9
  tensions, 232–40
  top–bottom integration, 180–3, 255
  top-down approach, 179, 255
information technology (IT), 47–51, 151–5
  integrated, 156–60
infrastructure, 90, 165–208
innovation, 35, 86, 91, 165, 187, 203, 245
interactivity, 47–8, 49
Intercontinental, 45
internal marketing, 145–9, 235
Internet, 50–1, 264
Ireland, 37, 91, 94, 112, 119, 144–5, 169, 218, 261–2
  tourism performance, 31, 33, 90, 246
  tourism policies, 64, 86–91, 245–6
  tourism quality initiatives, 13–15, 53
Irish Hotels Federation, 13, 53, 119
Irish Tourism Industry Confederation, 51, 186
ISO 9000, 126–30, 131, 133, 134, 219, 248

Juran, Joseph, 4, 6
Jurys Hotel Group, 37

LEADER programme, 89

loyalty, 67, 93, 160–1, 191, 244; *see also* customer satisfaction

Malcolm Baldrige Quality Award, 26, 35, 105, 211, 212
management, 2, 7,56–7, 175–9, 245
  competences, 56–7, 169, 261–2
  contracts, 43–5, 51
  quality, *see* quality management
  senior, 225–8, 229–30, 232
  style, 7, 184–5
manufacturing, 9, 10, 11, 97, 135, 138, 225
marketing, 47, 60, 64, 66, 83, 85, 86, 88, 89, 136, 147, 173, 219
  internal, *see* internal marketing
Marriott International, 21–2, 33, 37, 39, 50, 51, 55, 202, 228
mergers, *see* hospitality industry (consolidation)
middle management, 95, 148, 188, 190, 191, 225–8, 229, 234–5, 239, 241, 257
monitoring, 69

performance measurement, 116–22
personnel, *see* human resource management
Porter, Michael, 101, 105
Principal Hotels, 46
private sector, 73–4, 76, 91, 106
processes, internal, 5, 6, 19, 58, 111, 113, 254, 264
product
  development, 79, 85–6, 195
  quality, 11–12, 83

public sector, 72–4, 76, 85, 91,
174, 217
pubs, 107

quality, 1–30, 53–4, 59–60, 171,
247–50
as competitive advantage,
108–11
circles, 18
concept, 2, 4–8, 27–8
contemporary views on, 8–11
culture, 183–91, 211, 216, 218
definitions of, 2, 4–8, 18, 30
delivery, 68
documentation, 125, 126
evaluation criteria, 12–13, 20,
68, 231
failure, 15–16
full, 16
functional, 109
future challenges, 243–67
hard, 125–63, 251
human dimension, 8
implementation, *see*
implementation, quality
improvement, 7, 54, 65, 73
in tourism organisations, 19–
28
infrastructure, 87, 165–208
challenges to senior
management, 175–80
initiatives, 15–16, 53, 63, 66,
73, 86, 94, 96, 97–105, 117,
178, 180, 193, 197, 204, 215,
217, 228, 257, 263
management, 2, 3, 5, 7, 28, 93,
137, 165, 175, 195, 204, 213,
247–50
deficiencies in, 15–19
dynamics of, 94–6
evaluation, 209–42

"manufactured", 130–5
measurement, 3, 13, 14, 20–1,
25, 27, 116–22, 233, 236
partial, 15, 29, 239
perspectives on, 2, 3–4, 8–11,
29
philosophy, 1, 4, 6, 28, 30, 176,
210, 213, 218, 232, 240, 247,
254, 264
planning, 66, 68
policy, 3, 64, 61–92
rhetoric, 194
soft, 15, 125–63, 251, 263
competitive importance,
135–7
standards, 13, 54, 125, 126–30,
248; *see also* ISO 9000
strategic approach to, 25, 68,
69, 84, 97–104, 105–8, 176,
213–17, 247, 258–62, 266
questionnaires, 118

reengineering, 96, 259–60
regionalism, 71–5, 85, 89
research studies, 15–17, 22, 24–5,
27, 29, 55–8, 60, 92, 168, 224,
265–6
resources, 70, 148, 254
restaurants, 23–4, 32, 45–6, 130,
140, 194, 205, 260
Ritz-Carlton Hotel Company, 26,
35, 37, 55, 155, 202, 211, 212

Savoy Hotels, 38
service
characteristics, 9–10, 56, 57–8,
139
definition, 58
delivery, 1, 8, 18, 22–3, 47, 66,
77, 82, 143–5, 150, 151, 154,
160, 184, 196

service (cont'd)
   encounters, 22, 23, 159
   expectations, 1, 265
   integration, 156–61
   quality, 11–15, 49, 66, 83, 104,
      105–6, 109, 117, 136, 160,
      179, 180, 196, 219, 228; *see*
      also quality
   recovery, 249
   sector, 136–7, 152
SERVQUAL, 12, 13, 25
Sheraton Group, 35, 37, 104, 193
skills, 108, 115, 146, 160, 166,
   180–1, 187, 192, 246, 262; *see also*
   management; staff; training
Sofitel, 52
Spain, 64, 67, 91
   quality-oriented tourism
      policies, 71–5
staff
   empowerment of, 21, 138,
      144–5, 148, 151, 181, 183,
      185, 186, 190, 194, 198, 211,
      225, 229, 231, 236, 239, 263
   importance of, 81, 82, 108–9,
      143–5, 145–50, 171
   involvement, 28, 94, 159, 179,
      194, 195, 199, 201, 204, 225,
      229, 232, 239, 241, 255, 259,
      263
   motivation, 149, 152
   recruitment and retention, 82,
      102, 147
   resourcefulness, 196–206
   training and development, *see*
      training
   turnover, 134, 172, 203, 204,
      253
   see also human resource
      development; human
      resource management

strategic alliances, *see* hospitality
   industry
strategic quality, *see* quality
strategy, 97–108, 161, 166, 253,
   258–62, 266
   competitive, 101
   definitions, 98–9, 101
   integrated with human
      resources, 166, 172, 239
   see also quality

teamwork, 110, 202, 213, 223,
   226, 233
technology
   developments in, 1, 41, 47,
      140, 245
   impact of, 1, 47–51, 64, 143,
      156–8, 165, 216
   see also information
      technology
total quality management
   (TQM), 2, 6, 7, 8, 17, 19, 28, 94,
   105, 111, 125, 130, 131, 133, 135,
   137–43, 162, 165, 179, 182, 185,
   209, 210, 213, 219, 220, 221, 227,
   228, 230, 231, 234, 237, 242, 267
   failure of, 222
   techniques, 138
tour operators, 27, 53, 99–100,
   146, 160, 183
tourism
   as service industry, 10–11, 31,
      244
   employment in, 4, 31, 87, 170–
      1, 244
   expectations in, 66–7
   experience of, 66–7
   future challenges, 263–5
   growth in, 4, 31, 33–4, 71, 75,
      244
   importance of, 244–7

tourism (cont'd)
  industry, 1, 4, 61, 65–6, 70,
    243, 252; *see also* hospitality
    industry; hotels
  organisations, 19–28, 183
  policies, 63–92
    in Great Britain, 75–86
    in Ireland, 86–91
    in Spain, 71–5
  quality in, *see* quality
  strategies, 63–92
tourists, *see* customers
training, 75, 78, 79, 82–3, 85, 87–
  8, 103, 131, 132, 141, 145, 152,
  160, 166–7, 169–70, 174, 183,
  186, 192, 197, 203, 205, 217, 246,
  250, 253, 263

travel agencies, 11, 160

UK, *see* Great Britain
United States, 20, 32, 35, 37, 182,
  183, 185, 188, 193, 199, 205, 213,
  223, 249, 258, 263

variation, 9

wages, 79, 82
Westin, 35, 50, 55
World Tourist Organisation, 31

zero defects, 6